ROCK GARDEN
& ALPINE PLANTS

ROCK GARDEN & ALPINE PLANTS

Raymond Foster

David & Charles
Newton Abbot London North Pomfret (Vt)

The line drawings are by Rosemary Wise
Photographs are by courtesy of The Alpine Garden Society

British Library Cataloguing in Publication Data

Foster, Raymond
Rock garden and alpine plants.
1. Rock plants
2. Alpine flora
I. Title
635.9′672 SB421

ISBN 0 7153 8203 9

Library of Congress Catalog Card Number 81-67009

Typeset and printed in Great Britain by Ebenezer Baylis & Son Limited, The Trinity Press, Worcester and London for David & Charles (Publishers) Limited, Brunel House, Newton Abbot, Devon.

Published in the United States of America by David & Charles Inc. North Pomfret, Vermont 05053, USA

Contents

1
Earth and Stone

The design of a rockery is a personal matter which reflects individual taste, and no two people will share exactly the same views on all counts. Even the very term 'rockery' is open to controversy, for many gardeners who are primarily plantsmen, who set the welfare of their plants above other considerations, look on the word with suspicion, and tend to avoid it in favour of the broader term 'rock garden'. Certainly, it can conjure up images of a place where rocks come first and plants are obliged to trail in second place. Perhaps a rockery may be defined as an arrangement of rocks set with plants, whereas a rock garden is an arrangement of plants set with rocks. Both, in practice, should be places where plants of the kinds which appreciate mountain conditions can be grown in surroundings that, to some extent, simulate their natural habitat – places that satisfy both the needs of the plants and the critical observer's eye. In one's own garden, of course, the primary aim is to please oneself, but even this simple aim is not always easy to achieve unless a clear policy has been formulated from the start.

When this style of gardening first arose, rockeries tended to be sited in places that were not really suitable for anything else – certainly not for Alpine plants – and frequently they were constructed simply by tipping a cartload or two of rocks, to which were added a few barrowloads of soil. A rockery built along these lines could never have been described as a rock garden; the alternative name for an arranged heap of stones is a 'cairn', and this would have been a more apt description.

Cairns of both ancient and recent origin are to be seen scattered throughout hilly country in Britain and many other parts of the world, often to the extent that they form a traditional feature of mountain scenery. Useful and ornamental as they well may be, they are not structures upon which plants can reasonably be expected to grow. Rock plants like to have a fair depth of soil under their roots. We see such plants carpeting boulders and growing apparently actually on

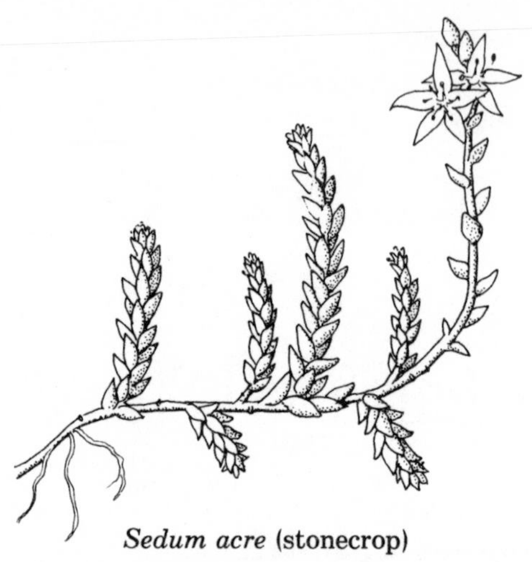

Sedum acre (stonecrop)

these inhospitable surfaces, and it is easy to assume that they are able to thrive with the merest anchorage – but this is rarely the case. The English climbing ivy grows so closely pressed to tree trunks and stone walls that it appears to draw sustenance from them, but this is an illusion: its health and continued existence depend entirely on the soil at its base. It is exactly the same in the case of a rock plant – only a few specialised kinds such as some of the stonecrops can manage, like the mosses, to grow in the merest scattering of debris on the surface of a stone. The great majority of plants need a deep, cool rootrun that is readily accessible to them between the rock crevices. Disconnected pockets of soil are subject to rapid desiccation – unless the rock they are in is particularly porous, such as tufa – and plants growing in them will rarely survive for long.

The cairn type of rockery, therefore, is able to support satisfactorily only those plants which are rooted nearby and are able to scramble over the stones. If, on the other hand, there is a central core of earth connecting all these pockets and running between the joints, such a rockery will have become in effect a circular retaining wall – even though it retains nothing except its own core – and the raised bed is a modification of this idea. Even in the case of dry stone walls, the introduced plant's connection with solid earth must be positive and unbroken.

My personal preference is for a rockery to imitate a natural outcrop of rock wherever possible – but plainly there are many instances where this idea is impractical. A 'plum pudding' type of rockery – consisting of a central earth mound decorated symmetrically with stone – will not look in the least like a work of nature, however tamed, but it may nevertheless form an attractive garden feature, and not necessarily a permanent repository for the ubiquitous *Alyssum saxatile* and *Cerastium tomentosum*; there are many possibilities for more adventurous planting schemes on such a limited scale. The 'plum pudding' has the immediate advantage of possessing roughly four micro-climatic zones, corresponding to the north, south, east and west faces, so that, already, a wide range of gardening possibilities is apparent.

If the rockery is intended to take on the appearance of a natural outcrop, the rocks must seem to originate from underlying strata which happen to emerge at that point. The effect will be easier to simulate if there is already a hillside or some other soil backing for an outcrop. Naturally outcropping rocks assume many and varied forms. In some parts of the world, the surrounding soil has become eroded over millions of years, leaving isolated pillars of piled rocks, like the African koppies. In their natural surroundings, these have a dramatic impact, but they are difficult to reproduce with any degree of realism; artifical koppies are apt to look as if a lorry has tipped the stone for a rockery, but no one has got around to arranging it yet. In a district where naturally occurring hills of this kind are commonplace, their miniature garden counterparts can readily be recognised and accepted as such; but in other areas it is safer to arrange for the rocks to emerge from the ground in more or less clearly defined strata.

A wise initial move when planning a rock garden is to inspect the district for any sign of natural rocks, occurring either as outcrops or fortuitously exposed in road cuttings or quarries, and note how the

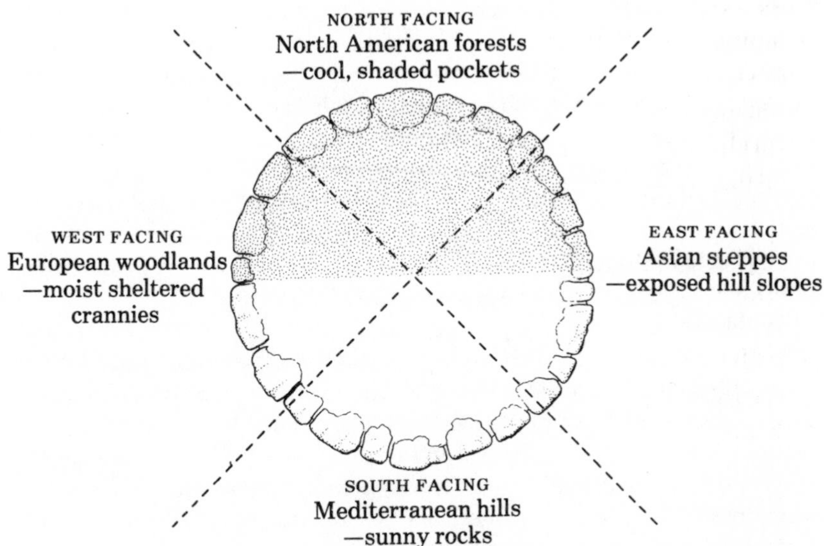

Micro-climate. A plant's natural habitat should decide its site in the garden

local stone behaves. In flat areas, of course, and in districts where the ground below topsoil level consists of deep sand, clay or gravel, though there will be no convenient guide, one's choice for a visually pleasing rockery is that much wider, because there will be no danger of the results clashing with any of nature's productions. The most glaring mistakes, in my view, are made when, despite a district having numerous clearly visible outcrops of a distinctive local stone, garden rockeries are built from imported material of perhaps contrastingly different colour and texture. This is really flying in the face of nature, and such an antipathetic rockery can never look right, no matter how 'natural' the simulated strata: passers-by may not be able to put their fingers on the reason why a beautifully constructed and well planted rock garden gives them little satisfaction; but there will always be something vaguely disturbing about it.

There are districts, of course, where two or more highly contrasting types of stone occur virtually side by side. In my home county of Shropshire, for instance, there are places where either white limestone or warm red sandstone would be equally acceptable, for both look quite at home. The rule to follow here is to make sure that no natural outcrop is visible from the garden – or from the viewpoint of the passer-by. If it is, the type of stone visible must set the tone for the rockery, but if no outcrop is in sight, choice of stone becomes a matter for personal preference and expediency.

A few very well-known types of stone – Westmorland, Cotswold, York – seem to hold a magnetic attraction for many people when planning not only semi-wild rockeries, but also more formal gardens with stone-built features. One needs to be practical about it: it would be a shame to use any other in districts where these types of stone occur naturally, but elsewhere in the country their use is liable to result only in incongruity – not to mention unnecessary expense. Stone from the northern fells, with its picturesquely weather and water-worn surfaces, cannot reasonably be expected to look at home in London or south-east England. It might be justifiable to use it in such areas provided the immediate locality is sufficiently expansive and rural but, all too often, the effect is suburban and artifical.

To these disadvantages may be added the every-increasing difficulty and expense of obtaining weather-worn surface stone, for its collection has been banned in many areas, and a major source of supply nowadays stems from unwanted rockeries in gardens that are being reconstructed or built over. A further point against using weathered Westmorland or other similar limestones in towns that suffer from any great degree of industrial pollution – and the 'clean air' regulations, while reducing the amount of smoke and soot, have scarcely diluted the concentration of harmful chemicals that become

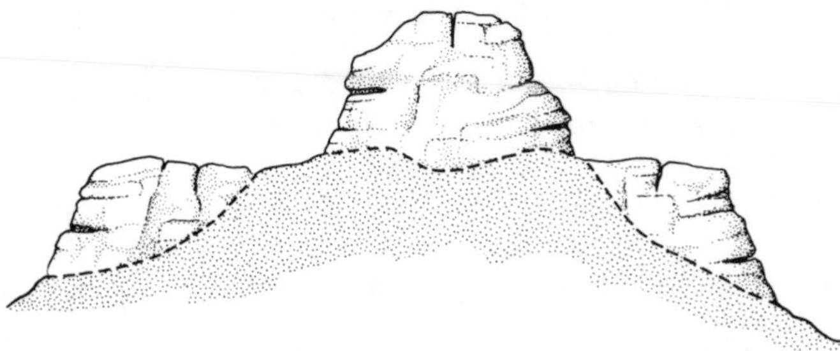

Weathered limestone. Pieces may readily be found to cap a free-standing rockery

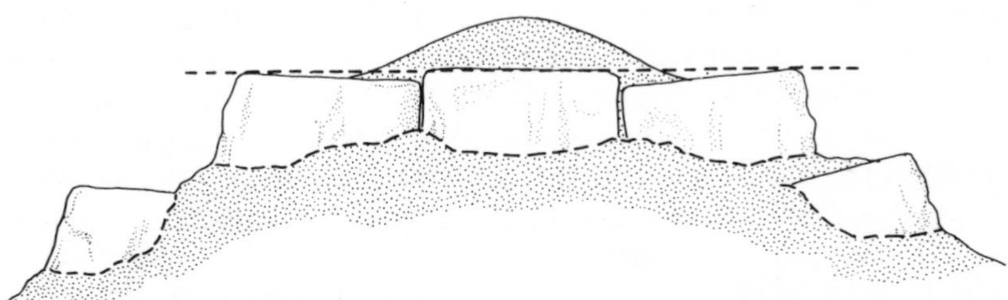

Quarried stone. On free-standing rockeries the topmost stratum should protrude from a dome of soil

airborne – is the progressive whitening that is apt to take place: the centuries of mellowing are cancelled out, and the surface of the stone rapidly becomes bleached from acid accretions until it is as white and staring as marble.

The advantages, provided the air is clean and there are no local rock outcrops with which weathered Westmorland stone can clash, are the very beautiful, picturesque shapes and textures which these rocks display, and the comparative simplicity with which they can be made to simulate a natural feature: having lain on the surface for countless years, they have no distinct arrangement of strata, so they may be placed, within reason, in almost any attitude and still retain their naturally aligned appearance. Because of this absence of strata or any noticeable lines of deposition, rocks of this sort often look best when the rockery is of the free-standing type – that is, when it is intended to represent a natural mound or hummock protruding through the surface soil, like the peak of a mountain. It will fall readily into the dome-shaped pattern required for this type of arrangement, and looks good from all angles when crowning a peak. Pieces of Westmorland may readily be found which will project their bulk upwards, so as to give the impression of towering height and thus add drama to the garden. This is often difficult to achieve with quarried rock, which normally demands a single-faced shelf formation, either stepped out of the hillside (as it was in the quarry), or thrusting upward with canted strata as though the result of some prehistoric upheaval. As a rule, therefore, surface-gleaned rock is best limited to dome-shaped capping arrangements, and quarried rock should be used for one-aspect rockeries. If quarried material is to be worked into a free-standing mound, it will nearly always be necessary to build a topmost dome with soil, and allow the uppermost stratum to protrude from this.

Rockery stone which derives from solitary rocks that have been uncovered during excavations usually resembles surface-gleaned stones, as such material frequently has rounded edges and lacks a definite face. These characteristics make it difficult to place effectively in some situations, but it takes happily to the moraine style of rock garden. This formation involves the use of half-buried, rounded or smooth-surfaced boulders intended to represent, not an outcrop of rocks protruding from the surface, but the ancient debris deposited by a glacier. Slate and granite lend themselves well to this type of arrangement.

With any load of sizable boulders there will inevitably be included a fair proportion of small pieces of stone, and these may be difficult to place so that they look neither fussy nor inconsequential. One way of using them is to arrange them closely together so that they take on the appearance of a single larger piece and, once well clothed with carpeting plants, will soon become indistinguishable from the rest. Another method is to site them in the scree bed. Screes occur in nature as the result of a breaking up and gradual erosion of stone particles of various sizes, often through the action of streams seasonably swollen by melting snow, and forming the familiar smooth delta-shaped aprons which clothe the sides of many hills. Garden screes provide conditions that are ideal for growing many Alpine plants, and they need not necessarily be associated with built-up rockeries. Sometimes they are constructed on flat ground, though a slight slope at least is desirable, as this ensures perfect drainage and more nearly approximates the natural qualities of a mountain scree.

There is no reason why these different styles of rock gardening should not be combined. A rock garden that includes outcrops, scree and moraine will not look in the least complicated or overdone. One system flows quite naturally into another, and the whole offers the widest range of possibilities for both choice and display of mountain plants.

Artificial rock outcrops frequently have a backing of some sort – a wall, a bank or a hillside. In cases where a rockery is to back on to a low wall – perhaps the retaining wall of a terrace or patio along the front of a house – quite obviously it is not going to fool anyone into believing it to be a natural rock formation. In just such a situation,

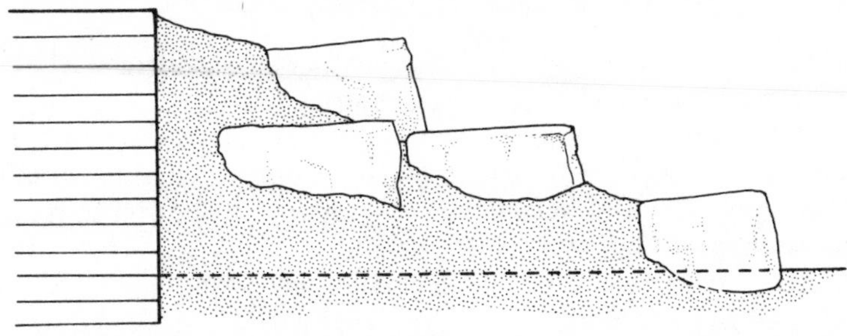

A lean-to rockery built against a retaining wall needs an apparently solid outcrop with clearly defined strata

however – when the completed rockery is to be viewed as the foreground to a building – a random, meaningless jumble of stones can do the householder the worst possible service: a rock formation emerging from beneath a house is going to represent a continuation of the house foundations, and it follows that an unbalanced, unstable layout will carry the impression that the whole building is about to slide away and collapse. Thus it is really important in these circumstances to create an apparently solid rock outcrop with clearly defined strata. This will bestow an air of peaceful stability – provided the stone appears to be of authentic local origin.

A word of warning should be added here about building directly against house walls: the damp proof course usually found two brick courses above ground level should always be kept clear, and earth must never be piled above it or damp will penetrate the wall and damage the mortar.

When designing a rock garden to front a house, the intended shape of the rockery should first be marked on the ground. If the area is covered with turf, this could be lifted and stacked in heaps, upside down, to correspond with the highest points of the intended design. These highest points should normally abut the wall or background slope, though there may of course be other peaks at a distance, separated by miniature valleys, if the area is broad enough. Nine times out of ten, however, for this 'lean-to' type of rockery, a straightforward front-to-rear arrangement will be preferable.

If perennial weeds are present, the ground base should be forked over so that they can be removed. The extra trouble involved is well worthwhile when compared with the continually recurring annoyance of trying to eliminate such weeds once they have established themselves beneath the rocks. If a weedkiller is used, it should be of a non-persistent type such as the chemical glyphosate (Murphy Tumbleweed or Monsanto Roundup), which does not entail a season's wait for the soil to recover from the effects. Paraquat-based chemicals such as ICI Weedol leave no trace in the soil and may give an immediate kill of top growth, but pernicious weeds such as docks and ground elder are sure to recover and shoot again.

Mountain tops, though the rainfall may be high, are very free draining, and most Alpine and rock-loving plants prefer a dryish soil in which to grow. Ground beneath a rockery that is allowed to remain damp after planting will not permit moisture to drain away thoroughly, and few plants will ever thrive there. If the basal area of an intended site is wet and unlikely to drain satisfactorily, it may be necessary to dig deeper than a mere fork's spit, and lay a land drain leading away to a lower dispersal area. Such drainage, however, will rarely be necessary and, provided the ground beneath consists of normal garden soil, construction of the rockery can commence without further precautions. With certain soils, minerals from the top few inches tend to wash down to the lower layers, an action which sometimes results in a hard iron pan forming at two or three spades' depth. This might prove an effective barrier against roots as well as water, and partial double digging – the bottom spit can merely be agitated with a fork – should break up any mineral pan.

Compost for the rockery is best made up of loamy soil with an admixture of peat and sharp, gritty sand. For average use, the proportions could be: 1 pt peat, 1 pt sharp sand, 3 pts topsoil. If the mixture can be sterilised to kill the weed seeds and pieces of root in it, so much the better.

Some confusion exists as to what constitutes a loamy soil: the description refers to the size of the mineral particles, and not to the percentage of animal and vegetable matter that may be present. A loamy soil when rubbed between the fingers will feel moderately gritty, neither too coarse nor too greasy. A quick test might be carried out by sampling the proportions of coarse and fine particles it contains: up to a cupful of soil should be placed in a clear glass jar – the screwtop jam jar type is convenient – topped up with water and shaken thoroughly, then allowed to settle. The soil will rearrange its pattern according to the size and weight of the particles of which it is composed; thus, the gravel will sink first to the bottom, the coarse sand will settle on this, then the fine sand, then finally the silt and the clay. All will be clearly stratified, and it is then possible to make a rough mechanical analysis of the nature of the soil. Soil particles are graded according to an international scale:

Above 2mm (1/12in)	= Gravel
Below 2 down to 0·2mm	= Coarse sand
Below 0·2 down to 0·02mm	= Fine sand
Below 0·02 down to 0·002mm	= Silt
Below 0·002mm	= Clay

Without micrometer work, it is easy to see the main divisions into coarse, medium and fine particles in the various strata that will have formed. Soils are graded into thirteen grades, ranging from (1) loamy coarse sand to (13) heavy clay. The loams themselves comprise the middle grades, ranging from a minimum of 15 per cent silt/clay and 65 per cent sand, to a maximum of 65 per cent silt/clay and 25 per cent sand. Within this scale, an average loam will contain about 40 per cent silt/clay, 10 per cent gravel, and 50 per cent sand.

If distilled water has been used to separate the particles, a simple test of acidity can now be made using a cheap soil pH test kit – simply a matter of adding a small quantity of chemical indicator to the water, and comparing the resultant colour of the solution with the colour chart that will have been supplied with the chemical. As a rough guide, in the case of Universal pH Indicator, the colour green represents a neutral reaction; alkaline reactions produce shades of blue merging into purple; and acid reactions produce yellows, shading into red. Litmus can also be used as a rough and ready acid/alkali test but, whichever method is used, the water must have been distilled or purified, otherwise the results will be biased.

The Table of Rock Plants (page 204) includes columns indicating the preferences of each plant. Most enjoy a slightly limy – that is, an alkaline – soil, but are able to grow perfectly satisfactorily when there is no lime, and the reaction is neutral or slightly acid. Only a few refuse to grow without lime in the soil, but there are several which cannot survive even a trace of lime, and plants such as these should be provided with their own pockets of the appropriate compost mix. A planting scheme should take careful note of this factor, so that, for instance, all the acid-loving plants can be limited to certain lime-free areas. In this respect, it should be remembered that lime gradually becomes washed out of the soil and deposits itself lower down the slope, so that lime-free areas must not be sited where they are liable to catch any run-off.

If topsoil or compost has to be bought and imported into a garden, the quantity required will need to be estimated by finding the cubic measure of the area to be filled. A 10 tonne load will give about 6cu m of average soil, but the old Imperial measure is more convenient to use. With this method, it can be estimated that 1cu yd of soil equals 1 ton in weight and, if the area is paced out in yards, this means that the length, times the breadth, times the average height of fill, all in yards, will result in a round figure of tons. Thus, an area measuring 10 paces by 2½ paces (25sq yd) and averaging 18in (half a yard) deep, will require $25 \times \frac{1}{2} = 12\frac{1}{2}$ tons to fill. In another example, an area measuring 9yd by 2yd by 1ft average depth ($9 \times 2 \div 3$) will require 6 tons of soil.

The rockery stones themselves will, of course, take up some room within this cubic area, and stone, on average, weighs about 2 tonnes per cubic metre. Here again, the old Imperial measure is convenient to use when estimating the quantity required, because 1cu ft of stone on average weighs 1cwt and 1cu ft is a very convenient average size for rockery stones, so there should be about twenty stones to the ton.

If the new rockery area is sited on sloping ground, and the imported soil is to be used merely to infill behind each stone as it is set in place, correspondingly far less soil will be needed, and much of the completed rockery will be planted actually at ground level. A very handsome rockery averaging say 10yd × 3yd, and rising from ground level against a solid retaining wall to a height of 18in or so, may well be built using no more than 2 tonnes of rock and 3 tonnes of compost fill.

Quarried stone will usually provide the square face and flattened base needed to reconstruct the solid rock strata which are to protrude apparently from the base of a retaining background wall. When such a wall actually fronts a house, the non-stratiform surface-gleaned limestone can certainly be used and will take on the appearance of a natural outcrop but, unless the house is situated actually within fell country, such an outcrop is bound to look oddly misplaced protruding from beneath the foundations.

It is impossible to adhere to any precise plan for placing rockery stones, because every piece is unique, and it is really of great value to study natural rock outcrops of the appropriate type. After aeons of geological upheaval the strata – laid down, perhaps, as the silted bed of sea and lake – are no longer horizontal: they protrude from the surrounding landscape at all angles from near level to almost perpendicular, and there are possibilities for copying even the most dramatic formations in the garden; but by and large such outcrops, however eccentric, should be consistent. Flattish rocks should always be given a slight slope backwards towards the body of the rockery, both to allow rainwater to be directed into the soil pockets rather than away from them, and to impart a degree of stability. In nature, admittedly, many protruding strata are tilted outwards and downwards but, in the garden, such rocks would certainly give rise to barked shins, or even broken legs. The rockery will be trampled and climbed over in the course of normal weeding and tending, and every rock must remain firm when trodden on.

Both from the point of view of stability and for general appearance, part of each stone will have to be buried or at least hidden from view, and something of a mystique has grown up over this concept. Obviously, there is little point in paying today's prices for stone and then burying more than necessary, but the nature of the simulated rock outcrop should be borne in mind – the pieces are supposed to be growing, as it were, from the ground, and their latter ends at least must be concealed. Loose stones belong to the scree and the moraine, and the different types of formation need to be clearly differentiated.

Once an angle of cant is decided upon, it should be adhered to faithfully – within the limits of the odd-shaped pieces at our disposal – throughout the rockery. A change of angle halfway will give a chaotic appearance to the whole: if the stones slant upwards on one side of the rockery and downwards on the other, the whole structure will seem to droop and sag as though something inside has given way. Such a fate can be avoided by adopting a firm policy starting with the very first stone to be laid, and this keystone will normally be to the front of the arrangement. It need not necessarily be one of the largest pieces – often the most impressive rockeries have their bulkiest stones at the rear, or on the peak – but it should preferably have a good shape and a clearly defined surface plane. It should be placed with careful consideration, since it gives the angle which all the other stones must follow. While the surface stratum must be made to slope slightly away from the observer, it is optional whether or not it also slopes laterally; in that direction, too, it will act as the master key in positioning all the others.

A sidelong slant to the strata must be governed to a large extent by the nature of the backing wall, where one exists: if this is low, and clearly level, there may well be an awkward meeting of rock and wall, and it would be better to keep the lateral strata more or less level, although each rock will still have the compulsory slope – however slight – from front to rear. In cases where a pronounced lateral slant is to be given, practical experience shows that the work will have to proceed from the outermost downwards, so that as the rocks are positioned, each will dip away from the one previously firmed. Attempts to build strata on a rising angle will meet with snags.

As each stone is positioned, with the base made stable and the angle consistent, infill compost must be rammed firmly around the back and sides. It is important to leave no unfilled spaces, even in the narrowest crevices, for it is these crevices that allow the plant's roots to find the cool moisture beneath the rocks. Sensitive root tips that come up against an air pocket will die, and desiccation in hot weather is liable to prove sudden and final. Something like a piece of broomstick is needed to ram the compost firmly into the cracks and joins, and the compost itself needs to be neither too wet nor too dry: wet soil is squashy and may pack too tightly so that it sets like concrete: dry soil will not firm properly, nor can it cling within the narrow crevices as it should. A correctly balanced mixture, which contains both coarse sand and leaf mould or peat, will tend to retain a consistent degree of moisture, and the packing process should be able to proceed smoothly in all except the most extreme conditions.

When using quarried stone, it is not the aim to produce continuous, unbroken strata of rock, and it is a mistake to build an outcrop which looks like a series of stone steps or, for that matter, a row of gappy teeth. Now, more than ever, ecology-conscious gardeners have become aware of their environment to the extent that a rock outcrop of natural appearance will be appreciated and admired far more readily than was the case in the early days of rock gardening. Everybody, in other words, is much more aware of the landscape, and it has become easier to see what is right and what is not quite right in rockery construction. The more adventurous rockery design will make full use of pre-existing features. An adjacent slope of the ground might be dramatised by siting an outcrop so that it slants in an opposing direction, and such a canted line of strata can be set to rise far more steeply within a rockery sited on an existing bank than is possible when a retaining wall or building is in the background, or when the rockery is free-standing and unbacked.

In cases where the rock garden is to form the whole face of a bank, so that stones may be dug directly into the existing ground and comparatively little imported compost will be required, though the rule of consistent slant still applies, the choice is far wider, and any of a great variety of rock formation types may be imitated. A pronounced sideways cant of the strata where the foundation thus already exists will often give a very satisfying effect and there is scope for using both hard-edged quarry stone and surface-weathered rocks. The rules referring to the preferred use of local stone still hold good except that, where no building is sited directly to the rear and no natural outcrop is within view, weathered Westmorland and the like can be used quite happily, and will not seem out of place.

Mountain scale rockeries have sometimes been created by removing topsoil from the naturally underlying rocks on a hillside, so that the exposed outcrop which results is natural and truly random in its arrangement. There can be no guarantee, however, that earthworks such as this will be aesthetically pleasing; so much depends on the nature and cant of the exposed rock faces and, indeed, they may lack adequate pockets of soil for planting, and thus prove disappointing on their completion.

Grassy banks may be turned into very beautiful turfed rockeries, using only a modicum of stone – a system closely allied to island bed gardening, and eminently suitable for large areas. Turf, if it already exists, should be left intact, and a very careful sketch plan of the area needs to be made before deciding exactly where to site the outcrops, for mistakes in designing this type of garden are more difficult to rectify, and planning should be restricted to the sketch pad until the designer is quite satisfied.

A common fault in this type of design is over-symmetry and unnecessary uniformity. Outcrops must be of irregular shape and size and unevenly spaced if an artificial effect is to be avoided, but they must nevertheless balance the design as a whole. A few large stones are more effective for this type of formation than numerous small ones, and quite often no more than one, two or three separate outcrops are required. High on the slope there might be a large, prominently jutting outcrop, representing a headland or the tip of an underground formation. Near the observer at the foot of the slope might be sited a smoother protuberance, more mound-shaped, wide but not too high, as though worn down by centuries of scrambling feet. Two-thirds of the way up the bank, perhaps, and to the left of centre, there might be an intermediate outcrop, straight-faced but not deeply protuberant, such as might appear as the result of natural erosion.

While the outline of these rock masses will be angular and erratic, the surrounding turf edge must be smoothly rounded, made to follow the rock contours without being given any sharp angles. Sharp corners in turf tend to give the impression of having only recently been cut, and they will always look artificial. Smoothly rounded, flowing lines, on the other hand, following – but not too slavishly – the vagaries of hard stone, will give an impression of the weathering and mellowing, the gradual formation which has been taking place over a geologically immense time scale.

Planting, of course, may proceed as for continuous rock gardens. In effect, one has created a series of island beds and, like herbaceous islands, these may be extended at will. Simplicity must be the operative principle and, if more outcrops are added, the whole scene can look fussy and affected. If extension is needed, this should be limited to an increase in size of the existing outcrops, maintaining the proportions of the original beds, one island to another.

If the area is not already supporting turf, this can be laid as part of the same operation – after the rocks have been set into place, as it is not a good idea to trample newly laid turf by manoeuvring heavy rocks across it. The turfs should be laid slightly overlapping the actual planned edges of each outcrop, so that they can be cut to shape later, once the new grass has rooted itself firmly. Small pieces of turf set on the edge of an area will be sure to dry out and fail to root, besides which, isolated edges of whole turfs are liable to shrink or turn yellow, and trimming would in any case be needed after it is firmly established. A clean, straight edge cut with an edging tool, leaving a drop of a thumb's length between the surface of the grass and the soil, followed by regular trimming with edging shears, will show each island outcrop always at its best and, representing as it does the closely cropped mountain pastures above the forest line – the transitional zone where continuous vegetation starts to falter and bare rock formations increase – will stress vividly the contrast between mountain and lowland regions.

When turfing is done on a steep bank, each piece will need to be pegged for stability until the roots have had a chance to penetrate and grip, otherwise they will move down the slope when trodden on, or during the initial mowing. Hard twigs make the best pegs – chopped lengths of hazel, perhaps, or the dead lower branches of conifers such as the cypresses. They should be cut into convenient lengths of about 15cm and simply tapped into the ground through the upper edge of each piece of turf. Consolidation on a steep bank should be very firm. It is not always possible to pull a roller in such places, but a heavy rake head or similar tool can be used as a rammer so that the turfs can be thoroughly compacted.

2
Special Sites

Scree and Moraine

In nature, a scree consists of fragments of rock and pebbles that have eroded from the crags and washed downwards to form a skirt; when it has reached an angle of rest that has imparted a degree of stability, it has become colonised by plants adapted to the extremely thorough drainage and the poor supply of nutrients offered by such an immature soil, with little humus other than that deposited by the scree plants themselves.

A moraine, on the other hand, originated when a glacier finally melted after having carved a valley through the rocks, leaving a deposit of rock fragments of all sizes. Moraine plants, therefore, normally have an extensive root system capable of probing through and beneath the upper layer of deposited grit and stones, to reach the underlying soil. In this case, the surface layers alone are excessively well drained and, as the moraine is normally formed on gently sloping land, the constantly replenished trickle of water from melting snow and ice is present at a variable depth throughout the spring and the early part, at least, of the summer. The nutrient supply is usually better than that found in a scree.

Both types of formation can be incorporated into the rock garden, and will extend the range of growable mountain plants so as to include some of the trickiest Alpine subjects. The scree should commence near the highest point, preferably running between two peaks, and be allowed to slope as gently as stability requires to near ground level. The moraine will continue the sweep of this slope, perhaps along the bed of a miniature valley, where the underlying soil can receive all the run-off from rain and artificial watering. The compost mixture can be the same in both cases: 2 pts loam, 2 pts peat, 1 pt sharp sand and 4 pts stone chippings, will prove a satisfactory formula.

The foundations of a scree will need to be excavated – or built into the rockery – and large stones and rubble can be incorporated as a

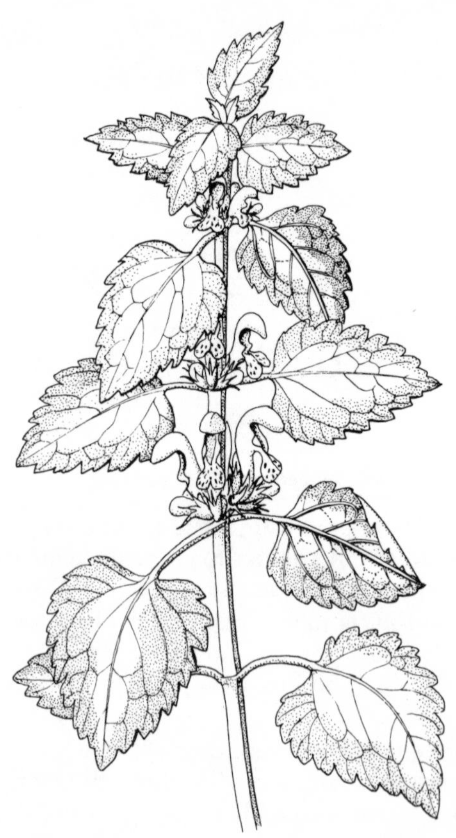

Lamium maculatum—excellent for linking the rockery to a border

drainage base. Inverted turfs are useful as a covering for the drainage material, to prevent the finer compost washing through. The whole scree depth at the finish will be around 75cm, about 50cm of which will consist of coarse drainage material, and 25cm of topping compost. The more specialised screes may be surfaced with pure grit or pea gravel, and this is surprisingly water-retentive – never becoming saturated, but less likely than standard composts ever to dry out completely. Pea gravel is the smallest size of gravel that is washed out in a sand quarry where different grades of sand and gravel are produced. Particles smaller than this constitute sharp sand (often described as concreting sand), and the smallest particle grade is classed as building sand, which feels fine and soft to the touch. Stone chippings consist of crushed rock: a limestone grit will be suitable only for lime-loving plants, and most rock plants enjoy or, at least, tolerate lime. For those that do not, such as the dwarf rhododendrons, a neutral type of stone such as flint or granite should be used.

Pea gravel is a good finishing surface for the moraine also, and in this type of site reasonably sized stones and boulders should be partially buried here and there. The more shapeless of the rockery stones are ideal for this purpose; they may be buried quite deeply, because they provide the perfect environment for many plants which enjoy the moisture retention and solid coolness of underground rock. The method also simulates the natural moraine, where large boulders have been carried by the ice and deposited at random, and imparts a harmonious appearance to the final planting. Ideally, such rocks should be buried to a depth, say, of 30cm, and should project above the surface for about 20cm, for these measurements would provide the optimum shelter, and allow the planting of shade-lovers against their northern faces.

If lime-hating moraine plants are to be used – and many North American plants fall into this category – it is best to plan a separate moraine area incorporating all lime-free materials, making sure that lime cannot wash down into the area from higher slopes, because this is sure to happen if the moraine is sited below a limestone outcrop, or at the base of a scree which contains standard John Innes compost or an alkaline topsoil.

The Raised Bed

This arrangement is a simplified modification of the rockery, and it has the advantage of versatility. It can be constructed on formal or informal lines, to present either an ornamental or a strictly utilitarian appearance. It can make use of whatever material is most easily obtainable: stone, brick, concrete blocks, peat blocks, planks, railway sleepers or rough-hewn logs can all be pressed into service. The raised bed can be adapted to suit any site or aspect, and the type of soil mixture it contains can be varied according to the needs of the plants that are to inhabit it. Its advantages over a ground level bed include freer drainage and ease of maintenance – provided all parts of its surface are readily within reach. To this end, the width of such beds should be limited to around 125cm, half this distance being far enough to reach efficiently when planting, weeding and tending small plants. In height, a raised bed can range from a mere step – to assist the drainage of a ground level scree – to almost waist height.

A dry stone construction for the supporting walls – preferably in the local quarried stone – will be cheaper than timber and probably no dearer overall than mortared concrete blocks; but the finished appearance, especially once the plants are established, will scarcely bear comparison. As with traditional rock gardening, local materials are usually cheapest and best, and, if the basic rock is limestone in character, this will suit the great majority of plants. Other methods, of course, may be preferable in specialised circumstances – a lean-to arrangement along a wall, for instance, and specially constructed frames and benches have been devised to accommodate disabled gardeners.

At ground level, the basal area should receive some preparation. Water must be able to pass freely through this surface, so it must be broken up by digging, and the perennial weeds removed, otherwise ground elder, couch grass, nettles and docks, if they are present, will be forever emerging here and there. The height of the bed is seldom great enough for there to be need of a foundation below the supporting stones, provided these are set slightly into the ground and at a gently backward-sloping angle – enough to allow water to run off them and into the bed area – so that there will be no movement as the soil is added and rammed behind them.

In beds of any depth, ordinary clean topsoil can be used for the basic fill up to the topmost 40cm or so. In the case of brick-built or solid-sided beds, even subsoil can be used, provided it is not too clayey. With a surrounding stone construction, however, especially when plants are to be sited to grow between these stones, good quality loamy garden soil is the best bulk filler to use. It must be added layer by layer as the stones are set into position, and firmly tamped behind and between so as to fill all the crevices. Air pockets would be no less disastrous here than in the rockery, and it is a good idea to spread a thin layer of soil between the stones so that they knit together firmly. This method of construction will, in any case, leave plenty of gaps to be filled with soil from the outside, so that any roots can enjoy a free run. If the stones are reasonably large, a fair proportion of them will be actually resting upon and partly supported by the infill compost, depending on their shape. Unlike a regular wall, the completed face of these supporting stones need not be symmetrical, and the results will resemble a rock garden in effect rather than a dry stone wall. Although they will be as firmly set as rockery stones, however, they should not need to be trampled on, provided every part of the raised bed can be reached comfortably by a person standing at ground level.

One of the more noticeable advantages of using a raised bed as distinct from a rockery in which to grow plants is the comparative ease with which various soil mixtures can be incorporated in its construction, so that all kinds of plants with widely differing requirements can be made to feel at home. In aspect, also, it may face in any or all directions, and offer habitat types ranging from the exposed scree to the sheltered, peaty hollow. A study of plant requirements will suggest that, within the northern hemisphere, acid soil conditions are most appropriate to north-facing beds, and alkaline composts should be provided for south-facers.

For moraine-loving plants in this type of site, provided the beds are not raised above, say, 40cm, a fill of 100 per cent pure pea gravel will provide an excellent growing medium. Pea gravel holds moisture during dry spells more efficiently than ordinary compost, and keeps many difficult subjects happy. It always draws water upwards by capillary action, and the vapour which arises from deep in the soil condenses among the cool pebbles, and remains trapped within the air spaces. This process of distillation means that the water held within pea gravel usually has a neutral pH reaction, and will support both calcifuge and calcicole plants. A dusting of bonemeal in the spring will normally provide all the nourishment necessary. In any case, the topmost 35-40cm should be filled with the appropriate compost. Lime-loving plants in general should be happy in a mixture consisting of 1 pt John Innes compost No 2; 1 pt coarse sand or limestone chippings; and 1 pt peat. For plants which shun limestone, this could be substituted by: 1 pt John Innes lime-free compost; 1 pt coarse peat; and 1 pt coarse sand or granite chippings. A simple pH test should be made if there is any doubt concerning the acidity of the materials.

In practice, provided a good quality loamy topsoil with a slightly acid reaction has been used, the other ingredients can be added in the form of a top-dressing, and worked into the upper levels simply by manoeuvring a garden fork through the mixture. A 5cm thick layer of peat and the same of grit – flint or granite for lime-haters, limestone for the others – lightly forked into a good loam, will give a final mixture at least 20cm deep to include 50 per cent loam, 25 per cent peat and 25 per cent grit, and this mixture will compact as it mixes, so that it will not raise the surface level of the bed by the whole 10cm. It will suffice for all the plants shown in the Table of Rock Plants (page 204) as enjoying a normal soil without other preferences.

If the supporting rock is a limestone of local origin, any chippings used to surface scree beds should preferably be from the same type of stone, as contrasting colours may look odd. Pea gravel too, if this is to be used as a pure surfacing material, should be checked against the rock for colour clashes before use. As pea gravel has been separated from coarse sand by washing, their colours should be closely similar, but sand colour itself varies greatly from quarry to quarry, and this is a point easily overlooked. The only really practical considerations, I suppose, are the size, the sharpness, and the pH reaction of the particles and, to some, they will be the only important factors – but I am a landscape gardener and, to me, the appearance of the completed bed is as important as the performance of the plants. Taste is an individual thing and there can be no sure formula for pleasing the eye, but it can be no bad thing to obtain samples, compare possibilities, and, if necessary, to compromise on the choice of plants.

Troughs and Sinks

The micro-environment of the sink and the rather larger trough gardens can be ideal for growing the smallest and most difficult Alpine plants successfully. They have the added advantage of bringing something of the mountain into the yard or on to the patio or balcony – and often provide the best possible camouflage for manhole covers.

They need rather more attention than raised beds, especially during hot weather, when there is the danger that they may dry out too drastically, and their compost filling should be both well drained and moisture retentive – that apparently contradictory combination. The standard mix of 50 per cent loamy topsoil, 25 per cent leafmould or peat, and 25 per cent sharp sand or grit should be supplemented with a surface of chippings or pea gravel. If lime-loving plants are to be used and the topsoil has an acid reaction, enough hydrated lime should be added to bring the pH up to 7, and, in any case, a sprinkling of bonemeal should be worked into the compost as a slow-release food.

Genuine old stone sinks have a beautiful, mellow appearance, and various methods have been tried to simulate this texture when using sinks made of synthetic materials. Old glazed sinks and troughs can be coated with a stone substitute known as hypertufa, after their surface has been roughened or scored with a hammer and chisel and coated with a concrete bonding agent. Hypertufa can be made by mixing 1 pt cement, 1 pt sphagnum moss peat, and 1 pt sharp concreting sand and, if the finished product is to match the local stone, cement colouring powder can be added – with discretion, for too strong a colour will be worse than none at all. Normally, the gamut of natural rock shades can be reproduced in hypertufa by using different concentrations of just two colours: buff and black. The buff will tint the finished product a pale Cotswold yellow, or a deep sandstone orange, depending on the concentration used – bearing in mind that the basic colour of the sand used in the mixture will also influence the results.

This coating of hypertufa should be as thin as possible – a mere skin a few centimetres thick, varying as it is moulded to resemble real stone – and it sticks best if the dry mix is made just tacky with water, but not too wet, otherwise it will run. There is no need to coat the inside, except for the top part that will show above the soil level.

Sinks can also be made from scratch, using a similar compound and a little ingenuity. A wooden box, or even one of stout cardboard, can be used to mould the outer shape, and a smaller but equally rigid box must be found to fit inside, with an all round clearance of 4 or 5cm. To be strong enough for the finished product to stand knocks, the mixture needs a larger proportion of sharp concreting sand to bind the concrete: 1 pt cement; 1 pt sphagnum moss peat; 3 pts sharp sand; and colouring matter can be added as before. A 5cm thick layer of the wet material is spread over the bottom of the larger box inside, and drainage holes must be built in at this stage. A convenient way of doing this is to cut pieces of the appropriate length from a cardboard tube – the insides of kitchen towel rolls are ideal – and two, three or four of them should be positioned, evenly spaced, leaving them hollow of course, but smoothing the concrete around them so that their height and the level of the mixture correspond. The inner box is now set in place, taking care not to disrupt the bottom layer with its cardboard 'holes', and the concrete mixture is dropped evenly all round. If the boxes are not rigid enough they will start to sag at this stage and, if cardboard ones are used, it is just as well to arrange some kind of bolster inside and out, with enough weight inside the inner box to prevent it riding up and allowing the concrete walls to ooze underneath. It is important not to have too wet a mix and, if it is on the dry side, it can very gently be tamped as the filling proceeds. When filled, the mould should be left a week or more before being turned out.

Finished garden sinks, whether concrete or tufa-coated are, by newly founded tradition, painted with water that rice has been boiled in, so as to provide an attractive surface for moss and algae to colonise, and quickly give them an air of maturity and permanence.

The completed sink, when filled with compost, will need a miniature rock arrangement before planting, and the stone really needs to blend with the sides of the container. One or two fairly large pieces are better than several small ones, and will lend the final planted effect a more serene and satisfying air; a scattering of small stones is liable to give the completed arrangement a fragmented, unsettled appearance. If the hypertufa has been successful and the synthetic sink is satisfactory, it might be convenient to synthesise miniature rock outcrops for it. This artificial rock can be made simply enough with a mixture of 1 pt cement, 1 pt sharp sand, and 2 pts sphagnum moss peat, again remembering that the basic sand colour will influence the final shade, which may be modified with a cement tinting agent. This mixture is wetted to a pastry-like consistency and dropped into a mould, which need be no more than a hole scraped in the ground.

Tufa

Real tufa is a naturally occurring substance, a kind of soft rock that is formed, like stalagmites and stalactites, through the evaporation of calcium-bearing water as it emerges from underground. When newly mined, it has a raw, starkly white appearance, but this soon weathers to a mellow grey, provided the air is not polluted with acid industrial fumes. As with hypertufa, it can be coated with glutinous rice water so as to encourage algae spores to settle and grow. The great advantage it enjoys over ordinary rock lies in its softness and porosity – it can be sawn or worked with other tools, and holes are easily drilled for planting – and its ability to support limestone-loving plants , which are able to root directly into the porous substance. As the chief component of a retaining wall with good topsoil directly behind it, tufa will support both surface-creeping and deep fibrous-rooting plants, and provide a sheltered environment for difficult Alpine subjects. Plants with thick, woody or carroty roots can grow in the crevices, rooted directly into the soil, and the calcicoles among them will enjoy the proximity of pure limestone.

The usual procedure when planting tufa is to drill holes of about 2 or 3cm diameter, sited about 10cm apart, depending on the expected size and spread of the subjects. An ordinary hand drill can be used, and the bit should be directed on a downward slant so as to retain soil and water. Small plants can then be inserted, and sandy soil worked among the roots and watered well in. The roots soon penetrate the porous tufa and enter the backing soil. The substance is very retentive of water, and artificial watering is necessary only in very dry weather, when the whole arrangement may be given a soak with a garden sprinkler for several hours.

Small pieces of tufa are excellent for simulating outcrops in miniature sink gardens, and large pieces may, of course, be used as free-standing rockery stones, but they are very expensive. A modestly sized tufa outcrop with a backing of soil makes a very fine Alpine feature for a corner of the patio, however, and offers a means whereby mountain plants can be made to grow and thrive happily without the necessity of a large garden to support them.

Walls

A wall which has become colonised by plants is, in effect, a rock face which chances to have an abundance of root-supporting crevices. Plant-supporting walls need not necessarily be of dry construction: old mortared walls frequently offer a secure home for lime-loving plants and, in wet climates at least, immigrant plants which require an extra sharp drainage at their roots may well be able to grow only on such structures. Plants such as lavender and rosemary, when planted in northern climes, are much longer lived when sited on a wall, and semi-hardy ones such as the maidenhair fern and many southern plants are able to thrive in this environment. Wallflowers and snap-dragons which have run wild are never so healthy and attractive as when able to seed themselves freely year after year on some wall.

A south-facing wall in the north temperate zones can have a microclimate nearer to the Mediterranean than the North Atlantic, and plants from the southern European countries, from the Middle East and eastern Europe, as well as the drier parts of South America and the western United States, will be able to survive on it. A north-facing wall duplicates the conditions found in stony woodland shade, and satisfies those many plants from Europe, Asia and North America that thrive in such a habitat. A west-facing wall resembles in many respects the woodland edge, with its indirect sunlight and moist pockets of soil, and suits such marginal plants as the violas and several euphorbias. An east-facing wall, on the other hand, presents extreme contrasts between summer and winter, with rapid temperature changes as the sun rises each morning; in this respect it resembles the steppe-like country of much of Asia, and makes a comfortable home for many hardy shrubs and bulbs that inhabit those regions.

Although old free-standing walls frequently accommodate plants, their roots running through the old mortar and grime between the stones or bricks, a newly built wall cannot be expected to do this. Retaining walls, on the other hand – walls which in effect lean-to against a bank of earth – may be planted immediately, and provide the type of environment many plants crave. Stone retaining walls for planting are normally constructed where banks are being cut back to widen driveways, extend gardens or make way for new buildings and, when earth is being dug out for this purpose, the excavation should be taken at least half a metre beyond the proposed line of the wall face. This will allow room not only for the stones, but also for the fill to be rammed behind each piece; if there is not enough room, this job can never be done satisfactorily, and all sorts of problems are liable to arise. The wall will need a gentle batter or back-slope, especially if it is of dry construction, and allowance in the excavation should also be made for this. It is usually advisable to telephone the appropriate local Electricity and Water Boards when initial excavation is being done by hired machine, so that they can check their plans for underground pipes and cables before the work commences. If these hidden supply lines exist, they must be uncovered by hand and made clearly visible, to avoid expensive accidents.

Surplus subsoil may need to be carted off the site, but there should always be plenty left to complete the job of infilling behind the wall, and the soil intended for this purpose should if possible be piled on the bank behind the excavation, ready to be shovelled straight in as the work progresses. This excavated soil can be replaced behind the wall unless it is of very poor quality, in which case a good fertile topsoil must be used—or a mixture of 2 pts loamy soil to 1 pt peat and 1 pt chippings, limestone or granite depending on the plant preferences.

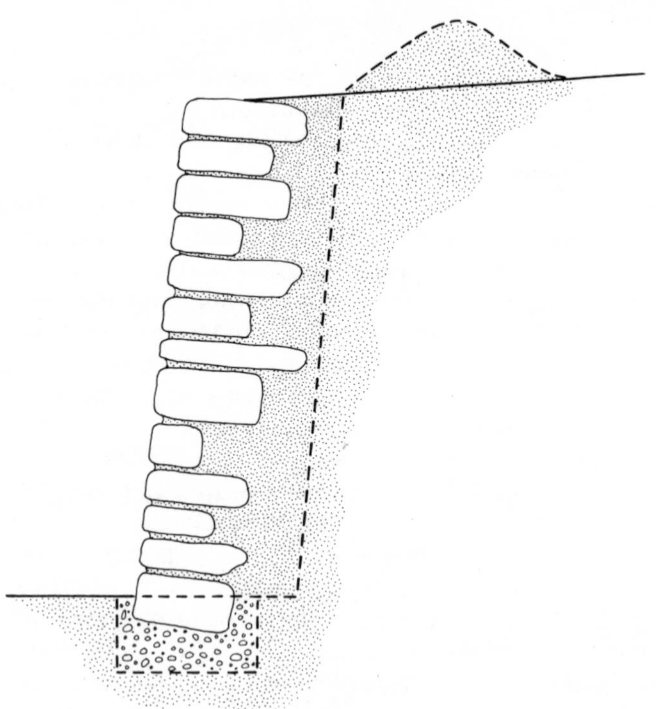

A retaining wall in section. The broken line shows the initial excavation and the soil retained for filling behind the wall. The lowest course has been set into concrete

Whatever the basic type of rock, the stone to be used is called walling stone, and consists of roughly quarried pieces which have a flat stratum and at least one reasonably flat face. When the wall is to have only a single face – a retaining, rather than a free-standing wall – one can estimate the amount of stone required by the formula: 10sq m of wall face to 4 tonnes of rock or, to use Imperial measure, 1 ton of stone to give 30sq ft of retaining wall.

Dry stone walls are best limited in height to one and a half metres, and, if kept below this limit, they should rarely need concrete foundations, provided the ground beneath them is solid. As a general rule, the largest stones are used for the lowest course, and these must be dug in a little way and given a slight backward slope, so as to bed them in firmly and at the same time set the angle of stability for the whole wall. If the ground is not firm, or the wall is to be mortared, or a greater height is needed, foundations should be provided: a strip 60cm wide should be dug out to a depth of about 20cm, and filled with a concrete mixture consisting of about 4 pts gravel, 2 pts sharp sand and 1 pt cement, and the lowest course of stones can be set in place while this concrete is still wet. If a retaining wall is to be mortared, whether spaces for plants are left or not, drainage holes should be built in near ground level.

In the majority of cases, a dry construction will be perfectly adequate for garden walls which back on to an earth bank, and the finished dry wall lends itself to colonisation by plants far more willingly than a mortared one. It is not normal practice to bed each stone on soil; every piece should sit firmly on the stones beneath, and several might be tried and rejected before the right one is found. The builder should stand in front of the wall line, even if there is room to stand behind it, and must check with his eye the alignment of each piece along the wall length, as the work progresses. Joins should never occur directly above other joins but must be offset in exactly the same way that bricks are offset, otherwise lines of weakness will be inbuilt, and the wall will never be firm. As each course is laid, soil should be shovelled in at the back and firmly rammed into every crevice, taking care not to disturb the stones. Periodically, suitably shaped pieces should be laid so that they extend inwards and key themselves firmly into the soil. It is as well to avoid the temptation to use up all the best shaped pieces first; the finished wall will look better, and the job of building it will go more smoothly, if they are distributed evenly throughout the structure, once the heaviest pieces have gone into the initial courses.

If the nature of the stone is such that adequate planting spaces are occurring automatically – sharp-edged stone tends to close up too neatly for this purpose – planting can perfectly well be carried out at any time after the wall is finished. If, on the other hand, the spaces are going to be too tight to get the plants in their places, the job must be done as building proceeds. With pot-grown plants especially, it might be advisable to do this, laying them in place as each course is completed and covering the rootball so that it makes unbroken contact with the backing soil. If the subsoil is being replaced, this method presents an opportunity to incorporate pockets of fertile planting medium where required. With most natural materials it is rarely necessary to leave obvious gaps for planting, as small plants can quite easily be manoeuvred into place, and planting compost introduced with the aid of a trowel and a stick. A lot depends also on whether the new plants are available at the time the wall is being built, and whether the person building the wall has a feeling for plants, as well as stone.

Paving

The paved area can offer a plant environment similar to the dry stone wall, and dwarf creeping plants, small enough not to trip anybody up, can often be seen at their best among paving stones. Plants such as the thymes and some veronicas, *Cotula squalida, Bellium minutum, Lippia canescens* and *Micromeria varia* might not be considered showy enough for a rock garden place of their own, but they will look charming underfoot. Others, such as the dwarf creeping heather Foxhole Wanderer and the cushion-forming Foxii Nana, can actually be used as path surfacing themselves, and may be mown annually like grass to produce a close, tough sward.

Most rockeries need a path to ensure that every part of them can be reached without having to trample over planted areas, and crazy paved paths usually look right in a rock garden. Care should be taken to see that the paving material does not clash with the rockery stones. Sometimes, the same stone may be used for the purpose, particularly if the source is a local quarry and the price is not prohibitive; a natural stone surface will inevitably be a little rough, but it will look right, especially if the sand used with the mortar mix is of an appropriate colour. Ordinary broken concrete paving slabs have a neutral shade which matches most materials, but some of the manufactured tinted and textured slabs can be chosen to match the stone perfectly. It may seem odd to buy sound slabs, only to smash them up for crazy paving. I have done it many times, and probably drawn a few wry glances but, if the effect is a planned one, there will be no anomaly, and the cost of the materials will be no more than for a formal path.

It is normal practice to lay crazy paving on sand, and to mortar the joints. These may be trowelled smooth and pointed, or the mortar may simply be 'dolloped' in and left rounded, so that the pattern of joins will stand proud of the paving surface – an especially suitable method if actual stone, or a roughly textured type of slab has been used. Alternatively, a dry mix consisting of 1 pt cement and 2 pts building sand can be swept into the joints and left to harden slowly; planting pockets are left where required, and may conveniently be filled with straight sand until planting time.

Crazy paving never looks right unless the joints are more or less equal in width. About 3 or 4cm apart should be the rule for every piece and, if the end product is to look informally haphazard, every piece of paving should match the space it is set into. If there are varying widths, and if square pieces are set into triangular spaces and so on, the completed path will have an artificially contrived appearance that will never match the rockery.

As a precaution against weeds penetrating the mortar, polythene – conveniently in the form of old fertilizer bags that have been opened out – can be laid along the path route beneath the sand. As a labour-saving gimmick, paths can even be laid across turf or weedy areas without initial excavation, by using this method. Planting spaces will

(Above) Silene acaulis, the moss campion, flowers best in a poor, gritty soil.
(Below) Saxifraga oppositifolia is found over much of the northern hemisphere

(Above) Saxifraga burseriana, an Alpine parent of many hybrids. *(Below) Saxifraga caesia* is neat enough for the trough garden

then have to be cut out of the polythene as required; but, if there are weeds underneath, the sheets will have to lie undisturbed for at least a full season before planting can take place, otherwise unwanted plants will grow through the holes. A path which has been laid on polythene like this will not drain readily if there are any hollows but, if puddling occurs, it is a simple matter to make a fresh planting spot at the lowest point of the hollow – by removing a piece of slab and cutting the polythene – and this will act as a drain.

There are numerous ways of making paths, of course, and a wide range of paving materials can be used; but a well laid path of appropriately coloured and textured crazy paving goes so naturally with the outcrops and strata of the matured rock garden, being a favoured rock plant habitat, and adaptable to hills and bends, that I personally would be content with nothing less.

3
Alpine Europe

All the high mountains of Europe are classified as Alpine. The Swiss Alps themselves represent a meeting point of plant types from central, western and eastern Europe and from the Mediterranean, and they have also a distinctive Alpine flora of their own. In botanical terms, the Pyrenees are closely related to the Alps: on their western slopes they experience a high rainfall, and the plants found there and to their north resemble those that occur in central Europe; to their east, the rainfall is low, and the plants are largely Mediterranean in character.

On all the high European mountains, the true Alpine plants have their stronghold in the area that lies between the altitudinal tree limit and the high, permanently snowbound regions. Perhaps they are plants which flourished over a wide range at a time when the glaciers were receding as the last Ice Age drew to a close. Adapted to exposed sites and the sun's glare, such plants would find it difficult to contend with the shade, the crowding, and the heavy humus deposits characteristic of the new forests which appeared and expanded as the climate meliorated. While some followed the ice sheets north, others must have retreated to the higher mountain slopes ahead of the advancing forests, and hold their own now above the high Alpine meadows.

Arctic and Alpine plants are often closely related, but their characteristics usually vary sufficiently to reflect the nature of their habitat, for, over many generations, slight changes have taken place to enable them to cope with conditions which, though they may appear superficially to be similar, are, in fact, very different. Arctic plants are adapted to a wet-cold climate with long, dark winters. Alpine plants have adjusted themselves to face dry-cold, intense light, and sudden extremes of temperature, an adaptation which often shows itself in the compact, mossy, cushion-like habit of growth that we see in *Androsace* and *Petrocallis.* Plants which are found in both the northern and the Alpine zones are often the easiest to please in the rock garden: some of the dwarf willows and junipers, silene, dryas, and many saxifrages fit into this category, as do some primulas such as *Primula farinosa,* which confines itself to the moist Alpine meadows and similar northern sites, and could not survive on the extreme higher slopes.

It is easy to appreciate some of the difficulties that arise when trying to grow cold-climate plants in more temperate zones. Far northern plants tend to undergo a long period of dormancy, and are stirred into activity when a certain surrounding temperature is reached. When transplanted further south, the same plants will wake up at the first mild spell of spring – only to be frosted, and perhaps killed, as winter weather closes in again. Alpine plants are able to lie dormant beneath a deep covering of snow which keeps them dry and free of frost, for what would at a lower altitude have been autumn rain has fallen as snow, so that the ground is not saturated. When spring arrives, the melting snow provides a never-failing and copious supply of water during those crucial early weeks of intense growth activity – water, moreover, that can drain freely into the gritty mountain soil, and be replenished daily as the summer develops. Alpine plants, then, experience a moist spring and summer on a site which dries out for the autumn and remains dry all winter. Small wonder that some Alpine subjects are considered difficult for, when transplanted to lower altitudes, they are liable to face saturated conditions all winter, followed by erratic rainfall or downright drought during the spring and early summer.

Among the dwarf willows that are found both on these high European mountains and on comparable sites in North America, in Scotland, and the far north, one of the commonest is *Salix herbacea*, a tiny creeping shrub which forms closely woven twiggy mats – quite ornamental with its glossy, rounded leaves in the summer and little buff catkins in the spring. Another mountain willow with a similar distribution is *S. reticulata*, which forms larger, denser mats. The hybrid *S.* ×*finnmarchica* occurs in many north European mountains, while the tiny-leaved *S. myrsinites* has a much wider distribution over uplands thoughout the north, and can scarcely qualify for the description 'Alpine'. The wide-carpeting *S. retusa*, on the other hand, though found on many high European mountains, does not occur in the Arctic, whilst *S. glaucosericea*, which has a covering of silky grey hairs that protect the young leaves in the spring, is easily grown in northern gardens. It makes an attractive rockery shrub, and is truly Alpine.

The dwarf buckthorn *Rhamnus pumila* is a tiny shrub of the high rock crevices, useful for its ornamental black berries in the autumn, and these can be used for propagation. Any shrub which creeps, and roots as it spreads, can be divided, of course, but the willows also take very readily from cuttings, and often a few twigs thrust together into the ground during the autumn will result in a healthy new plant for the following season.

A herb with a very wide natural range, both Alpine and Arctic, is the moss campion *Silene acaulis* – an easy plant to grow on the moraine, forming a 5cm high tufted cushion of tiny, bright green leaves, sprinkled with bright pink, notch-petalled flowers over a long season from June to August. It is usually more floriferous in the wild than it is in gardens, and some authorities claim that a poor, gritty soil produces the best flowering plants, provided the moisture supply is adequate during spring and summer. It is a fact that any plant, from a carpeting herb to a tree, will often attempt to produce seed by flowering more freely during times of hardship, so that, even if the individual plant should die, the survival of the species will be ensured. Besides growing readily from seed, silene may be propagated either by dividing the cushions and replanting the best pieces, or by taking soft shoot cuttings in the spring.

Cuttings of the moss campion and many other Alpine plants can be rooted without any special apparatus, using a clay pot completely enclosed in a polythene bag. A compost made up of John Innes No 1 and horticultural vermiculite, in equal parts, will provide the right balance of moisture retention, drainage, and temporary food supply, and the clay pot containing this should be given a thorough soaking and allowed to drain before the cuttings are inserted. Soft cuttings must not be allowed to touch one another before they have taken root, neither should they touch the polythene bag, which is kept wide and firm with about four pieces of cane inserted round the side of the pot. An arrangement of looped wire can be used equally well, but the water as it condenses on the inside of the bag must be allowed to trickle down and re-enter the compost and, to ensure this, the supporting canes are best sited inside the pot, with an elastic band holding the polythene closely in place. The whole pot is then placed on a windowsill – a north-facing aspect will probably be best, as it must not be allowed to overheat in the sun. There is no limit to the number of cuttings that may be set in one pot, but, as soon as growth starts – normally an indication that rooting has taken place – they should be removed and potted into their own individual containers. At this stage, a garden frame is the best place to keep them until they are large enough to plant out on the rock garden, allowing them by degrees to become accustomed to the open air.

Saxifraga is a vast genus of plants, and the two species *oppositifolia* and *aizoides* are relatively easy to please on the rock garden, for they are found not only in the high Alps, but also on rocky sites over much of the northern hemisphere as far north as the Arctic. Understandably, they have both given rise to several geographical and local variations, chiefly in flower colour. Typically, *S. aizoides* makes fairly low mats of tufty, interwoven stems bearing crowded, narrow, pea green leaves and small clusters of orange or yellow flowers in June and July. The stems also lie flat to make a mat in the case of *S. oppositifolia*, with tiny, odd-shaped leaves and pretty little solitary flowers, purple, red or pink, which appear in the early spring. It has been claimed that the best garden forms come from limestone areas, although both species occur naturally on many different kinds of rock.

More locally Alpine are the *Saxifraga* species *androsacea*, *burseriana* and *cuneifolia*. The first makes dense tufts of flatly rosetted leaves, and grows closely huddled into moist crevices beneath overhanging rocks where it finds shelter, if not shade, and sends out short stems of comparatively large bluish-white flowers in June and July. Enjoying similar conditions is *S. cuneifolia*, the parent of many varieties and hybrids. One of its local variations is found in the same mountains but lower down the slope, below the tree-line, where it chooses a mossy spot among the rocks beneath light shade. Typically, the species produces mats of rounded, healthily green leaves reminiscent of London Pride, and bears masses of dainty little white flowers, each petal with a yellow blotch at its base, which gives the whole plant a creamy appearance in late spring. From the limestone peaks of the eastern Alps, *S. burseriana* is also a parent of many hybrids, some of which are common garden plants as it adapts itself well to varied lowland conditions. Eventually, it makes large, compact cushions of tiny, silver, spine-tipped leaves arranged in crowded rosettes, from which spring short, reddish stems bearing the comparatively large white flowers. In some of its named forms the flowers have a soft yellow tone. The compactness of its silver cushions and the quality of its flowers make this plant a useful trough subject, though it will soon outgrow the average sink garden. Typical of the kabschia section of the genus – often claimed to be the most decorative kind of saxifrage – *S. burseriana* is best propagated by means of small cuttings removed from the edges of the cushions in the spring and given the polythene bag treatment, although on such neat plants as these, too drastic removal of cutting material will mar the appearance of the cushions.

Also from the kabschia section, *Saxifraga caesia* is a species found in both the Alps and the Pyrenees, and this also is neat and low enough for the trough garden, with its tiny leaf rosettes and small clusters of round, white flowers in May and June. In nature it favours deep crevices in the rock, where it makes tight little hummocks of greyish lichen-green. More locally distributed in the southern Alps, *S. cochlearis* builds silver-encrusted mounds of closely arranged rosettes, with pleasant little starry white flowers on red stems. It, too, is found in deep crevices of the rock, and is not averse to a shady or north-facing site in the rock garden.

Saxifrages found exclusively in the Pyrenees include *S. aspera*, *S. longifolia*, *S. geranioides* and the natural hybrid *S.* ×*geum*. The last-named is a plant of the London Pride group and is as easy to grow, forming extensive mats of rounded, long stalked, leathery leaves, usually tinged red underneath and arranged in loose rosettes, with a drift of dainty little red-spotted white flowers in the early summer. Like the London Pride itself, *S.* ×*geum* loves moist, shady places, and has no special preference with regard to soil mixtures. The silver-encrusted *S. longifolia* forms broad rosettes of long, fleshy leaves; a plant only for the larger crevices between rocks, because the flowering stems with their dense clusters of white flowers in June and July are rather tall and bulky. Its selected variety Tumbling Waters has been highly acclaimed as a wall plant. The greyish-white rosettes die after flowering, but the plant survives by sending out small offsets to provide the next season's display. From the mossy saxifrage section, a typical Pyrenean plant is *S. geranioides*, with daintily cut, fragrant leaves, and clusters of white flowers in the early summer.

The numerous cultivated varieties of mossy saxifrage are of very mixed origin, and they are usually easy to grow in garden surroundings, given a cool, moist, slightly limy soil and a lightly shaded site, such as they might find in a rocky, north-facing habitat. Their mountain ancestry suits them admirably for life between paving stones, to clothe dry stone walls, or to soften the hard outline of concrete steps. All the varieties flower between April and July, when they become sheeted with colour – but they are ornamental at other seasons too, with their flat mats or low mounds of finely cut mossy foliage. Among the crimson-flowered varieties, outstanding are: Ballawley Guardsman; Dubarry, very late flowering; Four Winds; Gnome, very late flowering; Peter Pan, dwarf; Pompadour; Sanguinea Superba; and Triumph. Among the scarlets are: Mrs Piper; and Red Admiral. Among the pinks are: Diana; Gaiety; Pixie, dwarf; and Winston Churchill. Carmine-flowered varieties include: Carnival; and Elf, very dwarf. White-flowered varieties include: Bob Hawkins, which has variegated foliage; James Bremner, very tall and robust; Pearly King, dwarf; and Stansfieldii. Flowers of Sulphur is a unique pale yellow. These saxifrages may be thought of, perhaps, as the moist-shade counterparts of the Alpine phloxes, and many of them are very useful for the deeply shaded retaining wall where suitable, attractive plants are rare. It is interesting to grow mossy saxifrages from seed: new plants will probably be no better than existing hybrids, and may be inferior, but there is always the chance of producing one worthy of a name. Old mats of foliage tend to become brown in the centre and, when dividing plants for new planting stock, these oldest, central parts should be discarded.

Leontopodium alpinum

Edelweiss – the Swiss national flower – is a typically Alpine plant, but geographical forms and closely related species are to be found on mountains in eastern Europe, in the Siberian steppes, and on the Himalayas. *Leontopodium alpinum* has grey woolly leaves, and flowers which are composed mainly of clustered bracts, for the flower-heads themselves are tiny. In spite of its mountain origin, it is very easy to grow in the garden, needing only a well drained sandy or gritty soil and an open position. Edelweiss is usually grown from seed and, following hot, dry summers, this is produced plentifully. Damp summers sometimes inhibit seed production, however, and when this happens, to increase the stock the plants may be lifted and divided early the following spring.

A Mediterranean plant which has found its way to the top of the Alps is *Globularia cordifolia*, which makes a flat mat of woody stems set with dark green rosetted leaves, very pretty from June to August when decorated with little blue balls of clustered flowers. It does best in a fairly dry, slightly limy soil in full sunshine, and may be propagated by division. Another which has climbed the Alps from the coast is the mountain toadflax, *Linaria alpina*, a pretty little trailing plant with miniature snapdragon flowers in violet with a honey-coloured centre, scattered among the pointed, greyish green leaves, and open throughout the summer and well into autumn. It enjoys a dry, sunny spot and is good on a wall, where it is not so rampageous as the common ivy-leaved toadflax, but is quite as easily grown and, like that species, may be divided in the spring.

A few houseleeks are limited to the high Alps and Pyrenees, and probably the best known of this very large and widespread genus is the cobweb houseleek, *Sempervivum arachnoideum*, so popular as a house plant in its numerous closely similar forms. All are very handsome, with their cobwebby, reddish leaves in tight rosettes, and stoutly stemmed, bright rose-red, starry flowers. Limited to the Swiss Alps, the slightly unpleasant smelling *S. grandiflorum* has huge, dull green rosettes and a large cluster of creamy yellow, purple-stained flowers opening in June. A rather similar local Alpine species is *S. wulfenii*, later to flower, and others of the genus found mainly in the eastern Alps include: *S. dolomiticum*, with tiny, fleshy rosettes of bright green, each leaf tipped with red and coated with sparse white hairs, producing drooping clusters of little purple-tipped white flowers; the closely related *Jovibarba hirta* with rosettes of sharp-pointed, brown-tipped leaves, and pale yellow flower clusters opening in August; and *S. kosaninii*, which has dull reddish purple flowers opening in July, a species also found in the Hungarian mountains. All these mountain houseleeks like to inhabit small clefts and holes in the rocks where the soil, though meagre, has been enriched with generations of rotted-down sempervivum leaves and stems. To keep them happy in the garden, their growing medium should consist of grit, plus a generous proportion of leafmould or other soil of plant origin. Propagation is usually a simple matter of separating the newly developing rosettes which appear around the base of the old ones, but sempervivums may be grown quite easily from seed, although the resulting offspring will not always be true to type.

Visitors to the Swiss Alps will know that the famous Alpine rose is in fact a rhododendron, and there are two species which bear this name: *Rhododendron ferrugineum* is a densely foliaged evergreen whose small, glossy leaves are coated with golden-brown scales. It produces clusters of tiny, deep scarlet-rose flowers from July to August, about a month later than the closely similar *R. hirsutum*, though the actual flowering season depends on altitude and exposure. Like most rhododendrons, the former species needs an acid soil and will not grow where lime is present, although occasionally when an acid humus has built up over a limestone base, the shallow roots of these shrubs will

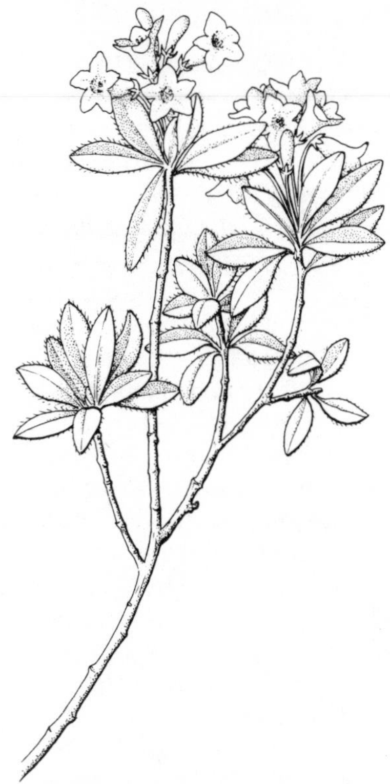

Rhododendron hirsutum

enable them to survive in the surface layers. *R. hirsutum*, on the other hand, prefers to grow in limestone areas.

Two fescue grasses typical of the high summer pastures are *Festuca alpina*, which makes low, non-invasive tufts of bright green, and *F. glacialis* – not limited to the Alps, but found on many high European mountains – which forms equally well behaved tufts of bluish green. It is not to everyone's taste to include plain grass in the rock garden, but there are many situations which call for this choice: a narrow drift of dwarf fine-leaved grass is excellent to delineate groups of mat-forming Alpines which might otherwise, once the flowering season has passed, prove too uninterestingly uniform.

A dry-slope plant that enjoys gritty, well drained conditions is the little mountain poppy, *Papaver alpinum*, a perennial, but best treated as an annual and grown afresh from seed each year, as it tends to be short lived. If the site is to its liking, it will seed itself regularly, and makes a pretty drift of white, pink or yellow flowers. There are several strains with distinct flower colours, and the variety *P.a.* Kerneri has larger, yellow flowers. Other typical plants of the dry slopes are the rock jessamines of the genus *Androsace*, allied to the primulas and producing somewhat similar flower clusters. The high European mountain species include *Androsace villosa*, a tufted plant whose overlapping leaves are arranged in rosettes and densely covered with white hair, and which bears fragrant little white or pink, yellow-eyed flowers in May. *A. pyrenaica*, limited to the Pyrenees, is another fairly easy to please little plant, which enjoys gritty soil in a sunny site and forms dense tufts of narrow, felted leaves, green in the spring but darkening as the season progresses, to a dark brown. It is well covered with tiny white, yellow-eyed flowers over a long summer season. A natural hybrid which occurs in the Austrian Alps is *A.* × *aretioides*, a rosetted, tufted plant bearing numerous short-stemmed pink flowers in the spring. Petite and well behaved enough for the trough garden, this hybrid prefers a gritty, lime-free soil, but the slightly larger *A. hausmanii* – almost as neat and equally pretty when in flower – is from the Austrian limestone mountains, and prefers lime. It is often possible to grow these species from seed and, in the case of *A. pyrenaica*, this is the only practical method. As an alternative for the others, the outside leaf rosettes may be removed as soon as flowering is finished and rooted under a polythene bag, or in a shaded frame.

Also neat and miniature enough for the sink garden is *Minuartia verna*, which makes a rounded mat of densly arranged bluish-green leaves, sprinkled in the spring with loose clusters of tiny white flowers. It occurs over a wide northern range, and has been recorded on British mountains, so it is in no way a truly Alpine plant, but it appreciates dry-winter scree conditions.

Cerastium uniflorum is an Alpine relative of the familiar snow-in-summer, *C. tomentosum*, and is much better behaved than that vigorous plant for a sunny spot high on the scree. It has tufts of bright grass-green, rounded leaves, sprinkled in July with 2.5cm wide white flowers. It is as easily increased as *C. tomentosum* by division or seed, or by summer cuttings. Another easy scree plant from the high Alps and Pyrenees is *Chrysanthemum alpinum*, which makes tufts of finely cut leaves with 3cm wide golden-eyed white daises in July and August. It is best increased by seed.

The Alpine gentians have a somewhat varied range. *Gentiana alpina* itself occurs in the Swiss mountains and the Pyrenees – a moraine plant, whose neat little rosettes of leathery leaves frame the gloriously deep blue, trumpet-shaped flowers in July. It is not as temperamental as some gentians, but nevertheless *A. alpina* needs care; division, when needed, should be carried out just as the plant is starting into new growth in the early spring, and the pieces replanted with as little root disturbance as possible. The same care needs to be accorded *G. angustifolia* from the western Alps, which flowers with clear sky-blue trumpets at the same time as *G. alpina*.

The rock beauty, *Petrocallis pyrenaica*, is not limited to the Pyrenees as the specific name might imply, but occurs also in the Swiss, French and Italian Alps, where it makes a densely tufted , close cushion up to 30cm wide, the little leaves sometimes hidden in May under a drift of tiny, fragrant, mauve or white flowers. It is more likely to succeed in pure grit than in ordinary garden soil, and is very much a plant for the high, sunny scree. Little tufts can quite easily be removed from the cushion's edge in late summer and early autumn, without disturbing the main rooting system, and these, though they may have a few roots attached, should be treated as cuttings and set in a sandy, gritty compost to develop.

The Alpine pennycress, *Thlaspi rotundifolium*, is a plant of the high scree tending towards moraine, and needs plenty of moisture in the spring and summer, for it roots deeply and spreads by underground stems, producing tufts of bright green, circular, waxy leaves and numerous flat clusters of fragrant carmine flowers in the spring. This pennycress sets seed readily in tiny, flat pods, but it may also be raised from shoot cuttings in the spring. Enjoying similar conditions, with a tendency to seek the permanent, deep-lying moisture supplied by the moraine, the prostrate *Spiraea lancifolia* is a downy little shrub that trails very pretty, loose clusters of tiny white flowers in June; a useful plant for the lower slopes. These trailing shoots can be layered in the spring or, alternatively, cuttings may be taken in late summer. Another creeping shrub of the southern Alps is *Anthyllis montana*, which forms a barely ankle-high carpet of tiny, pointed, silky-hairy leaves which give the whole plant a silvery appearance, very pretty in early summer when bearing its numerous round clusters of tiny pink flowers. The varieties *A.m.* Carminea with bright ruby red, and *A.m.* Rubra with deep rose flowers, are both improvements on the type. They are not difficult to grow, and relish an open, sunny spot in a well drained soil. Widespread throughout the southern Alps is a useful trailing plant of the sandwort genus, *Arenaria montana*, not limited to the high peaks but found also on the edges of the mountain forest, where it cascades over mossy rocks with trails of narrow, blue-green leaves, laden in May and June with comparatively large white flowers. It also is an easy plant to grow under normal garden conditions, and may be propagated by simple division.

A dwarf ericaceous shrub, *Rhodothamnus chamaecistus*, looks like a tiny rhododendron with its neat sprays of dark green foliage and bright pink flower clusters in April and May, and its compact, tufted habit enables it to be used in place of some of the dwarf rhododendrons for a sunny cleft in the rock.

One of the prettiest summer flowers of the southern Alps is *Aster alpinus*, which forms spreading tufts of pointed leaves like a

Michaelmas daisy, and is just as easy to divide. Typically it has 4cm wide bright purple flowers in July but, after centuries of cultivation in lowland gardens, several varieties have been selected over the years for the colour and size of their flowers. In bloom at the same time is the mountain pink *Dianthus alpinus*, from the Austrian Alps, and this makes bright green mats of finely arranged foliage with large, fairly short-stemmed but broad-petalled flowers ranging from pale rose to a deep purplish red. The flowers are disappointing in having no scent but, otherwise, this is one of the best of the wild dianthus species, and is comparatively easy to grow high on a moraine or low on a scree, with a good proportion of both leafmould and grit in the soil.

The narrow-leaved gypsophilas are related to dianthus, and the relationship is plain in the case of *Gypsophila repens*, with its large radiating tuft of sea-green leaves, and the small pink or white flowers which appear over a long season from June to August. In nature, it inhabits damp slopes overlying loose limestone bedrock into which its roots can penetrate deeply and, as with other damp-slope Alpines, it is easy to grow provided there is lime in the soil. Cultivated gypsophilas are by tradition given a proportion of old mortar rubble or brick dust in their growing medium, and this type of mixture will usually please *G. repens*, provided the soil is deep enough to accommodate the long, heavy roots. Cuttings may be taken at any time between April and September, and seed is usually set plentifully and germinates without difficulty.

Occasionally, closely related plants that prefer varying degrees of moisture may occur on the same mountain, but inhabiting different slopes. Most of the rock jessamines enjoy dry scree conditions, but one which appreciates a damp moraine is *Androsace carnea*, a densely tufted little plant with leaves similar to the moss phloxes, easy to grow in ordinary garden soils and situations, provided the spring moisture is adequate. It bears little clusters of pretty pink flowers in the spring, but there are several forms and hybrids which have flowers ranging from white to a rich rosy crimson.

Alpine plants from the damp slopes tend to be easier to grow in garden conditions than scree plants, but an exception to prove the rule is *Geum reptans*, the creeping mountain avens, with compound, toothed leaves in rosettes, rooting as it spreads in the manner of a strawberry. The 3cm flowers of a rich golden yellow are produced in July and August, at which season they must rank among the most striking of these high mountain plants. Its need for copious moisture coupled with thorough drainage makes this plant difficult to keep, and it has often been grown in pure grit, which usually tends to hold moisture more efficiently than humus-rich soil, but very good results have also been obtained by using a compost consisting of very coarse grit plus well rotted leafmould, such as might suit the more temperamental houseleeks. Once the plant is well established, propagation is no problem, as the rooted runners can simply be removed or layered direct into countersunk pots, and it usually grows willingly from seed.

The Alpine buttercups are easier moraine plants to please, including *Ranunculus montanus* with bright yellow flowers, and the white-flowered *R. amplexicaulis* and *R. alpestris*. Given an open, sunny site and a deep, moist, gritty compost – the richer the better – they will grow luxuriantly, producing neat tufts of bright green leaves and flowers which open in succession from March through till August. The best for general garden use is the variable *R. montanus* – there are several forms with selected flower structure – which will happily fill in between plants in the average border. For propagation, rooted pieces can usually be teased from the main plant, and it will also grow fairly well from seed.

Alpine meadows often have a strong accumulation of lime in their gritty soil, especially when the peaks above them are of limestone, and their comparative flatness means that they seldom dry out to the extent of scree formations. *Pulsatilla alpina*, a mountain 'anemone', is at home in such a site, and a limy moraine offers the best chance of success for this beautiful plant. The flowers, which open in May as the snow melts, are erect, almost tulip-like in stature, 6 or 7cm across the mouth, and pure white or sometimes flushed with purple. As they fade,

Pulsatilla vernalis

they are followed by attractive, fluffy seedheads. As with others of the genus, the tufted feathery foliage is rather similar to some of the anemones in general appearance. Of wider distribution, easier to grow and safer to transplant is the lady of the snow, *Pulsatilla vernalis*, a smaller plant with broadly bell-shaped, golden-centred white flowers, sometimes tinted on the outside with purple, and opening in April. Unlike *P. alpina*, *P. vernalis* keeps its green leaves throughout the winter, and the whole plant has a silky, downy appearance. The pulsatillas are normally grown from seed, and this is frequently the only effective method of propagating *P. vernalis*.

The Alpine soapwort, *Saponaria ocymoides*, is one of the most useful of general purpose rock plants, and seems quite as happy when trailing its bright green leafy stems over suburban rocks as it does at home in the high Alps and Pyrenees. With its very pretty pink flower clusters in the summer, this is an excellent subject for the dry stone wall. Selected forms and hybrids between this and other mountain soapworts include *S.* Olivana, which spreads less vigorously than *S. ocymoides* but has slightly larger pink flowers, and the very floriferous *S.* Bressingham Hybrid. The latter is as easy-going as *S. ocymoides* itself, but *S.* Olivana is rather more fussy, and insists on a gritty, lime-free soil.

4
Below the Tree-line

The boundary between Alpine and mountainous Europe is often sketched in by the upper limit of the mountain forests: larch, spruce and the pines, often nowadays in plantation form, but formerly the components of virgin coniferous forests which clothed vast areas from the Steppes to the Alpine limits; on the drier slopes, yew and the junipers. These have all, on occasion, given rise to dwarf forms, the best of which have been propagated and cultivated. Their stunted or prostrate habits of growth are redolent of the exposed mountain landscape and, when planted on the rock garden, they are in scale both with tiny Alpine plants and with artificially contrived miniature rock formations.

A typical European mountain tree is the larch, *Larix decidua*, and this is not normally a very variable subject. In the wild, aberrations of form are largely restricted to variations of coarseness in the crown, and the angle adopted by the branches as they grow from the stem. The variety *L.d.* Corley originated when twigs from a witches'-broom growth on a larch were propagated and grown on independently. Larch will not take from cuttings, and *L.d.* Corley has to be grafted on to normal seedlings. It makes a slowly expanding, rounded bush with congested twigs – not unattractive, but odd when you consider that witches'-brooms are caused by microscopic fungal bodies, and it is a colony of these that we are nurturing, in effect, when we plant *L.d.* Corley.

Norway spruce is found wild from the Austrian Alps to the Norwegian Arctic. Well known in Britain as the Christmas tree, *Picea abies* has given rise to a great many forms: Doone Valley, of tiny stature, a little bun of a bush admirably suited to the trough garden; and Echiniformis, which is equally short, but spreads proportionately to make a prickly little bush, perhaps 10cm high by 25cm wide after ten years of growth. More conical, but equally compact and densely foliaged, is the tiny *P.a.* Humilis and the very similar *P.a.* Pygmaea, both eminently suitable for the very small-scale rock garden where trees must not be allowed to exceed half a metre in height, even after fifty years or more of growth. Slightly larger but still exceedingly dwarf are: *P.a.* Effusa, a spiky, dark green globe of a bush; and *P.a.* Procumbens, which is a true 'dwarf' in the sense that branches are thrust outwards annually to a width of 2 or 3 metres, but upward growth is minimal – resulting after many years in a wide, flat-topped bush with prickly, upright needles. It has the same visual effect as some of the spreading junipers, but is not really suitable for the smaller rock garden. A similar shape is developed by the old variety *P.a.* Gregoryana, which will still be well under half a metre after many years, with rather spiky bluish-green needles in long, juniper-like sprays. *P.a.* Little Gem makes an almost perfectly round globe of tiny, closely congested, bright green needles, and the popular *P.a.* Nidiformis makes an unevenly tiered, radially branched bush of dark green, similar in some respects to *P.a.* Procumbens but not so spreading – after fifty years of garden growth, specimens of *P.a.* Nidiformis have not yet attained a metre in height. A larger, spiky-leaved version with almost twice the growth potential is the old variety *P.a.* Capitata. All these Norway spruce cultivars may be grown from cuttings, though good results are by no means assured. Small shoots should be pulled off with a heel and carefully trimmed to leave a base of clean, second-year wood. Early autumn seems to be the best season, but some growers have achieved good results from cuttings taken during April, and successful takes vary greatly from year to year; the field is wide open for experimental propagation work – but grafting is always an alternative possibility. The dwarf varieties will tolerate slightly alkaline conditions although, to succeed as a timber producer, Norway spruce needs an acid soil.

The Serbian spruce *Picea omorika* is a very similar tree, but of contrastingly restricted natural distribution, for it is limited to the limestone cliff forests of the River Drina in Yugoslavia. The nature of this habitat, and its fine proportions, make it a useful alternative to Norway spruce for commercial planting in alkaline soils. In the rock garden, the variety *P.o.* Nana makes a dense, rounded bush of spiky needles, barely a metre in height after ten years of cultivation, attractively dark green with conspicuous silvery lines below each leaf.

The Austrian pine, *Pinus nigra*, is a native of the southern European mountains, and well known elsewhere for its hardiness, and ability to grow in poor or chalky soils. Its variety Hornibrookiana is another example of a dwarf cultivar which was said to have originated from a witches'-broom – in this case from a tree growing in the United States, and propagated at some time between the World Wars. It makes a congested and rather untidy bush with twisted branchlets and stiff, dark green needles, and it will reach a metre's height after about

(Top left) A vigorous plant for the large rockery, *Saxifraga longifolia* Tumbling Waters is excellent for clothing a wall. *(Top right) Aster alpinus* is a parent of several garden varieties. *(Centre left)* Molten Gold, a selected form of the Alpine buttercup *Ranunculus montanus. (Centre right) Pinus mugo,* the wild dwarf mountain pine. *(Bottom right)* At home in the high screes, *Potentilla nitida* needs a gritty soil and full sun

twenty years. Pygmaea is a dwarf form of the lowland subspecies of this species, *Pinus nigra calabrica*, the Corsican pine; but the geographical races are very closely related, and this dwarf form was originally found growing wild in the Italian mountains. It makes a miniature pyramidal tree, and demonstrates its disturbed metabolism by the tendency to become chlorotic in the winter, as though it will not live to see the spring. So far, however, old trees have survived, and passed 3 metres in height after many years. Individual specimens of *P.n.* Pygmaea might well lend themselves to careful crown thinning in order to enhance their natural beauty.

The tree usually called the mountain pine is *Pinus mugo*, found wild in several European mountain ranges, where it usually inhabits limestone areas. The dwarf forms Gnom and Mops both make globular little bushes which have attained about half a metre in ten years, very suitable for small rock gardens, with stiff, dark green leaves closely set on intricately interwoven branches.

Pinus cembra is the arolla pine, which is found wild from the Alps to Siberia – where, it is said, the large seeds are collected for food. The one variety of *P. cembra* which is really valuable in the rock garden is Jermyns – named after the home base of Hilliers, the great British nursery firm which raised it. It forms a very ornamental cone of short, crowded, dark bluish-green needles, and will probably still be well under half a metre after ten years of growth.

The European coniferous forests are frequently fringed with large areas of the mountain heath, *Erica carnea* (often classified under the less familiar name of *Erica herbacea*), and which, like the common heather, forms close, weed-excluding communities but, unlike *Calluna*, inhabits alkaline as well as acid soils – a catholic taste which enables gardeners to enjoy a heather garden without the normally obligatory acid soil. The fact that *E. carnea* is probably the hardiest of all the heaths is borne out by its propensity for flowering in mid-winter. *E. carnea* Eileen Porter, with its bright carmine flowers, does have a reputation for slight tenderness, but there is more than a hint that this beautiful cultivar may, in fact, be a hybrid between *E. carnea* and the Iberian species *E. mediterranea*. The mountain heath is best known, perhaps, for the dwarf carpeting varieties Springwood White and Springwood Pink, which have deservedly become popular among those ground coverers which are perfectly agreeable to light shade. The white variety starts flowering in January, the pink a month later, and both stay in bloom right through the winter and well into April. Slightly earlier, from December until February, is the carmine

(Opposite) Ramonda myconi is a good plant for a north-facing site, or a shaded wall

Myosotis alpestris is a true mountain plant

December Red, of similar habit but taller by a few centimetres, and the slightly taller Ruby Glow, which flowers from December to April. These carpeting heaths rarely, if ever, need trimming to keep them low and compact.

One of the best known taller *Erica carnea* varieties, forming a solid, wide-spreading bush and flowering from February to April, is the bright pink King George V. Atrorubra is a very old spring-flowering cultivar with flowers of a deep carmine hue, and Praecox Rubra is also a very old variety, and one of the earliest of the group, the deep pink flowers opening before Christmas and lasting well into the New Year. Two varieties with coloured foliage are: Aurea, with pale pink flowers that fade as the flowering season progresses during winter and early spring, at which season the foliage turns bright gold and stays coloured until June; and Vivellii, with deep carmine flowers which open from January to March and contrast with the bright, bronzy-red foliage, which becomes green during the summer.

These heaths are well adapted to propagation by layering, if only a few extra plants are needed; otherwise cuttings can be rooted under a polythene bag, keeping them well shaded. They should be taken in June and July by breaking the tips off young shoots at the junction between the current and previous year's vegetation; these cuttings will be fairly tiny, depending on how much growth has been made, but the operation should not be left much after midsummer, otherwise flowering buds will have been formed, and the shoot's energy will be directed into producing a flower instead of roots. The rooting medium should incorporate a little soil taken from beneath an established erica colony, and the best results are achieved if there is a surface layer, about a centimetre thick, of pure silver sand.

The yew tree, *Taxus baccata*, can be said to typify in some respects the drier slopes of the European mountains, though its range extends far and wide and embraces northern Asia, the British Isles, the Middle East and parts of North Africa. The wild species has given rise to numerous forms which have found a niche in the rock gardens of many countries, among them the well known Irish yew and the much smaller *T.b.* Pygmaea – a conical shrub with densely compact, almost black foliage composed of tiny, glossy, bristly leaves. It should be still well under half a metre after ten years of growth, and deserves to be used more often in the small rock garden. Of more spreading habit, though little more than shin-high, *T.b.* Repandens eventually covers a large area with dark, drooping branches. It has an advantage over the spreading junipers in its ability to survive heavy shade – though it grows equally well in the sun. A similar ground-covering yew of equal spread, eventually reaching waist height, is the black-green *T.b.* Cavendishii. *T.b.* Decora forms a bun-shaped bush of somewhat spiky appearance, with long, upward curving leaves. One of the best yews for the medium sized rock garden, one that will probably take many years to reach a metre in height, is *T.b.* Argentea Minor, a variegated form with arching, drooping branches, each dark green leaf outlined in white, giving a silvery-grey tinge to the whole shrub.

The junipers are often associated with the yews in nature, especially *Juniperus communis,* which is widely distributed throughout Europe, North America and Asia. A more typically European species – though it is found as far east as the Caucasus – is *Juniperus sabina,* the savin, quite as variable a tree in the wild as *J. communis,* but usually adopting a low, ground-hugging form, itself very expressive of windswept mountain territory, and the poor, dry soil that usually typifies it. The lowest growing and neatest of those savin varieties that have been selected over the years for garden cultivation is *J.s.* Skandia, a truly dwarf creeping form with dark green, prickly leaves, not too vigorous for use on the small rock garden where, though it will span a good space between rocks, should not outgrow the site. *J.s.* Tamariscifolia is the best known variety of savin. It has sometimes been classified as a distinct species, for it comes true from seed and, as the Spanish juniper, is found in the Pyrenees. It is of a much brighter, more grass-like green than Skandia and, although it will not spread far horizontally, it forms a bulky bush approaching knee height after about fifteen years. There are many situations which call for Tamariscifolia, but it is a little too heavy for most rock gardens. There is a distinctively glaucous blue-green cultivar of Spanish juniper that is better behaved under garden conditions than the wild green form: it is hardier, and does not suffer from the tendency, sometimes found in the type, for branches to die back; as a rule the leaf sprays are better shaped, too, so that the overall impression is more picturesque. Blue Danube is the name given to a savin clone very similar to the glaucous form of Tamariscifolia, and they could well be one and the same. An unusual savin juniper for the large garden is Von Ehren, which after many years forms a densely-leaved table top, some 5 metres across, and little more than 1 metre high. Although it has a certain grace, with its prickly, firmly spreading foliage, the overall effect is too heavy and vigorous for any but the largest gardens.

Spreading junipers can quite readily be induced to form rooted layers by removing a few leaves from a convenient length of branch, and burying this portion shallowly, pegging it down if necessary. The free, foliaged part protruding from the ground need not be staked in an upright position, as is normal practice when layering deciduous shrubs, but may be allowed to lie along the surface as it would do in nature. Sometimes, ready-rooted stems can be found at the base of established plants, and these may be removed for replanting, but junipers usually grow fairly readily from cuttings. The best time of the year to take them is winter – at Christmas or early in the New Year – and they should be set under glass in a frame rather than given the polythene bag treatment. Cuttings taken with a heel usually seem more satisfactory than otherwise, and *J. s.* Tamariscifolia in particular will root readily the following spring when treated in this manner.

The cinquefoils, perhaps, are typical of the shrubs and shrubby herbs of the European mountains. *Potentilla fruticosa*, an upright shrub, is widespread throughout the northern hemisphere, and it is hardly surprising that such a cosmopolitan plant should have given rise to many garden varieties. The wild species itself is rather large for the rock garden, and most of the dwarf cultivars are best sited between sunny rocks at the foot of the rockery, although the red-tinged Tangerine and the very distinctive Red Ace should both be given partial shade; otherwise the flowers tend to lose their scarlet tinge, and fade to a dark yellow. A true sun-lover is the pure white-flowered dwarf Beanii, and so are the more typical sulphur-yellow forms Longacre and Moonlight, while the bright yellow Hurstbourne and Minstead Dwarf fill an intermediate category, and enjoy a site which offers them morning sunshine, with shade in the afternoon.

Propagation of the shrubby potentillas may be achieved by side-shoot cuttings taken in the early autumn, with a heel of older wood – the heel will tend to strip bark from the second year wood, and this needs to be trimmed. The cuttings should be kept under glass, well shaded from direct sunshine. Rooting success is unpredictable: I used to take numbers of them annually, sometimes with one hundred per cent success, but occasionally an entire batch would fail to root – possibly because the growth had not hardened sufficiently – and there is always room for experimentation with timing.

The herbaceous cinquefoils are more typically European Continental: *Potentilla alba* is a vigorous spreader with typical, five-segmented leaves, made conspicuous when young by the silky hairs on their undersurface outlining the shape with a white, haloed fringe. The flowers are quite striking – white with a yellow centre, each about 2.5cm across, in a short-stalked cluster of four or five together, in succession from April until August. Another mat-former is the richly yellow-flowered *P. aurea*, with slightly smaller flowers in loose clusters, appearing in July and August. There is a hybrid, *Potentilla* Fireflame, with brilliantly scarlet flowers in May and June contrasting vividly with the silvery foliage – a garden cultivar, of course, but the mountain species are just as easy to grow as this fine plant, given sunny, well drained sites, and *P. aurea* itself has selected forms with brighter, orange flowers. More difficult to grow is the Alpine *Potentilla nitida*, which makes a silky mat on the high screes, and scorns more homely surroundings. The species bears very short-stemmed, clear pink flowers in July and August, and there are a few selected cultivars, notably Rubra and Lissadell, with deep pink flowers. These varieties, like the species, demand scree treatment with a compost of almost pure grit in the full sun. There is a hybrid between a Himalayan species and the yellow-flowered *P. aurea*, which has been named *Potentilla*×*tonguei*, a dark green, compact mat with rich orange flowers, each petal marked with a crimson spot like a cistus flower. Other potentilla species include *P. ternata*, which forms a silky mat several centimetres across, with bright yellow flowers from June to August, and *P. tabernaemontani*, a widely ranging mat-former whose natural variety Nana is one of the best cinquefoils for the small rockery, dainty and tiny enough for the smallest sink garden – a tufted, downy plant with a miniature drift of 1.5cm wide buttercup-yellow flowers in May, June and July.

Associated sometimes with the potentillas are the thymes, a very mixed and freely hybridising genus. *Thymus lanuginosus* Hall's

Variety makes a very neat mat of greyish leaves, a free-flowering pink show which needs to be viewed from above, and takes well to a site between paving stones. The taller lemon thyme, *Thymus* × *citriodorus* and its varieties Argenteus, with silver-variegated leaves, and Aureus, with golden leaves, are very pleasant little plants to grow by the side of a path through the rockery. Aureus especially is highly aromatic, and may be used in the kitchen.

Senecio is a huge and cosmopolitan genus of plants, many of whose members are weeds, but there are several species native to the European mountains which are very useful in the garden. A sprawling shrub that looks at home at the foot of a rockery is *Senecio abrotanifolius,* with dark, glossy green leaves and heads of orange-yellow daisy-like flowers appearing from July to September, and *S. adonidifolius* is a similarly disposed plant, with deeply cut, dark green leaves and rather dull, orange flowers – also flowering from July to September. But best of the European senecio species are *S. incanus* and *S. uniflorus,* little silver-haired, tuft-forming plants whose amber daisy flowers form a summer succession – *S. uniflorus* in July and *S. incanus* in August. Both plants like to bask in the sun on a gritty scree, and both can be increased quite easily from late summer side-shoot cuttings, or from the rooted stems which can sometimes be teased from the tuft edges.

Erinus alpinus is a mountain plant which by nature flourishes in rock crevices, and translates very well to cool lowland climes if used as a wall plant, or allowed to nestle between paving stones. An old brick wall in which the mortar has crumbled can be made to support the fairy foxglove, as it is sometimes known from its rounded, hairy leaves and tiny spikes of purple or white flowers which appear throughout the spring. Seeds are produced and germinate so readily that they may be sown *in situ* as soon as they ripen.

Three campions from the southern mountains are *Silene alpestris, S. armeria* and *S. ciliata.* The wide-ranging *S. armeria,* which grows eagerly on old walls and has naturalised itself in many parts of the world, including Britain, is less permanent than the others, and often adopts the characteristics of an annual or biennial – but seeds itself so freely that it readily forms a permanent colony. It has rounded, olive-green leaves, and produces clusters of purple or bright pink flowers over a long season between May and September. The white-flowered *S. alpestris,* whose fringed petals open from June to August, is a tufted perennial with narrow leaves, and an easily grown plant which enjoys a fair amount of humus in the soil, and usually yields a small division or two in the autumn. More of a spreader is *S. ciliata,* which forms a thick, low mat of woody stems covered with small, pointed leaves, and little clusters of white flowers in the late summer.

The mossy saxifrages have many named varieties, and a selection of these was listed in Chapter Three, but many saxifrage species of this section are widely distributed over Europe. *Saxifraga moschata*, for instance, is found from Spain to western Asia, and forms bright green mossy tufts covered with purple flowers in the spring. It is a parent of many hybrids, among them Cloth of Gold, noted not so much for its pale pink flowers as for the foliage, which has a metallic golden colour all the year round, and forms dense, rapidly spreading mats. Also in the mossy section, but limited to the Spanish mountains, is *S. trifurcata*, with finely divided leaves and a good display of white flowers over a long summer season. Both species appreciate the light shade found beneath high rocks and, in more northerly climes, do best in a moist, north-facing site.

Saxifraga cotyledon, one of the silver-encrusted saxifrages, forms broad rosettes of rounded leaves and bears clusters of white flowers from May to July. It is found over a wide range in Europe, from the southern mountains to north of the Arctic Circle; so it is unquestionably hardy and tolerant of a wide range of sites although, as it occurs naturally only on non-limestone outcrops, it does not like lime in the soil. It is a very useful saxifrage for dry stone walls, though it is somewhat tall for most other rock garden situations. After seeding, the flowering rosettes die back for the autumn, and new ones appear at their base. There are many seedling varieties and, like others of the genus, *S. cotyledon* hybridises readily, so that plants grown from seed will be liable to vary widely in their characteristics. Another mountain saxifrage is *S. aspera*, which forms thick mats of finely divided foliage, the creeping stems rooting as they spread, making this an easy plant to propagate. It has pale yellow flowers minutely marked with orange. One of the most widespread of the genus is *Saxifraga aizoon*, to be found in many countries of the northern hemisphere – in Europe, extending from the Mediterranean to the Arctic. Understandably, it is an easy plant to please, and does well on dry walls – even in shady places where suitable wall plants are scarce, though shade is by no means necessary. The fleshy, silver-encrusted leaf rosettes measure about 10cm across, and the small, developing crowns can easily be detached as a convenient means of propagation. The pretty little flowers on a slender stalk are typically white with tiny purple markings, but there are numerous varieties and hybrids, and few plants are able to boast so many named garden cultivars, each varying only slightly in leaf, flower and habit.

The saxifrages often seem most at home in those rocks which rise immediately above the boggy, peaty lands that collect the moisture run-off that seeps beneath the shallow mountain topsoil. On these moist plateau areas shrubby herbs like the bastard box, *Polygala chamaebuxus*, find a stronghold. Bastard box was thought attractive enough to have been introduced into gardens centuries ago – it was known in England as long ago as 1650 – and has small, hard, box-like leaves and tiny, fragrant flowers shaped like those of the pea family, white and yellow, or, in the variety Grandiflora, purple and yellow. The main flowering season is during April, May and June, but the odd flower appears until autumn. It may easily be increased by division, and flourishes in a peaty soil, either with or without light shade.

On the edges of woodland in these lower mountain reaches, a typical little ground-covering plant is *Omphalodes verna*, the blue-eyed Mary, whose spreading tufts of heart-shaped leaves and white-throated blue forget-me-not flowers in the spring make it a charming subject for a peaty soil in light shade, easily propagated by dividing the creeping runners. This type of site, between woodland and rock, is home also to *Ramonda myconi*, which has rosetted leaves like a strawberry plant, covered with reddish hairs, and very pretty five-petalled purple flowers which last from May until July. It is a good plant for a shaded wall, provided the soil is not too dry: a north-facing site with an acid, peaty soil will be ideal. The varieties Alba with white, and Rosea with pink flowers are very attractive. In eastern Europe, its place is taken by *Ramonda nathaliae*, which has bright glossy green leaves, and orange-eyed, four-petalled lavender-blue flowers.

Semi-shaded mountain woodland is a typical habitat for several European violets. *Viola alpina*, a tufted plant whose rich purple flowers open in May and June, looks splendid on its own beneath the overhang of a rock, fairly high on the rock garden. All the group are easy to grow in a gritty compost which has a good proportion of leafmould, and the creeping violas – *V. biflora*, *V. calcarata* and *V. cornuta* especially – will thrive in any reasonably good soil. The last-named is a prolific mat-former which produces large violet flowers during the summer months but, although it luxuriates once established, it does not always take readily. New plants should be allowed generous growing time before winter sets in – divided portions should be replanted in September as soon as they are detached, otherwise division must wait until April. Easier to establish, and just as willing to spread, by underground runners, once it has a toe-hold, is the variably flowered *V. calcarata*. The flowers open successively from March to July, and may be purple, yellow or white. *Viola biflora* is very much at home in these transitional woodland zones, and has a wide distribution throughout the northern hemisphere. With its bright yellow puce-veined flowers, it makes a cheerful cover if allowed to run around the stems of shrubs or, just as efficiently, to clothe the higher north-facing slopes of the rock garden.

Soldanella, a genus of the primula family, is typical of midway moraine conditions. 'Shady' is too strong a description for the type of site soldanellas prefer: a cool spot where the soil is gritty and moist, and from where they can see the sun for part of the day, will be ideal. Given the right conditions, the soldanella species form spreading mats of glossy green, rounded leaves, with a drift of dainty, bell-shaped flowers in the spring, each petal delicately fringed. They are found on many mountain ranges in southern Europe, and the most garden worthy include: *Soldanella alpina*, whose wide, bluish-mauve flowers have crimson markings inside the drooping cup; *S. austriaca*, bluish-lilac on the outside, streaked with violet within; *S. hungarica*, with wide, purple-blue flowers; *S. minima*, the smallest, with delicate, pale blue flowers, lined with purple streaks; *S. montana*, the largest and most easily obtainable, with lilac-blue, widely bell-shaped flowers; *S. pindicola*, the most eastern in range, with large pink flowers; *S. pusilla*, with narrow blue flowers and notably dark, glossy leaves; and *S. villosa*, with broad lilac-blue flowers.

Primula carniolica also enjoys these mountain woodland borders where there is light shade and humus-rich, moist soil. It carries clusters of rosy-purple bell-shaped flowers in May, and its auricula-like leaves are smooth and glossy. *Primula auricula* itself has a much more widespread distribution in the southern European mountains and, with its hybrids, has given rise to innumerable cultivated forms which have been grown in the garden for centuries. Typically, *P. auricula* has fragrant, bell-shaped yellow flowers, ten or twelve to the cluster, the stem rising from a symmetrical rosette of fleshy leaves. Other primulas of the auricula type originating from the lower Alpine regions include: *P. glutinosa*, with fragrant violet flowers; *P. marginata*, with short-stemmed, violet-blue, campanula-like flowers; *P. palinuri*, from the Italian mountains, with large clusters of fragrant, nodding, deep yellow flowers; and *P. spectabilis*, with hard, glossy little leaves and large, bright pink flowers in threes or fours on a short stem. All the mountain auriculas enjoy a crevice in the rock where there is summer moisture but free drainage for the winter. A compost containing a good proportion of peat and sharp sand is best and, in the case of *P. marginata, P. palinuri* and *P. spectabilis* at least, this could profitably contain up to a quarter part of crushed brick or potsherds. If the rain tends to come from one definite direction during the winter – in Britain it usually arrives from the south-west – it is a good idea to allow these plants to face away from the weather beneath the protection of a small rock overhang; but they are not difficult to grow if the restrictions of their natural habitat are respected. They do not always provide distinct crowns for division and, when new plants are needed, seed should be collected as soon as it ripens and sown straight away, before it loses viability. The auricula primulas associate well with the clear blue, spring-flowering *Anemone apennina*, and its pale blue and white variety Alba, if they are allowed to colonise together.

Tunica saxifraga has the appearance of a dianthus with its narrow, spreading leaves, a few pale pink flowers together in a loose cluster during the summer months. It is sometimes given the alternative generic name of *Petrorhagia*. Found over a wide range in southern Europe, it loves a well-drained, sunny site, and is excellent on a south-facing wall. The mountain wallflower, *Erysimum alpinum*, is an excellent plant for the coarser reaches of the rock garden and looks right against a background of dark rock, though it is a little large for the Alpine scale. A variable species which has given rise to several garden forms and hybrids, *E. alpinum* typically forms tufts of pointed leaves with clusters of fragrant, primrose-yellow flowers in the spring. Much smaller, and neater in all its parts, is *Erysimum helveticum*, a little tuft of greyish green, pointed leaves with very pretty, fragrant pale yellow flowers in July and August. This species is better suited both for the small rock garden and the retaining wall, but really prefers a gritty soil and a sunny spot fairly high on the scree.

The drier mountain slopes typically support a somewhat shrubby-herbaceous carpeting vegetation, typified by the veronicas. The truly shrubby hebes – often termed veronicas – tend to be rather tender, whereas the ground-covering veronicas themselves are nearly all fully hardy, coming as they do from mountainous terrain. The herbaceous species may be increased quite easily by division, either in the spring or after flowering is finished in the late summer. They may also be propagated from short shoot cuttings taken at any time during the growing season. Of the European mountain species, *Veronica allionii* is a typical mat-former, covered in the spring with dense spikes of tiny, deep purple flowers; *V. alpina* also creeps from the roots, and bears small spikes of pale blue flowers in the spring; *V. fruticans*, known as the rock speedwell and distributed widely throughout the European mountain areas, has bright blue, red-eyed flowers which do not appear until July and last till autumn; and *V. nummularia* is limited to the Pyrenean region, a pretty little creeper which can be used to great effect between paving stones, bright with tiny blue flowers in June.

A few valerians also haunt this type of habitat, such as the fragrant *Valeriana celtica*, which is collected and dried like lavender. It has small, rounded leaves on creeping, underground stems, and loose clusters of yellowish flowers throughout the summer. *Valeriana supina*, on the other hand, colonises the damper spots and should be given moraine treatment. It makes a neat mat of tiny, glossy, dark green leaves, with clusters of pale pink flowers over a long summer season. Both plants may be propagated very easily by dividing the creeping shoots.

There is a mountain clover which also typifies the lower slopes, with their mat-forming vegetation – *Trifolium alpinum*, which creeps through the sparse turf with short, thick underground stems. With its trefoil leaves and purplish-pink flower clusters in July, it makes a pleasant patch which will grow anywhere. The much smaller *Trifolium uniflorum* has a wider natural range, and is perhaps the better plant for rock garden use, being more at home on the dry scree. The bright purple pea-family flowers are on display from early summer until the first frosts.

5
European Hill Plants

The drier hills of Europe in spring and summer are well typified by the bright yellow splashes of flower colour from the brooms and gorses of the genera *Genista*, *Cytisus* and *Ulex*. The species vary from large shrubs to fleshy, ground-hugging plants like *Genista* (or *Chamaespartium*) *sagittalis* Minor, which is only a few centimetres high. The typical *G. sagittalis* is capable of quite considerable spread, has no objection to partial shade, and is probably the best broom for ground cover, with its vigorous, evergreen stems and erect clusters of yellow flowers. *G.s.* Minor, which shares these characteristics in miniature, is ideal for the smallest rock garden. A similar species from the southern hills is *Genista sylvestris*, and both are excellent summer flowers for a dry, sunny wall,

The spiny gorses of the genus *Ulex* are not really suitable for the rock garden. Spanish gorse is *Genista hispanica*, a very spiny plant with bright golden-yellow flower clusters during the summer. It needs a sunny position, and is liable to be damaged by very severe winter weather. Less well known, perhaps, although it has a much wider distribution over the whole of Europe, including the British Isles, is *Genista pilosa*, a neat little shrub which is a picture of golden blossom in May. Both these species will grow fairly readily from cuttings taken during May and June.

Shrubs of the genus *Cytisus* include some useful species, among them *C. ardoinii*, a fine mat-former from the southern French hills, with bright yellow flowers in the spring; and *C. austriacus*, with finely leaved foliage of a silky, silvery appearance, which is unusual among the brooms in flowering late, the bright yellow flowers opening in August and remaining showy until the first frosts. The most prostrate of the genus is the southern European *C. decumbens*, introduced into more northerly gardens two centuries back, a shrub which hugs the rocks closely, and is covered with bright yellow flowers in the spring.

Many of the best garden brooms are hybrids, some raised at Kew, like *C.×beanii*, a graceful little shrub with golden yellow spring flowers, and *C.×kewensis*, a dainty spreader with creamy yellow flowers. These hybrids share *C. ardoinii* as one parent. The hybrid *Cytisus×praecox* is known as the Warminster broom, a popular garden variety which is spectacular in the spring when covered with cascading cream flowers, and there are variations in white and yellow. Most of the cytisus brooms can be propagated from shoot cuttings taken with a heel of older wood. In the case of the true species, this operation is best performed as soon as the new growth is long enough, in early summer; but the hybrids may be left until late summer or after. Among the wild brooms, the odd one out is *Cytisus purpureus*, the purple broom, a shrub from the hills of central Europe, recognised by its small purple flowers. For garden use, it is sometimes grafted on a standard stem to make a small tree, and this practice, when a common laburnum stock is used, gives rise to the strange graft-chimera +*Laburnocytisus adamii*, which simultaneously produces yellow laburnum and purple broom flowers.

Few plants associate better with the dwarf rock brooms than the prostrate veronicas, for both enjoy dryish, sunny situations, and their

Genista sagittalis

Veronica teucrium

foliage, though very different, blends harmoniously. Many of the veronicas, furthermore, especially the varieties of *V. prostrata*, are well into flower before the brooms have finished, and few colour combinations are more tastefully telling than shades of yellow and blue. *Veronica prostrata* itself has a very wide range over the hills of Europe from Spain to Siberia. It follows that few climes will be able to daunt this hardy spreader, which is able to grow and flower freely almost anywhere. It is the sort of plant which happily colonises a stone wall or a path edge, pretty at all seasons, but especially so in May and June when covered with clusters of deep blue flowers. Selected varieties include: Alba, with white flowers; Mrs Holt, with pink flowers; Royal Blue, with flowers, as the name suggests, of a rich, dark blue; Silver Queen, with ice-blue flowers; Spode Blue, with clear, light blue flowers; and the very dwarf blue-flowered Nana, suitable especially for paths, where it will happily run between paving stones, though it will tend to become a permanent acquisition, as it roots beneath the slabs. There is no problem with propagation of any variety, as pieces lifted at any time will re-root quickly. Plants grown from seed may result in unpredictable colour breaks, though most of the progeny will be similar to the wild species.

Veronica teucrium is a widespread, very variable plant, and it also has given rise to many named garden varieties. It has a more tufted habit and does not spread to the same extent as *V. prostrata*, and the blue flowers are larger and later, appearing in July. Some of the best cultivars include: Royal Blue, again with royal blue flowers; Trehane, with bright blue flowers and attractive greenish-yellow leaves; and Rosea, with pink flowers. The varieties of *V. teucrium* may be increased by using short cuttings of non-flowering shoots, taken in the late summer and potted under a polythene bag. *V. teucrium* associates well with the dwarf yarrows such as *Achillea tomentosa*, with dark yellow flowers, and the buff-flowered hybrid *Achillea* King Edward.

The capacity of some of the veronicas for spreading rapidly is shared by the dwarf creeping shrub *Coronilla varia*. A leguminous plant, it carries large clusters of very pretty pea-type flowers, followed by slender pods, and makes a vigorous cover for any sunny spot. It has been grown in northern European gardens for three centuries or more,

Achillea tomentosa

and is usually admired, but sometimes cursed, for if it likes a site too well it is liable to take on the status of a weed.

Some of the heaths, of course, are colonisers *par excellence*, and if *Erica carnea* is the true mountain heath, the hill heaths must be: *Erica cinerea*, the bell heather, widespread throughout the hills of western Europe from Spain to Norway, including the British Isles; *E. ciliaris*, from western Europe and extending across the Channel to appear in Dorset and Cornwall; *E. tetralix*, the cross-leaved heath, from Spain to Scandinavia, and also occurring in the British Isles; *E. vagans*, from the coastal areas of southern and western Europe, extending into parts of North Africa and Asia, and reaching its northernmost limit on the Lizard in Cornwall; and *E. mediterranea*, found, not near the Mediterranean Sea, but in the hills of Spain and Portugal – the home also of the tall *E. australis*. The best known plant of this type is probably the common heather, *Calluna vulgaris*, found from southern Europe north to Norway and Lapland, but so inescapably a plant of the British uplands that it has found its way into the next chapter.

Erica australis is not a plant for the rock garden, unless the site is immense, for it will attain a height of 2 metres. Nevertheless, varieties of *E. australis* are often very useful for giving height or a central focus to an extensive area of heaths. The species is not a spreader like the other heaths, but retains a pyramidal grey-green bush-like form. Two excellent varieties are Mr Robert, with large white flowers, and Riverslea with deep pink; during April and May, both plants become laden with bloom. *Erica mediterranea* is not so tall, but still very much a centrepiece, not outstandingly hardy, but valuable for its ability to grow in limy soils. The type has rather dull pink flowers, but the variety Superba is a much more colourful plant, with slightly fragrant, bright purple-pink flowers from March to May.

Erica ciliaris flowers are a rich, clear pink, without a hint of the purple that touches most heaths. A spreading plant of acid moorland, it will not grow where there is a trace of lime, and prefers mild, moist climates to cold, dry ones. A cultivated variety of *E. ciliaris*, propagated from a wild plant collected in Portugal a century ago, is Maweana, a vigorous spreader with bright pink flower spikes. Mrs C. H. Gill is a dwarfer form of the type, with thicker, darker green foliage and good spikes of bright pink flower – the best cultivar of the species to form a small clump on the rockery. A full-sized variety with white flowers is Stoborough; its huge white spikes from July to October blend beautifully with the light green leaves, and it makes a fine specimen bush for clumping between rocks.

The bell heather, *Erica cinerea*, by nature is less inclined than *E. ciliaris* to colonise large areas, and is usually found in small clumps on the drier, sandier and warmer parts of the moor – but it will not grow if there is a trace of lime in the soil. The wild plant bears bright purplish pink flowers that stand out against the sober purple of *Calluna* heather. Two very neat dwarf varieties suitable for the wild rock garden, with bright blood-red flowers, are Atrorubens and Atrosanguinea. Even dwarfer, forming a low, rounded bush no more than 10cm high, and also with blood-red bells, is Coccinea, one of the earliest to flower, the buds opening early in June, with the main display over before August. These flowers develop without the normal spikes, so that the low cushions become closely covered with bloom – a habit that fits Coccinea admirably for a non-tripping role between paving stones. Also low and neat enough for paving, or for a trough garden, is the bright pink-flowered Mrs Dill. If heaths are grown in the true Alpine fashion, with individual clumps, tufts and small drifts arranged for contrast and variety, these are cultivars that would be at home high on a south-facing rockery slope. More typical of the species in size and bushiness are the vigorous P. S. Patrick, with fine deep purple flowers produced over a long season; and Rose Queen, with deep pink bells which also last until autumn; Joyce Burfitt is a deep pink; Eden Valley, a bright lilac pink; Janet is a pale rosy lilac – a very pretty variety; and Apple Blossom is the palest shade of pink, almost white, with light apple-green foliage. The most unusual bell heather in flower colour is Velvet Night, a dark green bush with velvety maroon-black bells. Another odd variety is Domino, with white flowers which stand out against a dark foliage background – most white-flowered heaths have paler green leaves and stems. Ann Berry has bright greenish yellow foliage with typical pink flowers, and the dwarf Golden Drop has bronzy foliage throughout the summer, changing to brilliant red during the winter – quite ordinary flowers, but a spectacular foliage display. There are many instances when this plant could be used to powerful effect on the rock garden.

The cross-leaved heath, *Erica tetralix*, is a native of the wetter, more acid, and often lower-lying areas of moorland, a fairly dwarf plant, smaller on average than *E. cinerea*, and bearing clusters of drooping pink bells lasting from early summer to autumn. In nature it is not a very changeable species, plants varying chiefly in the degree of brightness in their flower colour, and the intensity of the silvery down that sometimes clothes their foliage. The variety Alba Mollis, as the name implies, has white flowers and leaves which are so silvery-silky that it qualifies as a foliage plant, and is quite attractive during the winter months. Con Underwood is not without a silvery tinge, and the flower bells are deep crimson and very striking. L. E. Underwood has quite distinctively coloured flowers of a salmon-pink, and strongly silvered foliage.

Erica vagans in nature makes a larger plant than *E. tetralix*, *E.*

ciliaris, *E. cinerea* or *E. carnea*, and is a true coloniser, enjoying milder west-coastal conditions than the others, and is also more tolerant of a trace of lime in the soil than any heath except *Erica carnea*. It is somewhat variable in flower colour, and specimens may be found of any shade between white and purple. There are few garden cultivars, but of those that I have grown, Lyonesse, Mrs D. F. Maxwell and St Keverne are outstanding. Pyrenees Pink is dwarfer than the others, but the flowers are not as good as the similar St Keverne, which is a strong coloniser with bright pink flowers appearing during the traditional heather season – August to October. Mrs D. F. Maxwell has deep cerise-pink flowers, and is a vigorous plant which has received several awards for garden worthiness. Lyonesse is a very floriferous white, also a sturdy plant which spreads well. None of them is really suitable for the small rockery, though for a specialised heather garden they are excellent – it is largely a matter of scale.

Not least among the qualities of erica species and varieties to give them value in the rock garden is their lengthy flowering season: if we include the mountain heath *E. carnea*, plants can be had in flower for every month of the year, and a rock garden need never be without colour. In nature, erica species frequently hybridise, and probably the commonest naturally occurring cross involves *E. tetralix* and *E. ciliaris*. Cultivated hybrids tend to grow more vigorously, and flower more freely over a longer period than the true species – a fact which points to their sterility, and demonstrates how much plant energy is normally involved in the process of setting seed. The larger hybrids, such as the winter-flowering Arthur Johnson, Darleyensis, N. R. Webster, and Silberschmelze, probably have *E. mediterranea* as one of their parents, and make very broad, dense bushes that will scarcely find a place on even the largest rockery, but they are capable of successfully bridging the gap between a herbaceous or shrub border in one part of the garden, and the heather-clad, rock-strewn slopes in another. George Rendall, also a winter-flowerer – the deep purplish pink flowers, crowded on the foliage, open at Christmas and continue until May – is of a more manageable size, and may be allowed on the lower rockery slopes. The summer-flowering hybrids are smaller in bulk, and resembles more closely the colonising *E. ciliaris* and *E. tetralix*, but their flowering season tends to be extended, and the flowers themselves are more prolifically produced. One that is small enough to take its place on the slope, or which can be allowed to carpet along the path edges, is Gwen, whose dainty pink flowers open in June and last until October. Almost as dwarf are: Dawn, with deep rose flowers, and an even longer flowering season; and *E. ciliaris* Hybrida, which becomes covered with bright pink bells throughout the summer and autumn. H. Maxwell is rather taller among the summer-flowering hybrids, an upright, spiky plant with bright pink flowers over a long season.

When propagating erica varieties, it is important to realise that, like some conifers and many other plants, heaths and heathers form a symbiotic, or mutually advantageous, relationship with tiny fungi that live in the soil. These soil fungi or mycorrhiza are indispensable to the health of the plant, and they are always associated in nature with the mature heath colonies. A plant brought from the moor, or bought from the nursery will have these tiny organisms already on its roots, and the relationship will continue unhindered, even though the garden soil that is to receive it has not grown heather before and does not contain mycorrhiza. On the other hand, when seed is sown or cuttings are set in a medium that does not include these minute fungi, though they may germinate or take root, the results will never be satisfactory. To supply the missing factor, then, is paramount, and this is simply a matter of collecting a little soil from beneath healthy, established heaths and heathers, and incorporating some of this when preparing compost for cuttings or seed. Open ground which is being prepared to receive nursery-grown plants does not need inoculation in this manner, because mycorrhiza will certainly be introduced along with the new plants. When older, well developed heathers are lifted, white threads of the fungus, like cobwebs, can be seen adhering to the roots.

Erica cuttings are best taken in August, and should consist of tiny side-shoots which may be pulled off with a heel of older wood, leaving all the leaves attached. Compost ingredients must be free from lime, and it is possible to buy special ericaceous seed and cutting compost which is suitable; if this is used, however, it should be surfaced with a layer of sharp sand enough to support the cuttings without burying them too deeply. A novel but effective method of rooting erica side-shoots is to establish a turf of sphagnum bog moss in a tray containing gravel and peaty water. The cuttings are simply pushed lightly into the moss, which is then sprinkled with mycorrhizal soil, and the whole tray is kept shaded until new growth starts. The young plants must be potted up without delay, however, when this method is used. Division is an alternative method of propagation when only a few plants are needed, but it may be necessary first to encourage the growth of new, fine roots, either by planting more deeply than normal, or by piling peaty soil among the shoots, and leaving the stock plant for a season before separating the rooted sprigs.

A common European plant which sometimes colonises poor, dry sites in the sun is *Antennaria dioica.* The pale greenish pink daisy flowers in June are not particularly striking, but the chief value of the plant lies in the woolly, grey foliage cover it produces. There is also a dwarf variety, Minima, which forms a very dense grey mat – an easy subject for any sunny situation, readily increased by division. *Valeriana saliunica* forms neat, dense little tufts of dark green leaves on similar sites in the southern hills, with scented clusters of tiny pink flowers in the summer, and this also is a very easy plant, which divides readily.

A densely tufted mat of leaves is also provided by *Iris pumila,* a spring-flowerer which has produced several garden forms and hybrids with very variably coloured blooms. The pinks also fall into this category: the maiden pink, *Dianthus deltoides,* is the progenitor of many named garden varieties with flowers of all shades from white to crimson. The wild plant forms grass-green mats of narrow leaves with long, thin stems which carry the variable little flowers over a long summer season, and occurs in many parts of Europe, including Britain. *Dianthus callizonus* from the central European hills, whose large and somewhat spikily fringed flowers in dense clusters are pink with purple markings, forms a pleasing mat that needs a gritty, limy soil, and is well enough behaved for a large trough. Not all dianthus species are so neat: one of the most widespread of the genus, *Dianthus superbus,* produces solitary, fragrant, feathery-fringed flowers of lilac-pink over a long season throughout the summer, but it is an untidy, sprawling plant that needs a wild corner of the rock garden. All these pinks are easy to grow from early summer cuttings, using the plumper, non-flowering shoots.

Two of the skullcaps are good mat-formers. *Scutellaria alpina* is widely distributed throughout the European hills, where it enjoys dryish, sunny sites, and forms a close cover of rounded, downy leaves. It blooms in August, producing clusters of purple- and yellow-lipped flowers, though there are several cultivated varieties with flower colours ranging from pure yellow to pink. *Scutellaria orientalis* has a more southerly range, and appreciates the warmest, sunniest positions between low rocks, where the creeping stems can lay a mat of downy grey, rounded leaves, decorated in July and August with symmetrical spikes of yellow- and puce-lipped flowers. Both these plants allow rooted sections of stem to be detached for replanting.

From the same family as the skullcaps – a relationship which shows in the spiked, lipped flowers – is the wall germander, *Teucrium chamaedrys,* well known over a wide European range, and naturalised in other parts of the world after having escaped from cultivation. It is not really suitable for domestic walls, and is more at home on wilder sites, for the rootstock creeps through the crevices so that it establishes itself immovably. It has upright sprays of dark green, rounded leaves, with spikes of pink and white flowers from July to September. Slightly better behaved is the trailing germander, *Teucrium pyrenaicum,* from the southern European hills – a neat little plant with round, silvery-downy leaves, and whorled clusters of pale purple and white flowers opening in June and lasting until August. A pleasant subject for the sunny retaining wall, or a steep site among rocks.

Among the sun-loving plants are two from the Spanish hills: *Linaria glacialis,* with fleshy, grey leaves and pale lavender flowers, like miniature violets, in the spring; and *Linaria tristis,* which has yellow, brown and purple flowers. The latter is the parent of several garden varieties, some of which are perennial, while others tend to seed themselves and die out annually. *Cerastium lanatum* is a dry-site carpeter with grey woolly leaves, better behaved than the rampageous *C. tomentosum,* and quite handsome throughout the summer when covered with its comparatively large white flowers. Equally sun-loving but, contrastingly, from the cold, northern regions, is the related *Lychnis alpina,* with dianthus-like tufts of dark green leaves and spikes of tiny, pale pink flowers during the spring and summer.

Gentians have a wide natural range throughout Europe and beyond. *Gentiana acaulis* is one of the easiest of the genus to grow, and loves open, sunny sites with plenty of moisture in the spring and summer and grit for drainage – but it will grow almost wherever it is planted, indicating whether it is happy or not by a proclivity either to flower generously, or not at all. Plants sometimes build up vegetative growth at the expense of flower, and this may be because the soil is too rich and moist. Flowering can sometimes be encouraged by transplanting to a poorer, drier site. *Gentiana acaulis* is a variable plant, and there are many named garden varieties whose flowers vary from white through different shades of blue; but typically the species produces deep blue trumpets in May and June. It is one of the few gentians that can conveniently and safely be propagated by division, and this should be done, when required, in the early spring. *Gentiana verna* is also easy to grow in a gritty medium, but it needs plenty of humus and does best with a modicum of lime in the soil. It does not divide so happily as *G. acaulis,* and is usually raised from seed. The colour of the short-stemmed trumpets – usually a deep sky blue – will be somewhat variable in seedling plants, and, as with *G. acaulis*, the flowers appear in May and June.

Some of the houseleeks are widespread and well known, having been cultivated or used as houseplants for many centuries. The best known European species, *Sempervivum montanum,* and *S. tectorum,* are traditionally encouraged in some countries to grow outside on the roof – an indication of the modesty of their soil requirements. Each species has its own charm, and each may be propagated simply by removing and potting up the numerous offsets that appear round the plant edges and, in the case of the closely related hen and chickens houseleek *Jovibarba sobolifera*, among the fleshy leaves of the stem. The soil in the tiny crevices and pockets in which these plants grow by nature consists wholly of gritty detritus washed down the rock face, plus the decayed annual leaf rosettes accumulated over many years, and this balance of humus and grit suggests the type of compost that should be aimed at when preparing an artificial environment for them.

Sempervivum tectorum

The closely related stonecrops often thrive in similar conditions, and many are found over an even wider range. The stone orpine, *Sedum reflexum*, with its tangled mats of fleshy blue leaves and cheerful yellow flowers, occurs in nature throughout the hills of central and western Europe. Even wider in distribution are *Sedum alpestre* – though it is most at home, perhaps, in the sunny mountain slopes of the south-east – and *S. sexangulare*, which reaches north into the British Isles, where it may be distinguished from the commoner native species by its tiny leaves being crowded into whorls, about six to the stem. This is a very decorative plant for a grey stone wall in the summer, when the flat heads of bright yellow flowers are set off charmingly by the bronzed foliage. Stonecrops which prefer the mountains and hills of Spain and Portugal include: *Sedum anacampseros*, with trailing, blue-green, fleshy foliage on reddish brown stems and, occasionally, clusters of purple flowers; *S. ochroleucum*, another mat-former with little red-tinged, spine-tipped leaves, and a summer display of pale yellow flowers; *S. hirsutum*, which makes flat little pads of tiny, crowded leaves, usually green but sometimes tinted red, with pinkish white flowers opening in June – a plant which enjoys a dry position on a raised bed or low stone wall; and *S. pruinatum*, with narrow green leaves and little clusters of pale yellow flowers in July, spreading by means of creeping shoots which root at their tips, before dying off in the autumn. All the stonecrops, of course, will root fairly readily, wherever they might be persuaded to remain in contact with the ground, and small leafy portions can be detached and dibbled in to their new planting positions at any time during the active growing season.

Creeping plants of the woodland edge are normally shade-bearers and when they would otherwise be suitable for the rock garden but there is no shade available for them, the same effect can often be obtained by allocating such plants an open aspect which faces north, so that they receive only the minimum of sunshine. European plants which fall into this category include the periwinkles, and *Vinca minor* is often of use on or near the rock garden. The typical species with its pretty, purple-blue flowers, tends to spread too efficiently for our needs, and the otherwise excellent Bowles Variety – a strong shade-bearer – is even more exuberant. The double purple-flowered Multiplex and the white Alba are slightly less vigorous, and Variegata, with yellow-marked leaves, is definitely far less vigorous, and will make an unusual carpet between taller plants.

Vinca minor

Asarum europaeum, known as asarabacca or hazelwort, is another creeping woodland plant that will occasionally find a place at the base of a rockery where it can be allowed to drift between rock and bush, forming a shin-high cover of kidney-shaped leaves and curious but not showy drooping flowers in the early summer. *Hepatica × media* Ballardii is an anemone-like plant for this type of environment, also revelling in shade, and adapted to a deciduous woodland cover by remaining usefully wintergreen, but losing its leaves in early spring when the flowers, like tiny blue buttercups, put in an appearance.

Asarum europaeum

The wild daffodils are natives of Spain and Portugal, some extending their range beyond this area, like the wild British lent lily, *Narcissus pseudo-narcissus* – one of the prettiest of the genus with its pale frill and bright yellow trumpet, and one of the best for naturalising in grass near the woodland edge. *N. bulbocodium*, the hoop petticoat, so called from the shape of the bright orange-yellow broad tumpet with its very small frill, is an attractive species also suitable for naturalising; the variety Conspicuus is likely to do best, perhaps, in a dry situation among short grass, while Nivalis will succeed in damper sites. *N. cyclamineus* has one of the most distinctive of flower shapes, with its narrow lemon-yellow petals forming a streamlined silhouette, and this species is most at home when allowed to grow undisturbed in woodland shade – especially when it can spear through a warm covering of moss or a low carpeting herb, as it flowers very early in February and March, and appreciates the extra protection. Another very early flowerer is *N. asturiensis*; with its tiny, deep yellow flowers of the typical daffodil type, it makes a perfect miniature clump for the early spring.

A narcissus that will naturalise well is angel's tears, *N. triandrus.* The variety Albus, with creamy white flowers, is usually recommended for short grass areas, the golden yellow form Concolor preferring clearer ground beneath the light shade of taller shrubs. The vernacular name may be poetically descriptive of the delicate, drooping flowers, though legend has it that the botanist who first collected *N. triandrus* Albus in the wild named it angel's tears in recognition of his Spanish guide Angelo, whose eyes were streaming in the cold wind when he located it. One might infer from this that the flowering period is particularly early in the year but, in fact, the buds seldom open before April.

Narcissus lobularis has a pale lemon frill with a bright yellow trumpet, and the marginally dwarfer *N. nanus* has a cream frill and a primrose trumpet, but they are so similar botanically that they are

Narcissus pseudo-narcissus

probably, in fact, forms of the same species. For garden purposes they are distinct, however, and both make an attractive drift on the rock garden. Other narcissus species worthy of naturalising on the rockery include: *N. canaliculatus,* very dwarf, with a round yellow cup and white frill; *N. scaberulus,* with dainty little orange flowers; and *N. rupicola,* of the jonquil type, with fragrant, bright yellow flowers. Bambi is a garden hybrid, with a white frill and miniature yellow trumpet.

The winter aconite, *Eranthis hyemalis,* also from the western European hills, makes a perfect drift of bright yellow buttercup flowers in February and March. It is most at home beneath deciduous shrubs, for its green leaves, which have taken advantage of the shade-free winter months, start to wither in the spring as the overhead cover unfurls. The autumn crocus, *Colchicum autumnale,* has a different approach to the problem, flowering as it does directly from the bare ground in the autumn, the broad, lily-like leaves not appearing until early spring. Both the typical species and its white flowered variety Album are too large and leafy for most rock gardens, but a place could well be found for them nearby, where they would have no objection to light shade. If autumn crocuses are to be lifted and divided, this operation is best performed in July, replanting them in their new places immediately.

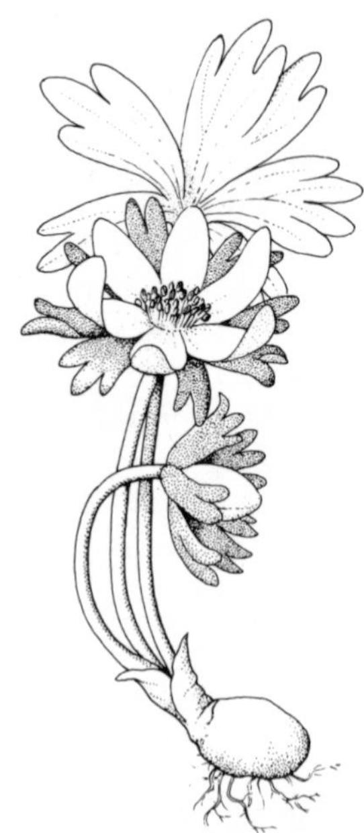

Eranthis hyemalis

Colchicum autumnale

The autumn squill, *Scilla autumnalis*, and the spring squill, *S. verna*, are both to be found near the south and west coasts in Britain, and also over a wide natural range in Europe. They are, perhaps, less spectacular than the similar but more familiar bluebell, being a rather pale lilac-blue, but are of value for their extended flowering season. The better known *S. campanulata* flowers in May, and is typically a rather purplish blue, though there are pink and white varieties. Rather tall for the rock garden, this clump-former is very much a plant for the intermediate reach between rock outcrop and woodland edge. The bright blue, star-like *S. monophylla* is dwarfer, flowering in the late spring, and can be sited higher on the rockery. They are all easy to grow, and eager to become naturalised.

6
A British Rockery

A visitor from southern Europe landing on the south coast of England on a sunny summer's day, and setting out to walk north between the stone walls of a country road, might be excused for thinking himself at home among homely plants. There on the wall he would recognise the familiar ivy-leaved toadflax, *Cymbalaria muralis.* If he looked closer he might notice a tuft or two of the tiny black-stemmed wedge leaves of the maidenhair fern, *Adiantum capillus-veneris.* Where the wall heightened and thickened, or ran into a cutting through the chalk, he would not need to peer closely to spot the vulgar pink flower clusters of the red valerian, *Kentranthus ruber.* All these plants are travellers which have neared their northernmost limit. In the case of ivy-leaved toadflax and red valerian at least, man has probably had a hand in carrying them across the Channel, and they luxuriate so long as there is a warm wall or protective cliff face for their roots to grip.

Maidenhair fern barely more than survives in such a dull northern clime as mainland Britain, and will not venture far from the limestone cliffs and warm walls of the south and west. In western Ireland it could be a different plant – strong, large-leaved and luxuriant – as it shares the rock crevices with the pretty little white-flowered Irish *Geranium celticum.* This inter-generic relationship is not so well balanced in England and Wales, for there the red stemmed herb robert, *Geranium robertianum,* with its bright pink flowers a cheerful splash of colour against the dull grey stones, often shares a site but tends to swamp the delicate fern fronds. Herb robert, though not confined to Britain, is very much at home in temperate northern climes, and can usefully be planted in a wall, provided there is some moisture all the year round and the garden setting is not too formal. *Geranium lucidum* is a very similar plant, also with a red tinge to its stems and leaves, and pink flowers which last successively over a long season. It will manage on a shaded wall, and seems to need less moisture than *G. robertianum.* Ripe seed capsules can be picked from midsummer on, and seed offers the easiest method of propagation for these native cranesbills.

Cymbalaria muralis

Old dry walls in southern England often display a modest patch of blue in spring and early summer from the tiny flowers of *Myosotis hispida*, the early forget-me-not, and dry banks sometimes support scattered colonies of the yellow and blue forget-me-not, *M. discolor*, whose little flowers are yellow when they open, and turn blue only as the season progresses. The best forget-me-not for the rock garden is *M. alpestris*, a true mountain plant, found in Britain and on many European hills. Cultivated varieties, of course, are well known, and the dwarf cultivars which come true from seed are ideal for forming drifts down the rockery slopes. They are biennial, and easily maintained in cycle by the simple and time-honoured expedient of shaking the old plants free of seed over the growing area each year.

Typical British wall plants include the biting stonecrop *Sedum acre*, whose bright green mat of tiny, fleshy leaves becomes starred with yellow flowers in June and July. It can be very invasive, but the yellow-leaved variety Aureum makes a temptingly cheerful patch of colour, especially in the spring, and it can be allowed to take over a narrow

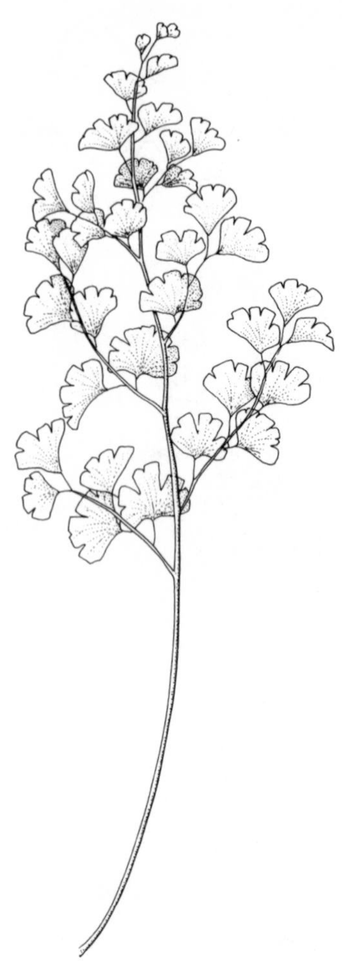

Adiantum capillus-veneris

gravelled path, with interesting results. For small rock garden use, however, there is a larger-leaved variety Majus, more conspicuous than the typical form, but which does not spread so rapidly or tenaciously. *S. anglicum* is better behaved and makes a mat of grey-green leaves, sometimes tinted with red, with pretty little flowers of the palest pink. The white stonecrop, *S. album,* has white flowers and a leaf colour usually midway between the other two, but sometimes this, also, becomes attractively tinged with yellow or purple.

The saxifrages are allied to the stonecrops, and perhaps the best known of these is London Pride – *Saxifraga umbrosa,* or a closely related hybrid; its origin is somewhat obscure, but it has been growing in Britain long enough to be called British. The closely carpeting leaf rosettes with their dainty pink-spotted starry flowers, stamens

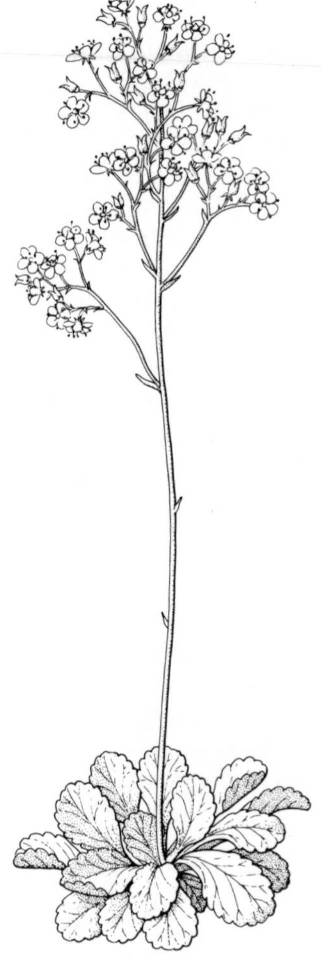

Saxifraga umbrosa

splayed like the legs and antennae of sprawling ants, make a charming drift in partial shade along the lower slopes of a comprehensive rock garden. For sunny spots in a similar situation there is the yellow-blotched variety Variegata Aurea, which makes a change from the normal green but looks a little odd, in my view, and can easily be overdone. The mossy saxifrages of the Continental hills are represented in Britain by *Saxifraga hypnoides,* in England called the Dovedale moss, which makes a compact, bright green cushion with clusters of miniature white flowers in the summer. It looks at home in any shady, moist, stony place.

A member of the same family is the pennywort, *Umbilicus rupestris,* a plant of damp shady spots, walls, and crevices in the rock. More typically a plant of the south-western European flora, it is limited in

British distribution to the milder south and west, where its curiously rounded, centrally stalked leaves, and spikes of small, greenish-white flowers make an interesting clump for siting beneath an overhanging rock. Cornish moneywort, *Sibthorpia europaea*, has a similar European range, and prefers the mild, moist south-western areas of mainland Britain and Ireland, to the drier east. It is an inconspicuous little plant with tiny pink flowers, but it makes a pleasant, unobtrusive carpet in moist places, rooting as it runs. There is an attractive variety Variegata with larger leaves, marked with golden green and silver, and this is well worth encouraging at the base of a wall, or to weld together clusters of small stones that have had perforce to take the place of proper rockery boulders. There is some similarity here to the carpets of sea heath, *Frankenia laevis*, whose tiny and densely clustered leaves, spangled during July with minute, tubular, pale pink flowers, can take the place of Cornish moneywort on poor, dry sites, perhaps on sandy areas, and is an excellent subject to run between paving stones where a healthy, evergreen appearance is so valuable in mid-winter. Frankenia is a natural associate along the south-eastern coastline with the sea campion, *Silene maritima*, a sprawling plant with rather fleshy, bluish grey leaves and stems, decorated from July to September with cut-petalled white flowers, each with a conspicuous, round, greenish bladder. There is a double-flowered form Flore Pleno, which is more decorative than the type, and this makes a reasonably good wall plant, never happier than when rooted in a shingly soil in the sun.

Armeria maritima

(Above) Primula auricula, the popular 'dusty miller', has innumerable forms. *(Below) Primula marginata* enjoys a peaty compost which contains crushed brick

One of the best known British seaside plants is the wild thrift or sea pink, *Armeria maritima,* with its familiar globular heads of mauve-pink flowers decorating the cliffs from June to August. The wild form is noticeably variable, and there are several named varieties with flower colours ranging from white to deep crimson-pink. The thick, woody rootstock can be cut and the pieces, with grass-like leaves attached, used as cuttings under glass during the growing season. Thrift is not limited in distribution to the sea coast: it is found in mountainous country too, in Wales and Scotland, where it makes a perfect flower colour blend with the dainty blue bells of the harebell, *Campanula rotundifolia,* a widespread plant of dry, hilly country; a clump of thrift surrounded by a small drift of the harebell is quietly effective when arranged at eye level, either on the rock garden or above a retaining wall.

The dry hills of southern England are home to several useful rock garden plants: marjoram, *Origanum vulgare,* grows wild there and makes an unusual clump of softly hairy, rounded leaves, with spikes of purple flowers in the summer. Its golden variety Aureum is more attractive, and might be found a place in the sun. Marjoram is closely related to thyme, and *Thymus serpyllum* is also found wild in dry, stony places, but it prefers cliffs and grassy banks near the sea where the cool, moist breezes help to keep the leafy carpet healthy and dense. The wild species has reddish flowers, and there are several very attractive cultivars, including Albus, with white flowers and light green leaves; Coccineus, with dark green leaves and rich crimson flowers; and Pink Chintz, again dark green, but with rose-pink flowers. All three are carpeters, making dense, prostrate mats of tiny leaves, but the pink-flowered Elfin forms tight little cushions of foliage that will not be out of place in the sink garden. All the thymes are ideal for gaps between the paving stones, and all are easy to grow on a sunny site in any light soil. They can be propagated by division either in the early spring or after flowering has finished or, when the stock plants are small and large numbers of new plants are needed, cuttings may be taken as soon as growth starts in the spring.

On sunny days, the rockrose *Helianthemum nummularium* displays a bright patch of yellow blossom, conspicuous among the sheep-cropped turf of the chalk downs – a natural habitat suggesting the type of garden treatment that will suit its many named varieties best: a sunny site on a dry bank, and a light clipping-over after flowering has finished in July – treatment which often results in a fresh crop of flowers before autumn, and ensures a neat, trim, carpeting habit. The

(Opposite) Veronica teucrium Trehane is one of the many garden varieties of this widespread speedwell

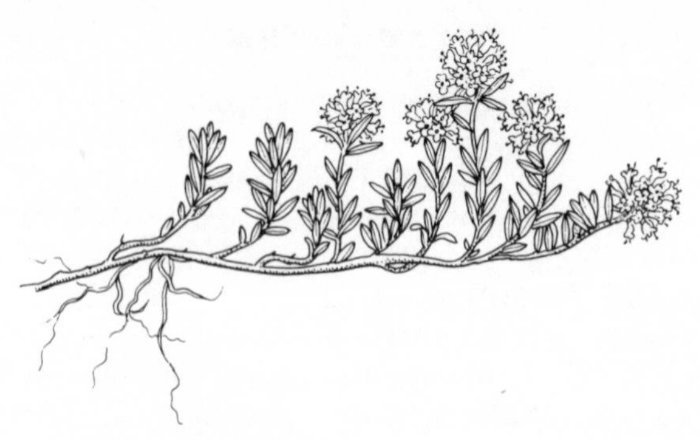

Thymus serpyllum

natural site of *H. nummularium* is nearly always chalky or limy, but, provided the texture is sandy and light, the varieties will thrive in soils as acid as pH 5, and there is no need to add lime for any reading higher than this. The Scottish Ben series includes some striking cultivars: Ben Dearg has mid-green foliage with coppery orange flowers; Ben Fhada, grey-green with orange and yellow flowers; Ben Hope, sage-green with carmine and orange flowers; Ben Ledi, dark green with brilliant pink flowers; Ben More, dark green with bright orange; and Ben Nevis, mid-green with bright yellow and crimson. Other favourite varieties include: Red Dragon, mid-green with yellow and scarlet; Rhodanthe Carneum, silver-grey foliage with flesh-pink and orange; The Bride, silver-grey with cream and yellow; Watergate Rose, sage-green with crimson and orange; and Wisley Primrose, greyish green with two-toned yellow flowers. Seed sowings will result in new, unnamed varieties which will probably not be as good as these, but they will all increase readily from shoot cuttings taken during the growing season and set in a frame, or under a polythene bag.

The drier British hills are often enlivened with the bold yellow splashes of broom and gorse – shrubs which are usually too large and coarse for garden use, though the small, drooping-branched *Cytisus prostratus* (it may be no more than a natural variety of the common *C. scoparius*) is of a useful garden size. Dyer's greenweed, *Genista tinctoria*, is also a very useful little shrub with bright golden yellow flowers, and the variety Plena especially, with its handsome double flowers, is dwarf and prostrate and takes its place with the best of the introduced species on the rock garden. It has to be propagated from cuttings, and these should be heeled side-shoots pulled off in the early autumn, and set in a frame to root over winter.

One of the most coveted plants of the chalk hills in southern England is the pasque flower, *Pulsatilla vulgaris,* whose anemone-like tufts of feathery leaves are decorated in April with short-stemmed flowers like broad-lipped violet crocuses. The wild form has suffered in the past from over-collection, but there are many named varieties with variously coloured flowers. As an interesting alternative to the crocuses, they make a charming drift on dry rockery slopes, and like to be left alone to increase slowly.

The pasque flower, of course, has its counterpart on the Continent, and so does the Cheddar pink, *Dianthus gratianopolitanus,* although its British distribution is limited to a small area of limestone cliff. Here again is a wild flower that has suffered from over-collection by gardeners lured, perhaps, as much by the name and aura of distinction, as by any qualities the plant may have. Cheddar pink forms a mat of blue-green leaves with fragrant, ragged-petalled, deep pink flowers from May to July, but several named garden varieties have arisen, some of which have darker or double flowers. Plants may be reared from plump shoot-tip cuttings taken early in the growing season, and I have found that three cuttings placed together to root in a paper pot under glass result in a sturdy, bushy little plant ready for planting out the following spring.

Another lover of limestone crags is the pretty legume *Anthyllis vulneraria,* commonly called lady's fingers. Inland, the pea-type flower clusters are yellow, but near the coast of Wales and the West Country, and in western Scotland, the flowers are red and the plant is given the varietal name Coccinea. It will come true from seed, and this is the best method to use when propagating this very neat little plant.

A weed may be defined as a plant growing where it is not wanted, and many wild flowers become weeds when they enter horticultural bounds. There are several unspectacular little plants, however, that are rarely noticed in the wild but which translate well to the rock garden, or which have a double-flowered form or a variegation that makes them desirable. The common daisy, *Bellis perennis,* is so prevalent as a lawn weed that it rarely receives the attention it deserves, but, high on the mountainside, the same plant has attraction, and a clump is not out of place on the rockery. Its giant double varieties are sheer Victoriana: the pink Alice; the red and white Victoria; the much dwarfer pink Dresden China. When these plants are used as a permanent feature, they will need lifting, dividing and replanting every second year to keep them healthy.

Chamomile, *Anthemis nobilis,* is very daisy-like in the flower, and this, too, has found a place for itself in the garden. Forming a close mat as it does, it has often been used to establish grass-free lawns in areas where the soil tends to dry out too severely for healthy turf, and it will make an unusual path. The best for these purposes is a non-flowering variety, Treneague, but there is also a double-flowered form which is quite ornamental as a rock plant. Rupturewort, *Herniaria glabra,* is an inconspicuous weed of dry, sandy places, but it has the virtue of remaining green and fresh in the driest weather and, with its close

Anthemis nobilis

carpet of tiny, rounded, dark green leaves, is often of use for running over rocks or covering a path. The sandwort, *Arenaria ciliata,* falls into the same category and, with its clusters of starry white flowers over a long summer season, is worthy of a place to itself at the foot of the scree. Another is the lesser stitchwort, *Stellaria graminea,* a common perennial of waste places, and this has a variety Aurea which makes a grassy yellow mat, well sprinkled in the spring and early summer with tiny, starry white flowers, All these creeping plants for sunny sites and dry soils have the attraction of easy propagation, for they will divide again and again.

The wild plants of hedgerow and woodland edge are not always such obvious candidates for the rock garden. Winter cress, *Barbarea vulgaris,* for instance, might grow unnoticed among lush vegetation, with its much-lobed, glossy, dark green leaves and cheerful if unremarkable yellow flowers, but the variety Variegata with cream-blotched leaves makes an attractive clump which, if there is no room on the rockery, might well be sited nearby as a link between mountain and lowland plants. Creeping Jenny, *Lysimachia nummularia*, is a favourite little plant – bright in the summer with starry yellow flowers – which spreads its trailers in moist, shady places, often inhabiting the shores of lakes and large ponds. The yellow-leaved variety Aurea is especially interesting, and useful for clothing a shaded wall.

One of the first plants to flower in the New Year is the celandine, *Ranunculus ficaria*, which carpets the ground with starry, deep glossy yellow flowers like many-petalled buttercups – a long naturalised introduction – and this is regarded by many as a weed when it invades the garden. Its bronzy orange-flowered variety Aurantiaca, however, is not invasive, and can provide a much needed late winter patch of colour for the foot of the rockery. Another unusual acquisition for a shaded patch below the outcrop is the green-flowered herb paris, *Paris quadrifolia*. The carpeting wintergreen, *Pyrola minor*, could be used to run around the clump as a stabiliser, with its rounded, leathery leaves and spikes of tiny pale pink flowers during the summer months. This wintergreen has creeping stolons which invite casual division, but divided portions do not take too kindly to replanting, and need careful nursing.

Selfheal, *Prunella vulgaris*, is a common plant of grassy places and can become a serious weed if allowed to invade the lawn, but there are several varieties or hybrids which can make a very attractive patch of carpet. Those of the 'Loveliness' series have dark purplish green leaves and flowers of selected colours, lilac, pink and white; the cultivar Red Riding Hood has rose-red flowers, and all are vigorous spreaders which are not likely to take over the garden.

Scarlet pimpernel is a tiny, well known wild flower common on wasteland and, while pretty, is not likely to be given garden space. The closely related bog pimpernel, *Anagallis tenella*, however, is well worth a place in a boggy patch at the base of the moraine, and the cultivated form Studland, though not always reliably hardy, makes an eye-catching carpet, with its tiny, fresh green leaves and delicate pink, fragrant bell flowers over the summer months.

Perhaps the best known British woodland plant is the bluebell, too hefty for most rock gardens. More suitable is the equally well-loved primrose, and *Primula vulgaris* is as valuable as any exotic species for a reasonably moist situation in the equivalent of light woodland shade. The wild pinkish purple 'Welsh' form looks very good when allowed to form a drift among large rocks. The cowslip, *Primula veris*, with its darker yellow and more tubular, sweetly scented flowers, prefers open meadowland and a drier soil, but it will also thrive in the

Primula vulgaris

light shade of the woodland edge. *Primula elatior*, the oxlip, is sometimes confused with an occasionally occurring natural hybrid between primrose and cowslip. Indeed, its characteristics are somewhat a blend of the two, for the pale yellow flowers, though in primrose-like clumps, are slightly tubular and nodding, and the leaves are similar to those of the cowslip. Purchased seed of *P. elatior* tends to be of hybrid origin, and includes strains with coloured flowers which, though they have pleasantly subdued tones, cannot escape an appearance of annual spring bedding, and rob the rock garden of its naturally wild atmosphere. In the north of England and in Scotland, the bird's-eye primrose *P. farinosa* is common – a plant which, like *P. veris*, prefers open meadows and banks to the woodland shade but, unlike that species, needs a moist soil on which to thrive. It has dusty leaves and mauve-pink, yellow-eyed flowers. *P. scotica* is similar but with darker purple flowers, a rare hill plant of northern Scotland which deserves a place on the high moraine where it can be admired from eye level.

The sweet violet, *Viola odorata*, ranks high on the list of popular woodland plants, and such a precious little flower deserves a shady pocket of its own on the rock garden. Brightest of the wild British violas is *V. lutea* which, with its yellow flowers – often varied with violet, mauve and white – has sired many garden hybrids over the years. Other woodland plants in Britain include several carpet-formers which can be put to good use in certain situations. The deadnettle family has *Lamiastrum galeobdolon* Variegatum, the yellow archangel – the little yellow flowers look in close-up like a traditional angel with arching wings – with silver-splashed leaves, and the pink-flowered, silver-striped *Lamium maculatum.* Both these plants make a splendid ground cover for light shade, and they may appropriately be sited as intermediate vegetation to link the rock garden with the shady border. The closely allied bugle, *Ajuga reptans,* which makes a close cover of crowded, narrow leaves, has several cultivated varieties selected from individuals with highly coloured leaves: Burgundy Glow, Multicolor (syn. Rainbow) and Pink Elf have striking variegations in shades of green, grey, bronze, purple, yellow and pink, while the flowers too are quite pleasant, in spikes of purple or blue during early summer. Each will make a striking clump or drift for a pocket among the rocks, and can easily be curtailed if it spreads too vigorously. *A. pyramidalis*, with blue flower spikes, is very similar.

Wood anemone is a favourite little plant that well deserves a lightly shaded place of its own. The typical *Anemone nemorosa* has white flowers veined and backed with pink, and selected varieties include: the double white Alba Plena; the pink Rosea; the lavender-blue Robinsoniana; the pale blue Allenii and Blue Bonnet; and the dark Royal Blue.

The ground ivy, *Glechoma hederacea,* makes a cover that runs too far, too vigorously, to be of much use in or around the rock garden, but its variety Variegata is far less vigorous, though it spreads extensively, and merely patterns the ground with its silver-marked leaves. It might be admissible to run around the stems of taller shrubs, or to carpet a heavily shaded area. The common ivy *Hedera helix* has

Viola lutea

two cultivars which originated from the stabilised, adult form of foliage that does not climb: Congesta, with three-lobed leaves, and Conglomerata, with rounded leaves. Both make dwarf, densely foliaged mounds that slowly pile up into a miniature bush. Cuttings taken from any topmost, flowering growth of the common ivy will grow into bushes that do not usually show a tendency to climb, but they will not be dwarf. Congesta and Conglomerata, on the other hand, are useful for clothing old walls in the shade, with the knowledge that they will not swamp their site. Irish ivy, *Hedera helix* Hibernica, does not normally climb, but it is not suitable for rock gardens. A cross between this plant and *Fatsia japonica*, however, produced the bigeneric hybrid × *Fatshedera lizei*, and this spreading evergreen is well behaved, and has proved useful for filling awkward gaps in the shade.

Ajuga reptans

Anemone nemorosa

Moist, rocky places in the woodland, old walls, or even tree trunks often develop an attractive cover of ferns. The oak fern, *Gymnocarpium dryopteris,* with its delicate, bright green fronds, as a rule carpets the ground. The polypody, *Polypodium vulgare,* on the other hand, will clothe almost any surface in the shade and will even grow quite high up trees, so it is an ideal subject for the shady wall. Both plants have creeping rootstocks which are easily divided, and small pieces replanted will soon start new colonies. Something of a fern-like appearance is exhibited by *Trientalis europaea,* the British equivalent of the American star flower which, like that plant, will make a spreading clump of thin stems, each surmounted by a star-like rosette of narrow leaves and, in June and July, little white starry flowers.

One of the most handsome shrubby woodland plants that have deservedly found their way into our gardens is the tutsan, *Hypericum androsaemum.* It is limited in natural distribution to the south and west of the country, where it prefers light, sandy soils. The 2cm wide yellow flowers that cover it in succession throughout the summer months quickly develop into red and black berries, so that flowers and fruit are displayed together. The flowers are not as impressive as some

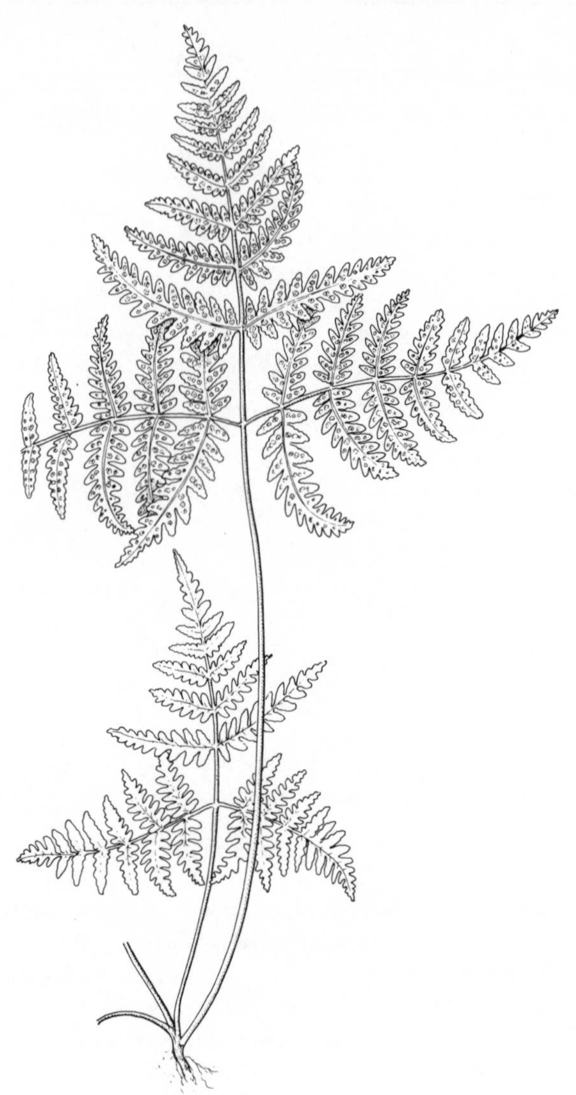

Gymnocarpium dryopteris

others of the genus, such as *H. patulum,* but the bush has a charm of its own, and is often the perfect answer when an ornamental, knee-high drift of shrubs is needed to fringe the rockery, or where trees and tall bushes are too closely adjacent. Tutsan grows readily from seed – there are usually self-sown seedlings to be dug up near established bushes – but it will also come readily from cuttings. The trailing St John's wort, *Hypericum humifusum,* is more truly a rock plant, and makes thin mats of trailing stems with rounded leaves, and little yellow or red-tinted flowers from June till September. It is not berrying, but, like tutsan, trailing St John's wort grows readily from cuttings taken at any time during the growing season.

In the hills of the west and north especially, the purple spires of the foxglove are a familiar sight. *Digitalis purpurea* is too tall for the average rock garden but, if a place can be found for a group of them at the base of the rocks, they will provide just that hint of mountain rising out of woodland that brings the rock garden to life. It is a biennial and needs sowing each year, simply shaking the tiny seeds from the dry capsules as soon as they are ripe; they germinate so readily that there is seldom need to give them nursery treatment.

Wood sorrel, *Oxalis acetosella*, is not only a woodlander but also a mountain plant, and it enjoys the shade and moisture within the lee of large boulders. Its shamrock leaves have the unusual habit of growing afresh during the autumn and lasting through the winter months – an adaptation to counter the summer shade of its native oak forests – and the pretty little purple-veined white flowers appear in the spring. There is a pink-flowered form, Rosea, and both this and the type make a useful bright yellowish green mat.

Boggy areas in the west and north are the habitat of the grass of parnassus, *Parnassia palustris*, a member of the saxifrage family, and a tuft-former with long-stalked, heart-shaped leaves and white, green-veined flowers on display from July to October. It makes an attractive clump for the foot of the moraine. There are several charming little plants which grow in the peat bogs, though few would be at home on the rock garden. An exception is *Wahlenbergia hederacea*, a pretty little creeping plant which might well find its way to a boggy spot at the base of the moraine. It has tiny, triangular leaves and campanula-like flowers of a clear, pale blue. At home in the peat bogs of western Europe and the British Isles and not always easy to keep in captivity, it sheds its seed in August and September among the sphagnum moss, where it germinates freely. This process might be imitated by establishing the bog moss in a shallow tray, as described for propagating erica heaths in Chapter Five, and simply scattering the fresh seed across the sphagnum turf.

A very local plant of northern England, which grows on limestone cliffs and looks even better on an old stone wall than the more widespread herb robert, is the crimson-flowered *Geranium sanguineum*, the bloody cranesbill. It has been a much-prized garden acquisition for centuries, and several cultivated varieties are in existence, their flower colours ranging from white through shades of pink to deep crimson-rose. A good companion for this, whether on the wild limestone rock face or a stone garden wall, is the hart's tongue fern, *Phyllitis scolopendrium*, unique among British ferns with its broad, dark green, strap-shaped leaves. When planted on a shady bank

Phyllitis scolopendrium

or in the crevices of a wall, hart's tongue will often seed itself but, if it does not, the hard green frond bases may be removed after the old leaves have withered and, when potted up under glass, usually produce tiny bulbils which grow into new plants.

Upland Britain – rough grazing land, mountain top and moorland – occupies a third of the area of these highly populated islands, and much of the moorland is covered by almost pure colonies of heather, *Calluna vulgaris.* Although the species enjoys a wide natural range through much of the northern hemisphere, it has a peculiarly British and Irish flavour, and it is from British horticulturists that most of the many named cultivars have originated. The mono-specific *Calluna vulgaris* is a determinedly lime-hating plant, although it sometimes grows on areas of peat that have built up over limestone rocks, or on chalk hills where the soil has become acid through the action of rain water washing the lime downhill. In size and habit, the cultivars range from the virtually flowerless path-carpeter The Pygmy, and Foxii Nana, to the waist-high Mair's Variety, with its long spikes of lucky white flower. Californian Midge is tiny and compact, with neat purple flowers, and makes an admirable trough plant. Foxhole Wanderer is a good flowerer with long spikes of purple flower, and also makes a dense, low cover of bright green, weed-proof foliage. Tom Thumb makes an unusual, almost juniper-like plant with pink flowers, and is small and neat enough for the trough garden. More closely resembling the wild species, but with a neater habit and finer flower spikes, there are: Alportii with crimson flowers; County Wicklow with bright pink, double flowers; Elegantissima, a late-flowering mauve-pink; H. E. Beale with double, silvery pink flowers; Hibernica, a late-flowering pink; J. H. Hamilton, double bright pink; Joan Sparkes, double bright purple; Mullion, a fairly low carpeter with deep pink flowers; Peter Sparkes with double flowers of deep pink; and Tib, double crimson and one of the earliest to flower. White heather varieties include: Alba Plena, the double white form; Alba Minor, an early dwarf; and Hammondii, a large and vigorous bush. Varieties with coloured foliage that gives a touch of colour outside the flowering season include: Cuprea, with bronzy, scarlet-tipped foliage, but with typical heather flowers; Golden Feather, rarely flowering, but with golden orange, feathery foliage; Gold Haze, with bright golden foliage and first-class white flower spikes; Mrs Pat, a dwarf bush with typical flowers and dark green, vividly pink-tipped foliage; Prostrate Orange, a good carpeter with golden orange foliage, though seldom flowering; Ruth Sparkes, with golden yellow foliage and double white flowers; and Sunset, with pink flowers, and brilliantly variegated orange, yellow and green foliage.

Calluna vulgaris and its cultivars are comparatively easy to root from cuttings: side-shoots about 2cm long should be pulled off the plants so as to retain a small heel of older wood, and the best time for the operation is the end of summer, around August. *Calluna* has a mycorrhizal association similar to *Erica*, and identical precautions should be taken when attempting to root cuttings or germinate seed of either genus: some soil should be collected from beneath established heathers, and incorporated in the rooting compost, or arranged below it in the container, so that the newly emerging roots can come into contact with the tiny fungal bodies in the soil. Although cuttings root fairly readily in a sandy compost, either within a polythene bag or under glass, they need very careful attention later when they are removed from this protected environment and potted on their own – the soil should be maintained at a constant moisture level, and they must be sheltered from scorching sunlight. Once properly established, however, and given an open, sunny site in a lime-free soil, heathers are among the sturdiest and hardiest of plants.

Daboecia cantabrica, the Connemara heath, may be found in many parts of south-west Europe besides western Ireland. It is not such a determined coloniser as the true heaths, is bushy, spreading, long-flowering, often rather large for the general rock garden – although

Porter's Variety is dwarf – and less hardy than either *Erica* or *Calluna*. Some of the best varieties include: Alba, with white flowers; Atropurpurea, with deep purple flowers; Bicolor, which includes white, pink and purple flowers on the same bush; Globosa, with large silvery purple flowers; and Praegerae, with salmon-pink flowers. Cuttings may be taken as for *Calluna* or, as with all heaths and heathers, layers pegged down during the summer and covered fairly deeply will usually produce new roots by the following year.

Several *Erica* species with a wide European distribution occur in Ireland, but *Erica hibernica* is uniquely Irish. Larger than most of the genus, and possibly hybrid in origin, the Irish heather has given rise to a few cultivated forms, notably: Brightness, which forms a thick clump of greyish green foliage with deep pink flower sprays from March to May; Coccinea, a similar early spring-flowering plant, but the flower colour is a deeper, more purplish pink; and W. T. Rackliff, which makes a thick, heavily foliaged, rounded bush with long sprays of pure white flowers in the spring.

Some of the conifers that associate particularly well with heathers are Irish in origin. Among the many common juniper varieties, *Juniperus communis* Hibernica is the Irish juniper, a compact, narrow column which resembles a dwarf version of the Mediterranean or

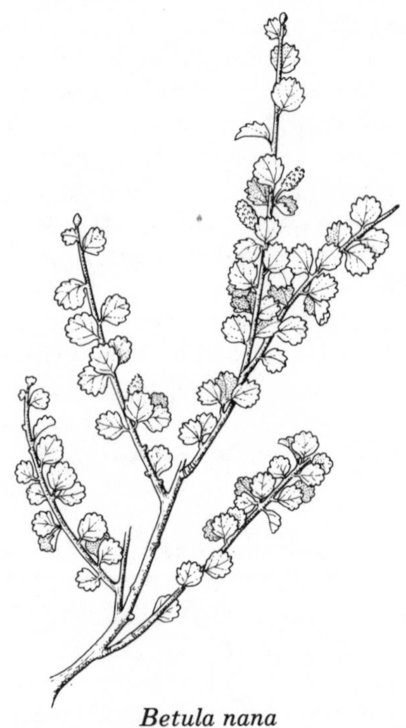

Betula nana

Italian cypress *J.c.* Compressa is an even dwarfer form, tiny and neat enough for the sink garden, and almost too small for the average rockery. Creeping varieties of *Juniperus communis* which originated in Ireland include: Hornibrookii, which makes an extremely close cover; and Repanda, scarcely taller, making a bronzy plume-like ground cover; while Montana, a naturally occurring form, is found not only in the mountains of the United Kingdom but also over the whole of the northern hemisphere from America to Siberia and Japan. It makes a dark green cover of thick foliage, and imparts a touch of wild grandeur to any craggy rock face. Cuttings taken from these junipers seem to root better after the bushes have experienced a touch of frost, and autumn or early winter is often the most successful time of year for taking them.

The Irish moors also gave rise, two centuries ago, to the upright form of the common yew, *Taxus baccata* Fastigiata. The golden Irish yew, *T.b.* Fastigiata Aurea, is very handsome and popular, but both these forms are really too large for any but the largest rock gardens. *T.b.* Standishii is a dwarfer, slower-growing type of golden Irish yew, and this is the best upright *Taxus* cultivar for the smaller garden.

The conifer perhaps most often associated with heather in the wild is the Scots pine, *Pinus sylvestris*, one of the most ornamental and garden-worthy of the pines. It has several dwarf forms eminently suitable for the rock garden, and probably the best of these is Beuvronensis – a dwarf replica of the mature, round-topped Scots pine of the ancient Caledonian forests, with glowing orange-barked limbs contrasting with the bluish green foliage. It is often worth trimming these dwarf trees very carefully so as to increase the amount of stem and branch visible, and enhance this miniature, almost bonsai

Linnaea borealis

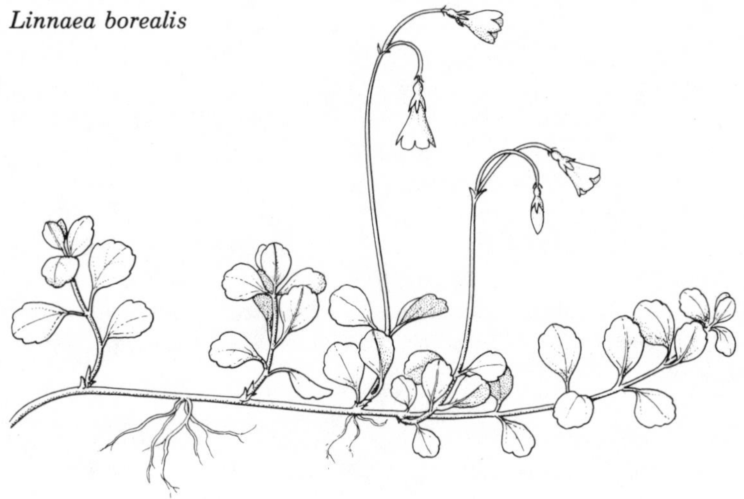

effect. The variety Windsor makes a congested bun of tangled branches and tiny blue-green needles; Compressa and Doone Valley both make rounded bushes with crowded, grey-green foliage.

Two dwarf trees – or shrubs – typical of the high moorland are *Betula nana*, the dwarf birch, and *Salix repens*, the creeping willow. Dwarf birch makes a neat bush with tiny, rounded, glossy green leaves, and little green catkins in the spring; creeping willow forms sometimes extensive carpets of small, silvery grey-green leaves, covered with tiny buff catkins in the early spring. Both are true species and will grow from seed – a necessity in the case of the birch, which will not root from cuttings. They are not the most attractive of shrubs available for the rock garden, but they have the valuable ability to grow and thrive in damp, boggy places.

Associates of heather on the drier reaches of upland moors are bilberry and the similar mountain cranberry, *Vaccinium vitis-idaea*. Centuries ago, mountain cranberry carpeted great areas of the Caledonian pine forests, and it is a useful ground-cover plant for lightly shaded sites today, with its close habit, its small, dark glossy green box-like leaves and little pinkish bells in the summer, and the sour but edible berries which follow. Another creeping evergreen which used to carpet the pine forests in many northern countries is the twin flower, *Linnaea borealis*. It is very pretty in May and June when the fragrant pink bells appear in distinctive pairs, and makes an attractive ground cover throughout the year in any peaty, lightly shaded spot. The long, trailing stems can be partially buried to induce rooting at the base of each shoot, and these can then be separated and replanted.

Sheep's fescue is a common grass of the dry mountain slopes, and the blue variety, *Festuca ovina* Glauca, makes a very attractive fine-leaved blue-grey tuft, non-invasive and well behaved. It might with advantage be allowed to form a drift on even the purist plantsman's rock garden. The truly Alpine flora of the Scottish Highlands includes the mountain avens, *Dryas octopetala*, a pretty little creeping plant with evergreen foliage and 4cm wide yellow-eyed white flowers in the spring. The woody stems root as they crawl between the rocks, and portions of these may be removed and replanted, but the fine roots are not always easy to dislodge without damage. Cuttings taken during the summer root fairly readily in a sandy soil, and the seed – the feathery seedheads are conspicuous – also germinates freely. There is a hybrid, *Dryas* × *suendermanii*, which is a larger plant with nodding, yellowish white flowers.

(Opposite) This spring-flowering gentian, *Gentiana verna*, is easy to grow in a gritty soil

(Top left) The shepherd's thyme, *Thymus serpyllum,* can be found growing wild in dry, stony places. *(Top right) Anagallis tenella* Studland, a pimpernel for a boggy patch at the foot of the moraine. *(Centre left) Geranium sanguineum,* a pale-flowered form of the British bloody cranesbill. *(Centre right)* A truly Alpine plant, *Dryas octopetala* is found wild in the Scottish Highlands. *(Bottom left) Euphorbia myrsinites,* a spurge which needs a sheltered spot among stones

The mountain lady's mantles, *Alchemilla alpina* and the similar *A. conjuncta*, are found in the Scottish Highlands, and they are much more suitable for the rock garden than the better known *Alchemilla vulgaris*, for they are smaller, more compact of leaf, and less inclined to spread beyond bounds. The greenish flower clusters are similar, but the deeply lobed leaves of *A. alpina* and *A. conjuncta* have a silvery, silken sheen. Another mountain plant with a well known counterpart is *Cerastium alpinum*, much less vigorous than the ubiquitous snow-in-summer, *C. tomentosum*. It forms a mat of greyish green foliage, with clusters of white flowers during the summer. Being more at home, perhaps, in the dry-cold deep snow of the European Alps, and flourishing in the drier, more easterly parts of the Scottish Highlands, it is sometimes apt to suffer when planted in wet-winter areas.

The mountain pearlworts *Sagina glabra* and *S. boydii* make very useful little cushions. The larger of the two is *S. glabra*, a spreading tangle of narrow-leaved shoots with nodding white flowers in the summer, and there is also a yellow-leaved variety which looks good on a sunny ledge. *Sagina boydii* is neat enough for the sink garden with its closely matted, dark glossy green leaves, though the flowers are inconspicuous. It is available from some nurseries although, following its introduction to horticulture during the nineteenth century, it is said to have disappeared from its Scottish mountain home, and has never since been recorded as a wild plant.

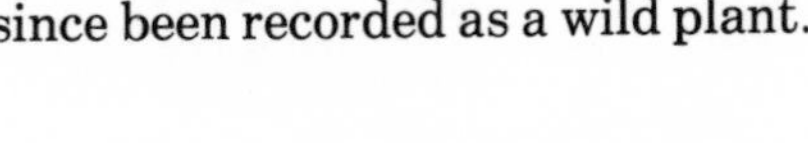

Dryas octopetala

Alchemilla alpina

7
The Mediterranean Influence

Plants of the Mediterranean type are accustomed to long months of summer dryness and heat, with rain in the winter, and the specialised flora produced by this type of climate may be found in similar zones at some distance north and south of the Mediterranean Sea itself. The Straits of Gibraltar – the traditional gateway to the Mediterranean – are narrow enough for many plants to have crossed by natural means. Cat thyme, *Teucrium marum*, is found on both continents, and is typical, perhaps, of a plant well adapted to its environment, with moisture-conserving woolly white leaves, and clusters of purple flowers in midsummer – a useful little shrub for the driest, sunniest sites but, often, an irresistible invitation to all the neighbourhood cats.

The Mediterranean influence extends south and west to the Moroccan Atlas Mountains, and several good rock garden plants hardy in northern climes – provided the summers are not too wet, nor the winters too cold – have been assembled from that region: the pretty little mountain daisy, *Anacyclus depressus*, for instance, whose prostrate stems with their tiny, ferny leaves carry yellow-eyed white flowers which are crimson in the bud; and a dwarf orange daisy, *Senecio doronicum hosmariensis* – one of that vast, almost worldwide genus that so loves warm, dry situations, with species to be found decorating hilltops throughout Africa, though few of them would be thought worthy of a garden place. The larger version of the species, *Senecio doronicum*, is less a Mediterranean plant, extending north as it does into central Europe.

From these dry North African mountains comes a fleshy-rooted buttercup, *Ranunculus calandrinioides*, whose greyish green leaves emerge, hosta-like, from the stony ground, with stems of 5cm wide, broad-petalled pale pink flowers in the spring. Two spring-flowering bulbous plants are *Tulipa celsiana* with starry yellow, red-tinted flowers, and *Narcissus watieri*, a dainty little daffodil with pure white flowers; while the winter-flowering *Iris unguicularis* from Algeria is an example of a plant – belonging to a moisture-loving genus – which has adapted itself to arid conditions.

The fleshy plants of the *Crassulaceae* would seem well adapted to withstand the lack of summer moisture, but few have established themselves in the region. Of those that have, the houseleek *Sempervivum atlanticum* probably stemmed originally from the common European *S. tectorum*, but now inhabits the western Atlas, where its red-tipped, sage-green rosettes cluster within rock crevices to produce their sprays of tiny white flowers – the petals minutely marked with purple, so that the overall effect is pale pink. From further east on the same mountain range there is also a stonecrop, *Sedum multiceps*, which makes tiny tufts of fleshy leaves with rather sparse clusters of starry yellow flowers in July.

At a lower elevation, the North African vegetation soon takes on desert characteristics, and if we seek lowland Mediterranean plants, we need to return to the European coastline. Cistus is a name that comes readily to mind when considering plants typical of south-west Europe, and some of the hybrids and named varieties are among the most useful of shrubs, and reasonably hardy for northern gardens. Best of all, perhaps, is the hybrid *Cistus*×*cyprius*, with crimson-blotched white flowers, but this, like many of the others, is too large for the average rock garden. One of the smallest is *Cistus* Peggy Sannons, with delicate pink flowers, but even this will eventually make a metre in height. For really hot, sunny spots, however, cultivars such as these are indispensable, and all are quite easily propagated by shoot cuttings 5-10cm long, taken in August and placed under a polythene bag or in a mildly heated frame. Other species and fine varieties which keep within reasonable bounds of growth include: *C. laurifolius* – probably the hardiest species, with leathery, laurel-like leaves and yellow-centred white flowers; *C. populifolius*, also hardy, with similar flowers and small, poplar-like leaves; *C.* Pat, with long, pointed leaves and crimson-spotted white flowers; and *C.* Silver Pink, with pointed leaves and clear silvery pink flowers – one of the hardiest of the hybrids and also one of the smallest and most compact. Silver Pink will usually survive a British winter, but it is always as well to take a few cuttings and overwinter them under glass, in case replacements are needed in the spring.

More in scale with the smaller rock garden is the broom *Genista delphinensis*, a typical dwarf shrub of southern coastal Europe – a tiny mound of brilliant yellow from July to the end of August, neat and small enough to make an excellent wall plant in the sun. Another dwarf broom that will serve this purpose to good effect is *Genista pulchella*, with greyish green, sometimes spiny foliage and bright yellow flowers clustered at the branch tips in June and July.

Many excellent wall plants are of the Mediterranean type, for a wall frequently provides the summer warmth and free drainage such plants require. Many subjects which are only marginally hardy in a particular district can prove perfectly safe in the coldest winter when they are wall planted. Such a plant of the French Riviera is the trailing snapdragon *Asarina procumbens*, which clothes the stones with hairy, lobed, sage-green leaves, producing its large white snapdragon flowers, marked with purple and yellow, in succession from May to September. It will grow in light shade too, though this is by no means a condition for healthy growth.

Ivy-leaved toadflax is a Mediterranean plant which has spread, not only over rocks and walls in its native zone, but to old walls in many countries further north, including the British Isles. It has a close relative, *Cymbalaria aequitriloba*, which is an excellent and well behaved wall plant, quite happy also between paving stones, where it makes a dense, evergreen cover of small, dark green, heart-shaped leaves, covered with tiny purple flowers in June. Another of the genus, from Corsica, is *hepaticifolia*, with kidney-shaped greyish green leaves and tiny lavender flowers during the summer months – good in shade, where it will clothe a wall without spreading out of place, and is also eminently suitable for covering spaces between paving stones.

Two plants which need the shelter of stone to ensure their survival during heavy frost include a spurge, *Euphorbia myrsinites*, with trailing stems and fleshy, pale grey-green leaves, and large clusters of yellow flowers during the summer months; and a St John's wort, *Hypericum coris*, rightly prized in northern rock gardens, for it is a charming little plant with its evergreen whorled leaves and bright golden flowers in July and August. Both are often lost when planted in the open, and a warm niche in a stone wall is the best possible site for them.

Not all the wall plants from this zone are half-hardy, of course, and the aubrietas are possibly the best known hardy subjects in this category. The wild *Aubrieta deltoides* is a variable plant, and there are numerous named cultivars. Some of the most distinct include: Dr Mules, one of the oldest and best, with deep violet-blue flowers; Greencourt Purple, with semi-double flowers of a rich purple; Bressingham Pink, with double clear pink flowers; and Red Carpet, with deep, glowing red flowers. The more typical purple shades make a perfect foil for such yellow spring flowers as *Anemone palmata*, whose huge golden buttercups rising from their tuft of lobed leaves revel in the same type of site.

The shrubby candytuft *Iberis sempervirens*, its Pink Variety, and the selected large-flowered Snowflake, are also perfectly hardy, although some dwarf forms of the species may not survive heavy frost.

They are popular plants in England, where they are usually thought of as an associate for *Alyssum saxatile*. *Iberis sempervirens* is a perfectly acceptable plant for the larger rock garden, but it has become so commonly used as a front garden stopgap that its presence may tend to detract from any studied rockery effect.

Iberis sempervirens

The names *Lithospermum prostratum* Grace Ward and *L.p.* Heavenly Blue are better known than the botanical name of the wild creeping shrub now known as *Lithodora diffusa*, a beautiful mat-former for a dryish, sunny site, and excellent on a stone retaining wall. The named varieties are more vigorous and have larger flowers of a richer blue than the species, and there is also a white-flowered variety. It is as well to treat these plants like aubrietas, and clip them back after flowering so as to retain their neat, carpet-like proportions. Propagation is best achieved by taking firm shoot cuttings in late summer; they must be kept well shaded, and the compost must be peaty and moisture-retaining but not wet, otherwise they will fail to root.

Onosma taurica, from the eastern end of the Mediterranean, is a striking wall associate for *Lithodora diffusa* Grace Ward. It is a coarsely hairy, tufted plant, with tubular yellow summer flowers arranged in a one-sided, curving cluster like the head of a shepherd's crook. Leafy cuttings of this species have a tendency to rot, and care must be taken to ensure that the hairy leaves do not touch the surface of the compost, or the polythene, or each other; but if these hazards can be avoided, rooting takes place very quickly under shade in the summer. *Onosma* can equally well be grown with *Moltkia petraea*, a plant that occasionally accompanies it in nature, and which is closely related to *Lithodora*. It has small, narrow, leathery leaves of pale green, and numerous clusters of tiny, trumpet-shaped blue flowers – the pinkish tinge to be seen in newly-opened flowers deepens gradually to a dark violet as the season progresses. It will thrive in similar sites and may be propagated in the same way as *Lithodora*, and may also be trimmed after flowering to keep the low bushes compact.

Two shrubby, sun-loving plants with little blue powder puff flowers are *Globularia bellidifolia* and *G. incanescens*, both to be found on the hot, dry slopes of south-facing hills near the Mediterranean, and equally appreciating sunny, dry slopes when moved to more northerly gardens. They are happy on a stone retaining wall, provided there is a flavour of lime in the soil, and *G. bellidifolia* in particular is neat enough to occupy the gaps between paving slabs and the margins of stone steps. Their tangled stems can usually be divided into rooted portions, but they set seed reliably and this usually germinates well.

The lavenders bring a touch of the Mediterranean to northern gardens and, while varieties of the common *Lavandula spica* may be best for cutting, the dwarfer *L. stoechas* is more ornamental, with its large coloured bracts, and is the best species to choose when planning a lavender clump for a sunny jumble of rocks. For propagation, side-shoots may be pulled off with a heel, and rooted at any time during the growing season. A comparable-sized bush from Corsica is *Anthyllis hermanniae*, with little greyish green leaves on a compact dome of tangled branches, and small clusters of broom-like yellow flowers in the spring, and this will also make a neat thicket in a warm, dry, sunny spot. There is a dwarf variety, Compacta, which will not outgrow the average small rock garden.

Stachys corsica is a close relative of the well known lamb's tongue, but its mat of little rounded leaves is a glossy green, and quite unlike the white woolly *S. lanata*; it is covered in the summer with spikes of pale pink flowers – a handsome and useful cover for dry, sunny spots. Old plants of *S. corsica* tend to die in the centre and, when they are lifted and divided, the central portion should be discarded. Other Corsican plants which have proved valuable include the popular lavender cotton, *Santolina chamaecyparissus*, of typically Mediterranean appearance with its ferny, white, downy leaves – one of the best of shrubs for the sunny border, but rather large for most rock gardens. It can be propagated very readily from cuttings at any season, however, so there is no reason why young plants should not be used among the rocks wherever their effect is needed, and discarded when they outgrow their site.

The Corsican creeping peppermint, *Mentha requienii*, makes a pretty, scented carpet with its tiny, rounded leaves and short-stemmed clusters of pale purple flowers in the summer. It is a denizen of cool, moist spots and shuns the usual Mediterranean-plant site. At the base of a moraine or near the path edge – perhaps beneath an occasionally dripping tap – this is a much-admired acquisition, and can be used in the kitchen for its delicate peppermint flavour. *Mentha pulegium*, the pennyroyal, with its wide distribution over the whole of Europe, including Britain, and much of Asia and North Africa, also occurs in these regions. It has a variegated dwarf form peculiar to Gibraltar, and both this plant and *M. requienii* were formerly much used in carpet bedding schemes which called for close spacing and constant attention.

A very useful little carpeting plant that enjoys similar conditions, and flourishes if allowed to spread over cool, moist rocks, is *Arenaria balearica*, a sandwort from the western Mediterranean islands. It makes a dense mat of tiny, bright green, glossy leaves, with numerous solitary, short-stemmed white flowers over a long season from March to August. It grows well in shade, and can be established on old free-standing stone walls. Severe winters sometimes blacken the foliage but it usually recovers, and can be a menace to other plants nearby, as it is liable to smother them. There is a closely related sandwort, *Arenaria tetraquetra*, from the eastern slopes of the Spanish Sierra Nevada – still within the zone of Mediterranean influence – and this forms a dense grey-green mound of rounded leaves, and also bears little white flowers. It is contrastingly a plant of open habitat, and requires a dryish, gritty soil high on the sunny scree, where it will make a neat cushion. Another little carpeter of broader distribution along the Mediterranean shore is *Micromeria varia*, a thyme-like plant with tiny yellowish green leaves and purple flowers. This also will make a neat cushion on the sunny scree, and is equally at home between paving stones, where it will come to no harm if it is trodden on occasionally. It will grow quite readily from shoot cuttings taken at any time during the growing season. Like the cat thyme *Teucrium marum*, this little plant is sometimes apt to be clawed and spoiled by cats which are attracted to the thyme scent. Also making neat cushions of a quiet sage-green, petite enough for the trough garden and very striking in May and June when it produces large gentian-violet trumpets, a plant of the campanula family from the Balkan coast is *Edraianthus pumilio*. It is not easy to propagate vegetatively, and seed should be collected for sowing in the spring.

Coarser, tuft-forming plants from the region include a scabious, *Scabiosa graminifolia*, with silvery white, grass-like leaves and mauve-pink flowers with deeply divided petals. An easy plant to please, it thrives in a dryish, sunny spot, and is usually raised from seed, though the woody rootstock can be lifted and divided. Some of the flaxes are small clump-formers which enjoy a sunny spot but are not unduly fussy regarding soil or site: fairly widespread near the northern shore of the Mediterranean is *Linum campanulatum*, a shrubby plant with variably shaped leaves and clusters of yellow flowers over the summer months; *L. narbonense* is taller, with stiff, pointed leaves on erect stems, and clusters of blue flowers from May to July; Gemmell's Hybrid is a cross-bred flax which has thick, greyish green leaves and numerous yellow flowers which open in June – a more compact, lower-growing shrub than the others, and deserving of a sunny spot, fairly low down, perhaps, on the south-facing scree. They will all root fairly readily from cuttings taken as soon as flowering is finished in late summer, and placed under a polythene bag in the shade. *L. arboreum* is a rather more tender shrub from Crete, a beautiful little plant with large golden yellow flowers in the spring. It grows well while the weather stays mild, but is apt to be killed during northern winters.

Also from Crete, but originating high in the mountains, comes the very pretty little perennial *Anchusa caespitosa*, which makes a tuft of narrow, almost grass-like dark green leaves, bearing a cluster of deep blue, slit-skirted flowers in the spring. Shoot cuttings root very readily, but they should be taken in the spring no later than the middle of May, otherwise the resulting plants are liable to die back later in the season. This dainty plant approaches the Alpine in its requirements, and will not tolerate too much winter wet. A dwarf mullein bush from the same island, *Verbascum spinosum*, is a typical dry-land plant, each of its intricately intertwined grey twigs ending in a prickle above whorls of little ragged-toothed downy grey leaves, and attractive clusters of 2cm wide, orange-centred yellow flowers. There is a hybrid mullein named Letitia, one of whose parents is *V. spinosum*, and which is also eminently suitable for the rock garden and makes a bushy little shrub with sage-green downy leaves, and comparatively very large yellow flowers over the summer months. Both Letitia and *V. spinosum* will grow readily from shoot or root cuttings taken between spring and autumn.

Italy is often assumed to have a Mediterranean climate, thrusting south as it does into the warm sea; but much of the country is mountainous and, even in the south, the Apennines have snow lying on their central range from November to May. North of this mountain chain, the great plain of northern Italy is virtually enclosed between the Apennines and the Alps, and it experiences cold winters, although the summers are hot. The frontier between the Mediterranean and the central European climatic types is therefore the Apennine Range rather than the Alps, and many Italian plants are more typical of the European mountainous zone than the Mediterranean.

Some mountain stonecrops which descend, as it were, to the seashore and thus have a varied distribution are: *Sedum dasyphyllum*, a neatly compact little mound of tiny, fleshy leaves, flowering in June with comparatively large, white starry flowers; *S. tenuifolium*, with bright golden yellow flowers in July, and leaves that die off annually, spreading slowly as the shoot-tips root themselves; and the tall, evergreen *S. sediforme*, with fleshy, pointed, grey leaves and large clusters of greenish white flowers in July and August – a variable plant, with several forms showing differences in leaf and flower colour.

There is a dwarf mountain onion, *Allium pedemontanum*, which likes an intermediate position where it can enjoy the warm sunshine, but has no objection to extreme cold. In northern gardens – though expensive to buy – it establishes itself well on the rockery, and produces clusters of bright pinkish violet bell flowers in the early summer.

Italian mountainsides under the Mediterranean influence often support shrubs such as cistus and daphne, and these thrive in similar conditions when moved to more northerly gardens. *Daphne collina* is a handsome bush with glossy, leathery leaves, silky and downy on their undersides. It bears large clusters of dark pink, fragrant, cross-shaped flowers in late spring, extending into summer. Its variety Neapolitana is rather larger, but still dwarf enough for the rock garden, and has greyish leaves with clusters of fragrant, bright pink flowers in the spring. Both are reasonably hardy in Britain. The natural hybrid *Daphne*×*thauma*, which makes a low mound of narrow, dark green leaves, with clusters of bright pinkish purple flowers in May and June, is a valuable rock garden shrub. Best of them all, however, is the tiny *D. petraea* – a gnarled miniature bush only a few centimetres high, with closely crowded little leaves, dark green and glossy. It enjoys an Alpine winter and a Mediterranean summer, so perhaps it is difficult to please but, when the numerous clusters of fragrant rose-pink flowers are out in May, any effort to establish it will have been worth while. This dwarf daphne is ideal in a trough garden, in a nest of tufa, or on the high scree, where it needs a gritty soil which has a good proportion of humus and a touch of lime. All these daphnes are evergreen, and they are not easy to propagate from cuttings; if any seed is set, it should be collected avidly and sown in the spring.

The dwarf rock cherry, *Prunus prostrata*, grows in the Apennines, and its natural distribution extends across the Adriatic and into the

Balkan countries. It is a spreading shrub with gnarled, intertwining branches, and bright pink flowers appearing in April before the little leaves unfurl. The 2cm wide nodding flowers are usually arranged in pairs along the stem, and are sometimes succeeded by little red cherries. After many years, *P. prostrata* will reach a spread of 2-3m, though scarcely exceeding knee height.

The hot, dry hills of Greece support a Mediterranean type of flora, but plants of the Adriatic coastal regions tend towards the eastern European range. *Campanula garganica* is an intermediate plant, perhaps; sun-loving, but perfectly hardy and facing cold winters with equanimity; enjoying a moist, cool soil, but flourishing also in stone walls and rock crevices. The prostrate, radiating stems carry kidney-shaped leaves and broad bell-shaped flowers, blue with a white centre, borne over a long period from May right through the summer months. *Fritillaria bithynica* also occurs further east in the Turkish hills, and shows somewhat mixed characteristics; the greenish yellow bells, arising from scattered clumps of narrow, almost grass-like leaves, appear as early as February on sheltered slopes.

Hypericum olympicum

The dwarf St John's worts provide examples of this range: *Hypericum olympicum*, while touching on the Adriatic, is more truly a plant of eastern Europe and Asia Minor and, while loving the sun, is perfectly hardy and has become justly popular in north temperate gardens, where its glaucous little leaves and clusters of golden yellow flowers are greatly admired in midsummer; *H. empetrifolium*, on the other hand, while occurring in the same region as *H. olympicum*, is more truly a Mediterranean plant, its range extending through Greece to the Greek islands and, while it also is much admired as a perfect rock garden acquisition, with its evergreen mound of little whorled leaves and clusters of rich yellow flowers towards the summer's end, a hard winter will kill it unless it has been allocated a truly sheltered but sunny spot, high enough on the rockery to ensure freedom from long-standing frosty air. For the smaller garden, the prostrate *H. empetrifolium* Prostratum is best, and this flowers as prolifically as the type. *H. olympicum* has a very pleasant lemon-yellow form Citrinum, which I prefer to the typical plant – the softer flower colour blends beautifully with the bluish leaves – and both types may quite easily be propagated from fairly soft shoot cuttings, using the polythene bag method, but taking care that the slightly fleshy leaves are not allowed to touch the sides.

The dianthus-like tunicas, now often classified under the genus *Petrorhagia*, also illustrate the floral transition from Adriatic to Greek zones, although in this case both species are fully hardy in Britain at least; *Tunica illyrica*, with purple-marked white flowers, is of more northerly and easterly distribution and has fewer preferences regarding soil and site, making a broad, free-flowering clump almost anywhere; *T. graminea*, on the other hand, needs a gritty, dryish soil and, preferably, a sunnier site, where it will make a neat clump, with small clusters of pink flowers in midsummer.

A typically Greek relative of *Scabiosa* is the dwarf perennial *Pterocephalus parnassi*, a spreading tuft of grey, hairy little leaves, with scabious-like purple flowers in the summer, followed by fluffy round seedheads like powder-puffs. It makes an excellent subject for a stone retaining wall in full sun. Another little grey-leaved plant is the pretty *Alyssum olympicum* from the northern Greek hills, flowering in the summer with rounded clusters of deep yellow flowers, and neat enough for a sunny trough. The spiny little goat's thorn *Astragalus angustifolius* is a typical dwarf bush of the dry Greek hills. It makes a low, tangled, thorny mound of narrow leaves, downy white when they first open, becoming smooth and grey later, and decorated in June with little clusters of milk-white pea-family flowers. All the goat's thorns are best raised from seed and, once established on a sunny site, should not be disturbed, as they rarely survive transplanting.

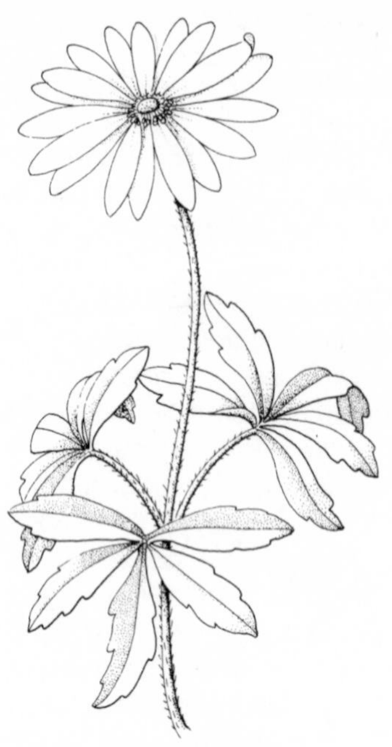

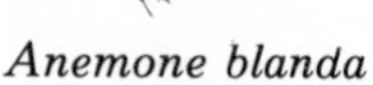

Anemone blanda

Cyclamen hederifolium

The well known *Anemone blanda* comes from these hills, where it produces its variable blue and pink flowers as early as February. Both the species and selected varieties, such as the deep blue Atrocoerulea and the clear pink Rosea, are splendid colonisers when transplanted to northern gardens.

One of the characteristic shrubs of the cool Olympus mountain range is *Cytisus demissus*, a perfect rock garden broom, which hugs the rocks with a finger-high mound. It is perfectly hardy, well inured to Alpine life above the tree-line, and loses its tiny trefoil leaves in the winter, the comparatively large, pale yellow flowers, keeled with tawny brown, making an eye-catching display in the late spring. The easiest way to grow *C. demissus* is from seed, though, if there are others of the genus nearby, the progeny may well turn out to be hybrid. If plants are to be raised from cuttings, the tiny side-shoots should be pulled off towards the end of summer and set under polythene bags. As soon as they root they should be potted individually, and planted out without disturbance, as they do not take kindly to transplanting.

A few saxifrages from the Greek and Albanian mountains have become very popular as garden plants. *Saxifraga grisebachii* has silver-grey leaf rosettes which mound up over the years to form a substantial cushion. Two forms are found in the wild, one with pink and the other with bright crimson flower clusters, and usually it is the latter which is cultivated. An early spring-flowerer, *S. grisebachii* appreciates the protection of a warm cleft in the rock, but is perfectly hardy in northern climes. Another species with a wide geographical range, centred on the Greek mountains and with slightly varying forms typical of its different localities, is *S. marginata*, which forms crowded mats of fleshy green leaves, the early spring flowers ranging from white and pale yellow to pink and purple.

The Grecian fir of these mountains, *Abies cephalonica*, is a large and handsome tree, but it has given rise to a dwarf form, Nana, which will still be well under half a metre in height after ten or fifteen years of garden cultivation, and is able to bring something of the atmosphere of a Greek mountain forest to the northern rock garden. It has short, stiff, bright green leaf sprays on tiered, spreading branches – an attractive little tree which grows well on limy sites but, being a true mountain plant, it will not take kindly to late spring frosts and needs to be planted fairly high up a steep slope so that the cold air can drain away.

Both the Mediterranean and Middle Eastern regions are rich in bulbous plants, for a hot dry summer suits their style of growth, provided there has been adequate moisture to swell the bulbs. The winter's rain is valuable especially to the spring-flowerers, and explains why most of them settle happily in the colder, damper northern climes. Autumn-flowering bulbs – or corms – from the area include the saffron, *Crocus sativus*, which is grown commercially in many countries. The large lilac-pink flowers are reluctant to appear until the plant is well established, and bulbs should be left undisturbed as long as possible. Closely similar crocuses are *C. elwesii*, also autumn-flowering with purple-marked lilac flowers, and *C. goulimyi*, whose flowers are more freely produced. Other autumn-flowering crocuses include the prohibitively expensive *C. niveus*, with orange-centred white flowers, and *C. salzmannii*, with large, yellow-throated lilac flowers.

The spring-flowering species include: *Crocus imperati*, in purple and brown; *C. sieberi*, very early-flowering, golden-centred lilac; and *C. versicolor*, with white and purple flowers. Young corms are formed round the old ones in the soil, and these may be lifted and replanted singly for propagation once the colony is firmly established. If the clumps do not seem to be spreading from year to year, however, they are best left undisturbed. Crocuses will grow fairly readily from seed, although the tiny seedling corms will not produce flowers for three or four years.

The same is true of the colchicums, but these can also be lifted and divided in midsummer, replanting them in their new sites immediately. *Colchicum agrippinum* flowers in the autumn, in fritillary-chequered purple and white, and is one of the easiest of the genus to grow in ordinary garden conditions. Summer-flowering *C.*

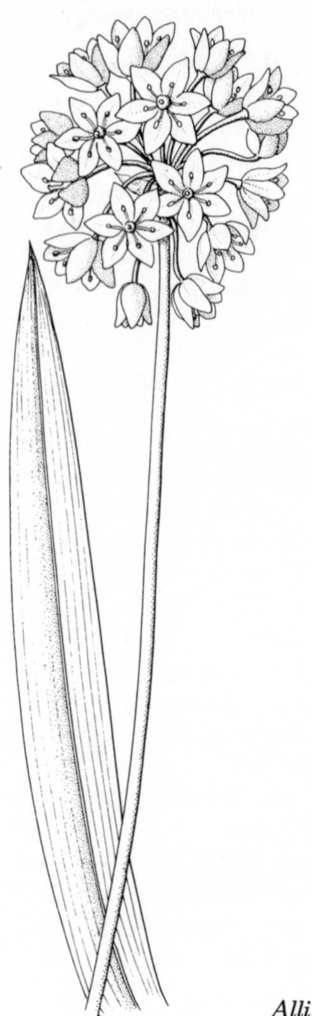

Allium moly

alpinum is perhaps better suited to the higher rockery slopes, but all the colchicums, with their bulky lily-like leaves, are a little too demanding of space in the spring, and their true place is in the herbaceous border.

Several of the Mediterranean onion species have well repaid their adoption by British and American gardeners. One species – *Allium triquetrum* – has naturalised itself in parts of Britain, where the clusters of white bell-like flowers in the summer look good in a shady spot, but this is a woodland plant, and may become invasive in the garden. The golden garlic is *A. moly,* with round heads of golden yellow flowers in June, not too tall to be allowed to drift among rocks, and eager to establish a colony in a sunny, moist situation. *A. napolitanum* is of a similar size, but it misses the warmth of the Mediterranean breezes, and does not do so well when transplanted to northern climes. The white flower clusters are very ornamental, however, and it is often used as a cut flower. Also good for cutting is the bright violet-pink *A. pulchellum*, flowering in the late summer, and its white-flowered variant Album, but they are both rather large for the rock garden.

Few rockeries are without a drift of grape hyacinths, not least of their attractions being their hardiness and the speed with which they spread, even under difficult conditions. The common blue kinds can be varied and augmented with the fragrant *Muscari macrocarpum*, whose flowers open purple but turn clear yellow, and the strongly fragrant *M. neglectum*, a dark royal blue with white markings.

The Mediterranean equivalent of the western European winter aconite is *Eranthis cilicica*, equally easy to grow and naturalise, but dwarfer, with attractive bronzy foliage and bright golden yellow flowers in February and March. In a group, they are happy in light shade, and should preferably be left alone once they are established. Seed can be collected as soon as it ripens and sown *in situ* around the old plants, to help extend the colony.

Cyclamens of the Mediterranean region can be relied upon to flower for eight months of the year: *Cyclamen repandum*, with bright carmine flowers and large, handsome leaves, is in bloom from March until May; *C. hederifolium*, with silvery, variably shaped leaves and crimson-blotched rose-pink flowers – there is also a white-flowered variety, Album – flowers from September to November; and *C. coum*, with its crimson flowers and small rounded leaves – its variety Roseum has paler pink flowers and lighter green leaves – flowers from January until March. Cyclamens prefer light shade and a well drained soil; their natural habitat beneath taller vegetation shields them from drying out during the summer months and so, more than most plants from the region, they object to extreme conditions, and usually take well to temperate northern climates. Colonies are best not disturbed once they are planted, and may take a few years to become firmly established. Of the three, *C. hederifolium* and *C. coum* are the hardiest, and the quickest to naturalise themselves when planted in the north.

8
Looking Eastwards

Many sun-loving plants of the Mediterranean type extend their distribution eastwards from Europe to Asia Minor and beyond. Some of the campanulas, for instance, may be said to have their roots in the west but to face east. From the Carpathian Mountains we have *Campanula carpatica*, one of the best known garden introductions; more than two centuries of Western cultivation have acquainted us with numerous varieties, both of garden origin and of natural occurrence in the wild, with flower colours ranging from pure white to deep blue and purple. Half the charm of *C. poscharskyana* and *C. portenschlagiana* lies in the acquired ability to pronounce their names, but they are both excellent and very popular in the garden, and make admirable wall plants. *C. portenschlagiana* (syn. *muralis*) is easy to grow in most situations, forming a low carpet covered with purple-blue bells which open in June and continue through the summer months. More vigorous, and suitable for slightly wilder surroundings, *C. poscharskyana* will make a tangled ground cover of trailing stems and little heart-shaped leaves, covered from June to November with clusters of starry, lavender-blue flowers. The latter is not a plant for introducing into stone retaining walls without much thought, for it is liable to take over and swamp the opposition. Another creeping campanula that will root itself beneath the stones and appear here and there on a stone wall or between paving slabs is the neat *C. cochlearifolia*, which bears nodding blue bells from June to September.

To propagate these campanulas, little rooted portions can be detached or, alternatively, they will grow quite readily from soft shoot cuttings taken during the growing season and rooted under a polythene bag. When several of the species are grown together, collecting and sowing seed will often result in new hybrid forms which may, or may not, be an improvement on the parents. Hybrids which have been named and acclaimed include: Hallii, a tufted plant with pure white bells; Peter Nix, a vigorous spreader with nodding, light

Campanula carpatica

blue bells on long stalks; and Birch Hybrid, a rather rampageous spreader which produces numerous light purple flowers during the summer. Both Birch Hybrid and the species *C. portenschlagiana* will grow well in light shade, provided they are getting enough moisture during the growing season.

A lightly shaded site of this sort will suit *Corydalis solida*, an unusual plant of the poppy family, with striking purple flowers in April and May – a tuberous perennial that may be treated like a bulb. *Soldanella hungarica* is also a European plant with an easterly range, enjoying cool, lightly shaded sites, but with no objection to sunlight, provided the roots have a cool pocket in which to delve. A north-facing niche between rocks will be admirable. Like the campanulas, this little plant produces blue bells, but they are distinctively fringed almost to the petal base like a traditional pixie's hat, and clustered in a sizable clump above the rounded, tufted leaves.

Scutellaria is a genus that occurs both in Asia and Europe, where it is known as skullcap after the shape of the domed and lipped flowers, and two species from the Balkan and Caucasus area – *S. hirta* and *S. virens* – are mat-formers suitable for sunny spots. Their styles of growth differ fairly widely, however, for the purple and white flowered *Scutellaria hirta* has lax, trailing flower stems, giving the plant a minimal overall height, and making it an ideal subject to dangle over a low ledge; the yellow flowered *S. virens*, on the other hand, has upright stems, and is very much a plant for the transitional zone between rock garden and herbaceous border.

Equivalent in some ways to the heather of the west and north, *Bruckenthalia spiculifolia* is an evergreen, spreading, colonising shrub with spikes of pink flower from May to July. It is more a plant of the rock garden than many of the heaths by virtue of its dwarf stature, and will make a hardy, spreading clump for a lime-free slope, but it needs dividing every three years or so, otherwise the central part tends to die back.

More typically a rock plant among the sun-loving mountain dwellers of the Balkans is *Wahlenbergia serpyllifolia* – by which name it is usually known, although botanists prefer to classify it as *Edraianthus serpyllifolius*. This is a very neat little mat-former with thyme-like leaves and large, solitary, violet-blue trumpets, crimson in the bud, which open in June. Not very hardy, it likes a sunny scree site, and thrives when given a warm ledge furnished with a limy, gritty soil, and a good proportion of humus a short distance below the surface. It can be grown successfully from seed or, alternatively, cuttings of non-flowering shoots may be taken early in the summer, and these root readily in a polythene bag.

The mountains of eastern Europe are a sempervivum stronghold. Nearest, perhaps, to the common houseleek *Sempervivum tectorum* is the Balkan *S. schlehanii*, but it is a neater plant with smaller rosettes, the fleshy leaves flushed with red – though there are several slightly differing forms with varying degrees of redness in the leaves – and stout leaf stalks bearing a few large, purplish red, white-margined flowers in August. *S. erythraeum* has small, flattened rosettes of a soft purplish green hue, and thickly leaved stems bearing small clusters of purplish pink flowers in July. Very similar to *S. erythraeum* in leaf and flower is *S. macedonicum*, whose habit of growth, however, is quite different, for it is a sprawler, with prostrate leafy stems carrying self-rooting offsets. The variable *S. reginae-amaliae* has pink flowers and crowded rosettes of olive-green leaves which become purplish in hot weather. Some of the yellow-flowered houseleeks from these mountains include: *Jovibarba arenaria*, with small rosettes of tiny, crowded, light green leaves, often tipped with reddish-brown, and a slender stem which carries a small cluster of straw-yellow flowers in August; *Jovibarba heuffelii*, which has pale yellow flowers in August, variably-sized rosettes of bluish green, brown-tipped leaves, and is unusual in not producing removable offsets – to increase the species, the hard, woody rootstock must be divided into pieces, each with a small rosette attached; *Sempervivum leucanthum*, with crowded little rosettes of purple-tipped leaves, and slender-stemmed clusters of large yellow flowers in July; *Sempervivum ruthenicum*, with pale yellow flowers in July, and pink-tinged leaves arranged in large rosettes which contract in the winter and expand in the summer.

A relative of the British wild ragged robin from these Eastern mountains, *Lychnis flos-jovis* is a sun-lover which forms a neat tuft of pointed, white woolly leaves, and bears numerous deeply fringed purplish pink flowers in June and July. It is an easily grown plant, best propagated from seed, though it might be persuaded to divide in the early spring. White woolly tufting plants always suggest dry, sunny sites, and one of the best known garden plants of this kind is the lamb's tongue, *Stachys lanata*, from the dry Middle Eastern hills. The species is a little too coarse and rampant for rock garden use, and the flowers are rather weedy, but the non-flowering variety Silver Carpet makes a useful low cover for the foot of the rockery. *Stachys discolor* from the same region is rather more dainty, with small, crinkly leaves – green above and white woolly beneath – and the spikes of whorled white or pale pink flowers are more attractive than those of *S. lanata*, and make a pleasant drift. It can be divided in early spring but, when this is done, the older, central parts of the plant should be discarded, as it is not particularly longlived and soon deteriorates.

Genista lydia is a charming dwarf broom which extends across the Bosphorus into Asia Minor; rarely more than knee-high, its slenderly pendulous branches form a firm mound, covered in May and June with bright, buttercup-yellow flowers. As the flowers fade, side-shoot cuttings may be taken with a heel of older wood, and these will root fairly readily. When flowering brooms are surrounded by the local creeping *Veronica filiformis*, though this can be a terrible weed, the colour combination is striking; although the veronica has a longer flowering season, the clear sky-blue flowers first open with the broom, and they stay in harmony for several weeks. Another flowering companion for the veronica is the brilliant yellow creeping *Hypericum rhodopeum*, and the two plants are compatible also in vigour. *Veronica filiformis* can be very invasive in the garden, the prostrate stems rooting at every node as they touch the ground, and it is sometimes best restricted to an isolated bed or grassy verge where it can be allowed to colonise freely. Flowering at the same time, but better behaved on the rock garden is the mat-forming *Veronica pectinata*, with hairy grey leaves and small spikes of deep blue, white-centred flowers, and there is also a pink flowered form which is very attractive. Propagation presents no problem in the case of *V. filiformis*, for rooted portions of stem can always be removed, but *V. pectinata* may not divide readily, and is best increased by means of shoot cuttings taken after flowering has finished.

One of the best known – and best loved – of spring-flowering mat-formers from this area is *Alyssum saxatile*, especially the typical species with its bright yellow flowers, but there are several slightly varying cultivars: Citrinum makes a pleasant change from the normal with its lemon-yellow flowers; Dudley Neville sports an unusual shade of yellow-buff; and Tom Thumb is like the type but smaller in all its parts, and better proportioned than the others for the average rockery. The varieties, including Tom Thumb, can be increased with cuttings of the new shoots taken as soon as flowering has finished, and potted under a polythene bag. Arabis is commonly associated in gardens with alyssum, and *Arabis caucasica* is the common white rock which ranges in nature from south-east Europe to Iran. The form Variegata has a yellow variegation of the leaves which gives the plant some interest over the non-flowering months, but the best species – from the southern Turkish mountains – is *Arabis androsacea*, with tiny silky-silvery leaves in a dense tuft, and clusters of white flowers in the summer. This is no front garden stopgap, but a precious little Alpine plant that needs some cosseting in a sunny pocket of gritty soil.

The Taurus Mountains where these plants are found rise from the Mediterranean, clad with fir and oak forests which are fringed, like those of the European Alps, with well-watered grazing meadows. There is quite an extreme range from the olives and figs of the coastal zone, and the date palms and citrus of the south-facing valleys in the foothills, to the high plateau land beyond the mountains. Here, the climate is Asian Continental; the temperature range is extreme; and the vegetation, except near the stream courses, sparse. Some of the plants here share the characteristics of Mediterranean and Alpine flora: *Phuopsis stylosa* forms a musky scented, bright green mat of tiny whorled leaves, with clusters of small, rose-pink trumpet flowers from June to August – a plant which enjoys a warm, sunny spot, but fully hardy and able to grow in ordinary garden conditions without complaint; *Omphalodes cappadocica* is a creeping, tufted plant with long-stalked, heart-shaped leaves, and dainty sprays of starry, deep blue flowers opening in May and lasting till July – an explorer which enjoys creeping between the stones of a dry retaining wall and which, like the *Phuopsis*, appreciates a sunny spot, but is perfectly hardy and easy to grow. Propagation can be achieved by transplanting a portion of the rhizome with shoots attached.

Further east, Turkey is protected to some extent from cold Russian winds by the bulk of the Caucasian Mountains. The effect of these cold winds can be well seen in the Caucasus itself, for the interior and the north-facing slopes of these mountain ranges experience deep snow and ice, and the vegetation is very poor. The south-facing slopes of the Caucasus, on the other hand, are well clothed by nature with luxuriant forests, both evergreen and deciduous. The Caucasian fir, *Abies nordmanniana*, forms impressive stands of timber on these well-watered slopes and, like many plants of the region, has found the climate in the British Isles a suitable alternative for healthy growth. It has a rather unusual dwarf variety, Golden Spreader, a low, wide-spreading form with pale yellow leaves, eventually covering a considerable area, though reaching barely more than knee-high after many years.

Some of the plants which form the bulk of this mountain vegetation are familiar to European and American gardeners: the much-travelled *Rhododendron ponticum*; pyracantha; philadelphus; viburnum; the tall tree heather *Erica arborea* (the variety usually seen in gardens is *E.a.* Alpina, from the southern European mountains), which makes a heather garden centrepiece similar to *Erica australis*; and *Inula ensifolia*, a bright yellow summer-flowering daisy which chooses a sunny spot between other plants.

Silene schafta, a dwarf catchfly from the Caucasus, makes a very useful patch of carpet for a sunny, rocky spot, producing its pink-magenta flowers freely in succession from June until the end of October. It is a good wall plant, too, satisfied with ordinary soil and easily raised from seed – or it can be increased by taking shoots with pieces of the woody rootstock attached, during either autumn or spring.

A speedwell from the western Caucasus is *Veronica peduncularis*, a spreading herb with variable leaves and pinkish white flowers, and this is often grown in the rock garden, but the English cultivated form Nymans Variety is better, with bronzy foliage and large clusters of pale blue flowers in May and June. It may be propagated quite easily from short cuttings taken as soon as the flowers fade. From the lower south and west-facing mountain slopes comes the prickly thrift, *Acantholimon glumaceum*, which makes a dense, dark green tuft of prickly leaves and carries spikes of very pretty little bright pink flowers over a long summer season. Most other species of *Acantholimon* are rather tender, coming as they do from the hotter, drier parts of the Middle East, but *A. glumaceum* is as hardy as the primulas which often associate with it, and equally easy to grow.

The common European *Primula vulgaris* occurs in the region, though its flower colour may differ from the familiar northern and western primroses. The tiny *P. juliae* also comes from the area – a well known carpeter, covered in April with short-stemmed, bright purple flowers. It is inevitable that such a small, moisture-loving plant should revel in light shade, creeping as it does around the stems of taller plants, and spreading quickly enough to ensure an adequate supply of new crowns for division. *P. amoena* is also an easily grown plant which enjoys a cool, moist site. It produces rather small leaves which have a white woolly down on their undersides, and tight clusters of as many as ten 2cm wide early spring flowers, usually bright violet with a yellow eye, but varying from white through shades of lavender. The primulas associate well with the yellow-flowered *Anemone ranunculoides*, which has bronzy, cut leaves, and produces its buttercup flowers in April and May.

Several species of stonecrop are native to the Caucasus Mountains, and some of them have become firmly established in Western rock gardens. Probably the best known of these is *Sedum spurium*, for it has naturalised itself in many parts of Europe, and has several cultivated varieties. The typical species forms an evergreen mat of creeping stems and flat leaves, and bears dense heads of tiny pink flowers in July and August. The variety Schorbusser Blut has crimson flowers, and makes an excellent cover for a patch of poor soil in the sun. Very closely related is *Sedum stoloniferum*, smaller in every part, with light green leaves and clusters of pink flowers in June and July. A much daintier stonecrop, suitable for a rocky niche, is *S. gracile*, which makes a bright green patch of narrow, fleshy leaves, with little clusters of pinkish white flowers in June. Not connected with Spain in spite of its specific name, *S. hispanicum* is an annual stonecrop with fairly large, flat, reddish grey leaves and loose clusters of starry white flowers in June. Although it dies after flowering, when it is sited in very dry places the flowers tend not to appear, and in such sites *S. hispanicum* becomes perennial. There is a dwarf form, however, which is said to be truly perennial. Probably not found in the Caucasus, but a native of the Turkish hills further west, *S. lydium* is an evergreen mat-former with tiny, red-tinged leaves – the red tint deepening during hot, dry weather – and clusters of little, pale pink flowers in June; it is an easy plant to propagate, for the creeping stems root as they touch the ground. Most of the stonecrops, of course, root very readily from cuttings, and mere leaves will often grow independently if they are sown like seeds in moist, sandy soil. *Sedum sempervivoides*, as its name implies, has something of the appearance of a sempervivum, with its heavy rosettes of red-flushed leaves. It is a biennial, and dies after producing its clusters of scarlet flowers in June and July. Sempervivum proper also has a toehold in the Caucasus, but this must be nearing the eastern limit for the genus. One of the few Caucasian houseleeks to have found their way to Western gardens is *Sempervivum pumilum*, with little green rosettes which become tinged with red during the hot, dry season, and a leafy-stemmed cluster of rosy-purple flowers in July.

South of the Caucasus, the inland hills are dry and climatically extreme, and the plant type resembles that of the steppes of central Asia. Tulips more typical of the central Asian regions are to be found growing here, among them: the dwarf *Tulipa urumiensis*, excellent for the small rock garden, with spreading tufts of olive-green leaves and richly golden yellow flowers in April; the March-flowering *T. pulchella*, small enough for a clump or drift on the face of a rockery, with two distinct forms sometimes classed as separate species – *T.p. humilis*, with yellow-centred mauve flowers, and *T.p. violacea*, also yellow-centred, but with rich violet-blue petals, both forms rather expensive to buy; and *T. hageri*, with black-centred, coppery scarlet flowers marked with buff and yellow blotches, whose bell-shaped flowers in April, and broad, dark green leaves make a pleasant clump for a sunny spot with good drainage, sheltered from cold winds.

The Mediterranean influence is noticeable on the western slopes of these hills, becoming more pronounced as the elevation decreases westwards through Syria and the Lebanon to the coastline itself. Retracing this sequence from the eastern Mediterranean coast, the Lebanese hills have a scrubby cover characterised by locust trees and umbrella-shaped pines. At a higher altitude there is somewhat stunted forest with scrubby oaks, maples and the strawberry tree. Between this level and the highest peaks there are dwarfish mountain pines, rhododendrons, cypresses, silver firs and the cedar of Lebanon. A dwarf form of this cedar, *Cedrus libani* Nana, has been cultivated in our gardens since early in the nineteenth century. If left with unthinned crown, it will form a very dense, almost globular bush with a dark greyish green foliage – on the limit of size for trees admissible to a reasonably-sized rock garden, for it will have topped a metre after ten years. Slightly less tall is the more recently introduced Comte de Dijon, which eventually makes a slightly narrower cone, and lends itself well to crown thinning so as to expose the miniature limbs. The weeping dwarf Sargentii is an extraordinarily elegant little tree, whose pendulous mound of blue-green foliage likes to drape itself over large rocks. The yellow-leaved Aurea Prostrata will also do this to a certain extent, but it has very stiff, almost horizontal branches, and is not so graceful. These dwarf cedars are very difficult to propagate from cuttings, and the usual practice is to graft them, using normal seedling stocks.

At an altitude that limits the trees to junipers and a few other stunted species, which survive between thorny little bushes of berberis, goat's thorn and genista broom, there is a rich spring-flowering vegetation, but this 'Alpine' flora has more in common with the low-altitude plants of eastern Asia than the European Alpines, with their counterparts in the Arctic regions. There are some connections with the European mountains, however – *Saponaria pulvinaris,* for instance, is a soapwort which grows on sunny, west-facing slopes, where it forms tight little cushions of bright green, covered in the summer with familiar rose-pink flowers. In northern gardens this needs the Alpine treatment of a south-facing scree with thorough drainage, and gives excellent results in a trough. From the same hills, and also suitable for a small corner in a trough garden, comes a tiny daisy, *Bellium minutum* – a flat pad of minute leaves sprinkled in June with typical yellow-eyed white daisies, purple in the bud and on the petal reverse. An easier plant to handle than the soapwort, it nevertheless needs a warm niche and a well-drained soil. Often it can find a comfortable home between paving slabs, where the close cover will keep out weed seeds. There is no problem with propagation, which is simply a matter of division. A rather more exotic plant from the same region is *Fritillaria crassifolia,* a pretty little spring-flowerer that fits readily into rock garden schemes. It is a plant to be admired in detail, with its broad bells of deep burgundy, chequered with green, and a raised bed will often provide an ideal site.

Aethionema grandiflorum has been named the Persian candytuft to indicate its close relationship with iberis and their similar appearance, and its natural distribution from the lower Lebanese hills to Iran. This and the similar *Aethionema pulchellum,* which occurs both here and to the north, are never happier than when given a hot, dry site on a sunny stone wall. The larger of the two, *A. grandiflorum,* has sprawling, twiggy stems which bear rounded, grey-green leaves and masses of bright rose-pink flowers from June to August. The more compact *A. pulchellum* makes a neat mound of narrow, greyish green leaves, with closely packed clusters of clear pale pink flowers over the same season. *Aethionema* Warley Rose is a named variety which arose in England many years ago, and is superior to the others for general garden use, with its long season of brilliant pink blossom, and compact cushion of neat, blue-green leaves. They are all best in a limy, gritty soil but, without the protection of a stone wall or a sheltered rockery, cold winters will sometimes kill them. Because of this, it is always as well to take a few cuttings during the summer and keep these over winter under glass, in case replacements are required.

The Middle East, including Asia Minor and the Caucasus, is an area particularly rich in bulbous plants, and new kinds are still being discovered and introduced to Western gardens. The spring-flowering crocuses enjoy a sunny site where they can bake and ripen during the summer months. They include: *Crocus ancyrensis,* very early to flower, with little dark orange cups; *C. aureus,* from which the Dutch hybrid yellow crocuses have evolved; *C. biflorus,* flowering in February with two-toned purple flowers – especially handsome on the rockery are the varieties Alexandri in deep purple and white, and Weldenii, with pure white interiors to the large, grey cups; *C. chrysanthus,* the well known bronzy orange February-flowerer with numerous cultivated forms, such as Cream Beauty, with creamy yellow flowers, E. P. Bowles, with yellow and purple, Zwanenberg Bronze, with yellow and bronze, the pure white Snow Bunting, the purple and white Lady Killer, the blue and white Blue Bird and the purple and gold Blue Peter. Other species include: *C. dalmaticus,* with clear pale blue flowers; *C. fleischeri,* with small white, orange-centred flowers; *C. susianus* Cloth of Gold, with deep yellow and bronze flowers; *C. tomasinianus*, with lavender and silver, and its variety Whitewell Purple with crimson-purple flowers. Autumn-flowering crocuses from the area include: *C. iridiflorus,* a highly prized and highly priced species with orange-centred purple flowers; and *C. zonatus* with large, orange-spotted lilac flowers. Many of the crocus species will naturalise themselves well in northern temperate gardens, and should be left alone as long as they are growing healthily.

The so-called autumn crocuses, colchicum, are represented in the region by at least two species, *Colchicum byzantium* and *C. speciosum,* both with large, pinkish purple flowers which appear from the bare ground in the autumn, the young leaves not appearing until the spring and withering by the end of the summer. The leaves are large and somewhat untidy on the rock garden. More suitable where space is restricted is the closely related *Merendera sobolifera,* whose solitary pinkish lilac starry flowers appear before the leaves in February and March.

The sternbergias also are crocus-like flowers, with moderately unobtrusive foliage dying down soon after the flowering season has finished. *Sternbergia clusiana* has a large, globular yellow flower in the autumn; *S. fischeriana* has bright yellow flowers in the spring, and rather larger leaves; *S. lutea* has glossy yellow cup-shaped flowers in the autumn, and narrow dark green leaves that persist throughout the summer. They are all plants that like to be left alone to increase their colonies slowly, but they are often reluctant to come into flower.

We sometimes tend to think of snowdrops as northern flowers, but their natural range extends through southern Europe, Asia Minor and the Caucasus. The familiar *Galanthus nivalis* is the one with the widest range, and is probably the best for naturalising. Its varieties include the double Plena, the vigorous, large-flowered S. Arnott, and the green-tipped Viridapicis, but the type species always looks right

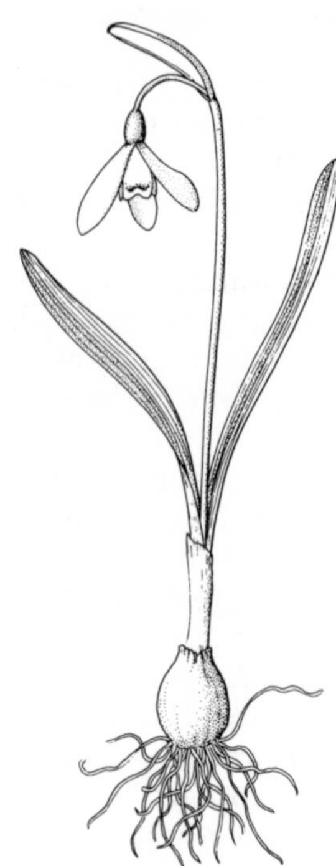

Galanthus nivalis

on the rock garden. The large-flowered *Galanthus elwesii* and *G. plicatus* are limited to the Middle Eastern region, are later to come into flower, and are probably the least permanent colonisers when transplanted further north – although the *G. elwesii* variety Cassaba is remarkably floriferous, and effective when a flowering drift is to be seen from some distance.

The Iranian equivalent of the British bluebell is *Scilla tubergeniana*, a pleasant little clump-forming plant with starry flowers of pale streaky blue, quite hardy but spreading more slowly than the robust bluebell. The spring-flowering grape hyacinths are well represented in Asia Minor and Iran: *Muscari ambrosiacum* has honey-scented pale creamy lilac flowers; *M. armeniacum* has spikes of deep blue globular flowers; *M. azureum* has bright blue bell-shaped flowers; and *M. tubergenianum* has spikes of flower which are pale blue at the top and dark blue lower down the cluster. They all colonise satisfactorily and should be allowed to develop undisturbed in a sunny spot, or on the edge of light shade, until they show signs of becoming too crowded, when they may be lifted and divided.

Comparatively few bulbous plants flower in the summer, and the Caucasian flowering onion *Allium oreophilum* is of interest in producing its globular heads of carmine-pink flowers in June. it naturalises well in British gardens, and spreads quite rapidly without becoming invasive.

Truly Alpine, from the high Turkish mountains, are the chionodoxas, called glory of the snow from their flowering season, which corresponds with the melting of the snows. They need no special conditions on the rock garden, apart from good drainage during the winter months. Their fine, unobtrusive foliage dies down and disappears for the summer, and they can happily be placed so as to spear through creeping plants without swamping them. Favourite of the genus, perhaps, is the March-flowering *Chionodoxa luciliae,* with bright sky-blue, white-centred flowers, and its variety Rosea, with pink flowers; *C. sardensis* is dark blue, without the white centre; *C. tmoli* has soft clear blue flowers with a white centre; and *C. gigantea* is larger than the others, with soft purplish blue, white-centred flowers, and this has a variety Alba with white flowers. They are best not mixed, but a drift of any of these species or varieties has a most cheerful effect. The very similar *Puschkinia libanotica,* with soft blue and white flowers – and its white-flowered variety Alba – can be used in exactly the same way as the chionodoxas, and their flowering seasons correspond.

9
Asian Hill Plants

Of those rock plants that have come to the West from the immense land mass of Asia, the majority originated in the Himalayas, in the mountainous regions of China and in Japan – the areas in which plant collectors have been most active in the past. Both the Chinese and the Japanese, of course, have a long and honourable tradition of plant selection and breeding which resulted in the acquisition of many varieties new to the West when these Oriental nations opened their doors to the world after centuries of Imperial isolation.

Some plants are widespread and of general occurrence throughout most of Asia, and a few have become household names, like the mother of thousands, *Saxifraga stolonifera*, the popular pot plant with rounded, marbled leaves and strawberry-like runners which hang from the parent plant like so many spiders – and which produces its long-stalked, distinctively pouting little red-speckled flowers in the summer. Mother of thousands has naturalised itself in many parts of Europe, and the only real climatic danger which it has to face when growing out of doors is the prematurely mild spell of spring weather inducing it to put out fresh, soft growth too early in the season, resulting in frostbite. It usually survives life in the open, provided it is not subjected to early morning sun, and a north-facing, shady position, perhaps on a wall or sheltered rock face, suits it best.

Sedum aizoon is another rock plant of wide distribution, with silvery rosettes of coarsely toothed leaves bearing clusters of bright yellow flowers in the spring. Two other plants of the stonecrop genus are Siberian in origin: *Sedum hybridum,* a creeping plant with tiny red-tipped leaves, and flat clusters of crowded, tiny yellow flowers in the summer; and *S. kamtschaticum,* which is more floriferous, with loose, drooping clusters of yellow flowers over a long summer season, on a close mat of dark green leaves. The latter has a form Variegatum with white-margined leaves, and this is more ornamental than the type and a good wall plant, especially colourful in the autumn when the drying flowers deepen to a striking crimson.

Erythronium dens-canis ranges from Britain to Japan

The far northern regions have given us the white-flowered *Dianthus squarrosus,* with fragrant, fringed blooms in the summer, carried over a dark green mat of foliage. *Tanacetum herderi* is a good foliage plant from western Asia, easy to grow and readily increased by simple division, producing neat little mounds of silvery rosettes; a relative of the chrysanthemums, it produces tiny, golden yellow flowers in the summer. The well known shrubby *Potentilla fruticosa* has a vast natural range over the northern hemisphere, and many good garden varieties have originated from wild central Asian forms. One of the dwarfest is *P.f. mandshurica,* with white flowers in a summer-long succession, while the hybrid seedling Gold Drop, with bright yellow flowers, its large-flowered variant Klondyke, and Buttercup, with small, dark yellow flowers, are among the best of the genus for all-round rock garden use.

A Far Eastern plant for sunny spots in any soil is the bellflower, *Platycodon grandiflorus,* a tuft-former whose ballooned buds open into 5cm wide campanula-like flowers of purple-blue – occasionally white – from July to September. It sets seed readily, and this may be collected and sown in the spring. The variety Apoyama has great merit, as it grows barely half as tall as the type, yet carries larger flowers of clear violet; Mariesii is intermediate in size between the two and has soft blue flowers; while Mother of Pearl is a full-sized plant with soft pink flowers. The varieties will not come true from seed, though many intermediate forms may appear from experimental sowings, but mature plants will divide very readily in the spring.

Related to the European bugles are plants of the genus *Scutellaria* – but whereas the ajuga species enjoy light shade, these prefer a more open situation. From the west of the Himalayas, *Scutellaria macrochlamys* is a trailing plant which basks happily in the sun, and spreads a carpet of felted grey leaves, brightened during the early summer weeks with spikes of purple-veined orange flowers. Another of the genus which has proved itself of value in Western rock gardens is *S. scordiifolia*, a spreader with bright blue flowers, originating in eastern Siberia and Korea. Both are ideal for running between rocks at the base of a sunny rockery, will thrive in ordinary soil, and are easily increased by division.

A very cheerful spreader for light shade, one that will run around tufted plants such as the bellflower and the Asian primulas, is *Waldsteinia ternata*, with rosetted three-lobed leaves and bright buttercup-yellow, saucer-shaped flowers in dainty clusters during April and May. If this plant has a fault, it is that the flowers tend to be produced at the edges of the carpet – that is from the youngest parts of the plant – but this tendency can be overcome by dividing it as soon as the flowers become sparse, and discarding the old central portion. The natural range of waldsteinia extends over much of northern Asia, and it may be found in forest land from eastern Europe, through Russia to Japan. Another plant which makes a mossy carpet, and is excellent also for clothing a shady wall, is *Selaginella helvetica*; the flowers are inconspicuous, but the evergreen foliage is a handsome, bright glossy green, turning coppery red in autumn.

Two fine candelabra primulas that need a moist site are: *Primula burmanica*, with yellow-eyed wine purple flowers in whorls; and *P. helodoxa*, with large, bright yellow flowers of sweet primrose fragrance – a handsome plant indeed, though rarely to be planted near the rock garden, for the flower stalks may approach waist height, often carrying five or six whorls of up to twenty 2.5cm wide flowers each. Candelabra primulas almost always set seed prolifically and this, provided it is fresh when sown, germinates rapidly. After two or three seasons, the vigorous tufts can be divided, for propagation when only a few extra plants are required. Of totally different calibre is the farinose *Primula clarkei*, a charming little plant neat enough for the sink garden. On the rockery it does best in moraine conditions, for it needs surface drainage coupled with cool moisture beneath, such as it finds in its native Kashmir. On a plant barely as tall as your thumb, the 2cm wide mauve-pink spring flowers are balanced proportionately by the neat rosettes of leaves, which are often tinged a coppery crimson shade.

The Asian rhododendrons are of course legion. Of widespread occurrence from Siberia to Japan is the dwarf *Rhododendron chrysanthum*, with bell-shaped lemon-yellow flowers in small clusters during the late spring. *R. cephalanthum* is of wide eastern range, extending southwards to the Burmese hills; its dwarf race *R.c. crebreflorum* is one of the best miniature evergreens for the rock garden, with its tiny, aromatic leaves and large clusters of bright pink, trumpet-shaped flowers in the spring. Also from the Burmese hills comes *R. nitens*, a summer-flowering evergreen, an upright little shrub with scented foliage and large purple flowers – not exactly a dwarf, but small and compact enough to find a place between boulders on a medium sized rock garden. As with most rhododendrons, an acid soil is essential, even if it is not basically peaty by nature, and the slightest trace of lime will cause yellowing of the foliage, and may kill the plant.

Most of the hybrid evergreen rhododendrons are the results of crosses between Asian species and, for a free-flowering show in their season, the hardy dwarf cultivars cannot be beaten. Spreaders which will run over and between rocks include: Aspansia, a brilliant red for the early spring; Carmen, which flowers later and is a deep crimson; Ethel, a brilliant scarlet in the early spring; Impeanum, with large violet flowers in the early summer; Jenny, with crimson trumpet flowers in the late spring; Little Ben, with bright scarlet trumpets in early spring; Pastel, a pleasant pink in late spring; Prostigiatum, a dense shrub with bright violet flowers in early spring; and Scarlet Wonder, which falls between the spreading and mound-forming categories, and whose bright red, frilly flowers appear in early summer. Mound-formers among the dwarf rhododendron cultivars include: Bluebird, a compact little shrub with clusters of bright violet-blue flowers in early spring; Chikor, which has pure yellow flowers in late spring; Chink, with flowers of a curious sulphury lime-green, borne in drooping clusters in early spring; Fittra, with bright rose-pink flowers in early summer, a very floriferous bush; Lady Primrose, flowering in the spring with neat clusters of pale yellow, speckled with blood red on the petal face; Pink Drift, with somewhat bluish pink flowers in the late spring; Red Cap, producing brilliant crimson flowers in the summer, one of the latest of the rock rhododendrons to show colour; Sapphire, bearing lavender-blue flowers in early spring; Sarled, with clusters of creamy white flowers in late spring; and Treasure, which carries large, dark pink flowers in the spring, and looks wirily tough with its gnarled twigs and bronzy foliage, though it is less hardy than most, and needs a sheltered spot between deep rocks.

With propagation in mind, the spreading types may be examined below surface level to see if any shoots have developed roots so that they can be detached and replanted; failing these, cuttings may be taken fairly early in the summer and given the polythene bag treatment. Propagating compost can consist of 2pts good topsoil, 1pt sphagnum moss peat and 1pt sharp sand, but the ingredients must be free from lime, and the topsoil is often best taken from among healthily established rhododendrons, as this is known to be satisfactory for their needs. Cuttings of suitable shoots will still be moderately soft in their tissue by the end of July and should be taken no later than this, preferably with a heel of older wood attached. Their length is irrelevant, but with these dwarf cultivars they will most likely be around the 2 to 3cm size. Leaves should be left on, though they may be trimmed if they are inconveniently large, for they should not be allowed to touch one another, or the polythene cover, while rooting is taking place. The pot should be stood in a light but not too sunny place – a north-facing window might be suitable.

Many cotoneasters familiar to Western gardeners had their origin in China and the Himalayas, and are discussed in Chapters 10 and 11, but one useful species from the Indian hills south of this range is *Cotoneaster buxifolius,* a rambling evergreen with dull green, orange-backed leaves, and the usual display of fine red berries from late summer onwards.

The dwarf Siberian pine, *Pinus pumila,* is a bushy little tree, and its variety Compacta is an even smaller, bushier version of the type. It makes an erect shrub with densely crowded greyish blue needles, and will lend itself admirably to careful pruning in order to enhance the miniature tree effect. Its natural home is on the most exposed slopes of the Siberian mountains and, similarly, it should be given the most exposed site available on the rockery.

Several juniper species range over the whole of Asia, and *Juniperus* ×*media* is a naturally occurring hybrid – a cross between the species *J. chinensis* and *J. sabina* – to be found in the wild wherever the ranges of these two junipers overlap. The wild form has given rise to many cultivated varieties of great value in the garden, and several are dwarf enough to use on the rockery. Best known of the group is Pfitzeriana, the pfitzer juniper – one of the most familiar of all garden conifers, and more at home, perhaps, as a lawn specimen. It is always handsome with its steeply ascending, splayed, drooping-tipped branches, eventually making a wide-spreading bush. The golden pfitzer, Pftizeriana Aurea, is only marginally smaller, and always arouses admiration in the garden. Old Gold is similar, but noticeably dwarfer and denser, and the golden-yellow foliage does not fade during the summer as the golden pfitzer tends to do. Pfitzeriana Glauca has grey foliage and is similar to the green type in size, but is slightly denser in texture and more compact. Blue Cloud is similar but markedly less

(Above) Lithodora diffusa (Lithospermum prostratum) Grace Ward here shares a sunny site on the corner of a path. *(Below) Daphne petraea* makes an exquisite miniature bush

vigorous, the foliage has a blue tinge, and the whole bush has a more graceful appearance. Plumosa is in keeping with the scale of an average rock garden, but even this bush is rather too vigorous when more compact types of juniper are available. It has plume-like sprays of green foliage that splay out at a shallow angle and eventually cover quite a wide area. Plumosa Aurea is a very attractive yellow-leaved form of this, especially striking during the winter months when the foliage takes on a deep bronzy gold tint.

Bulbous plants tend to have originated in fairly dry areas, and most of them benefit from a long, hot summer. The tulips are no exceptions, and some of the wild Asian species surpass the cultivated garden race for size and brilliance of flower. *Tulipa fosteriana* has immense flowers of brilliant scarlet and, though the wild type might be accommodated on most sites, its named varieties tend to be too tall for rock garden use. The mountain tulip *T. aitchisonii,* on the other hand, is really dwarf and, with its orange-tinted yellow stars opening in April, makes a very pleasant drift for a sunny site among rocks, though ruinously expensive to buy. *Tulipa biflora* bears small flowers in clusters of up to five, basically white with a yellow centre, but stained with shades of crimson and green – a March-flowering species for a sheltered spot. There are several cultivated varieties of the April-flowering bright scarlet *Tulipa greigii* from the central Asian plains, all showing varying degrees of the green and puce leaf-mottling typical of the species. Dwarfest of the *T. greigii* varieties for rock garden use include: Compostella, with brilliant orange and yellow flowers; Donna Bella, with a mottled flower in cream and pink; Perlina, in pale pink and primrose yellow; Plaisir, striped with primrose yellow and lilac; and Red Riding Hood, bright scarlet with a black centre. The well known peacock tulip range originates from *T. greigii,* but these, by and large, are too tall for the rock garden. One of the hardiest species for planting to establish a permanent colony under less than perfect conditions is *Tulipa kaufmanniana,* with flowers of the narrow-petalled water lily type, about 8cm long and reddish when closed, but opening into a broad, pale primrose star, quite un-tuliplike against the tufts of broad grey leaves. Selected cultivars of the species include: Ancilla, white, marked centrally with red; Fritz Kreisler, with large salmon-pink flowers; Gluck, primrose yellow shading to red; Scarlet Elegance, with yellow-centred scarlet flowers; and Shakespeare, with flowers shading from buff and salmon-pink to orange. *Tulipa linifolia* makes rosettes of narrow leaves, with red-stemmed flowers in May, of a brilliant scarlet centred with purple-black – a fine rock garden clump-former. Another late-flowering species is *Tulipa tarda,* which produces small flowers in

(Opposite) Verbascum Letitia, a hybrid dwarf mullein bush

bright yellow and white, shading to green, clustered as many as six on the same stem. It spreads by means of underground stolons to make a splendid drift suitable for a site high on the sunny face of the rockery.

The Siberian squill, *Scilla siberica*, is one of the most commonly seen Siberian plants in Western rock gardens, and a valuable early spring flowerer. Its variety Spring Beauty is slightly taller than the wild species, with rich blue flower spikes, and Taurica is the earliest to come into bloom, its light blue flowers sometimes opening before the end of February. A less well known bulb from central Asia is an onion, *Allium karataviense,* rather tall for most rock gardens, but often very useful on a site nearby, where it can strike an unusual note with its broad bluish grey leaves, often streaked with metallic red, and globular flower heads of pale lilac-pink in May. Rarer, and far more expensive to buy, is the Far Eastern fritillary *Fritillaria camschatcensis,* with dark wine-purple bells, and its variety The Black Knight, whose petals are almost black – a curious flower that loves to establish a small colony in a shady, moist corner where the soil is gritty or stony, a combination of circumstances that recalls its native habitat. As with most other fritillaries, the bulbs tend to hold water in their upper hollow if planted too neatly level, and it is a good idea to slant them on their sides, setting them about 8cm deep.

The dog's tooth violet, *Erythronium dens-canis,* is found over a vast natural range from the British Isles to Japan, and is a perfect coloniser for shady places. Some of the best garden varieties of this species originated from wild specimens collected in Siberia, especially the dark pink flower forms: Rose Beauty has such flowers, and broad leaves mottled with a deep shade of bronze; and White Splendour has similar leaves which show off its pure white flowers in April and May.

An anemone from Kashmir that deserves a place in Western rock gardens is *Anemone biflora,* whose nodding flowers in shades of pink and crimson open in late January and early February, when flowers of these colours are rare. Also from Kashmir is a dwarf shrub, *Jasminum parkeri,* the tiniest of jasmines – a dark green dome sprinkled with small yellow flowers during the summer, and a valuable garden acquisition. In hard winters it may lose its leaves, but the tangled stems retain a fresh, green appearance, so that it looks attractive at any time of the year.

10
The Himalayas

The Himalayas, like the European Alps, represent something of a meeting point between distinct botanical regions. Typically Chinese and Japanese plant forms reach the eastern end of the mountain chain, where the climate is largely warm and damp, and even plants of the sub-tropical type are able to flourish at what would, in Europe, be an Alpine altitude. Flora of the Mediterranean and Middle Eastern types reach the western end of the Himalayas, where the dry season is far more clearly defined, and variations in annual temperature are greater. Tender plants here cannot survive at any great altitude; the temperate forest finds its limit around the 3,000m (or 10,000ft) contour, and plants of the Alpine type find their full expression above this forest line.

So wide a range of plant habitat – from the tropically warm, moist valleys with their heavy rain and equally heavy evaporation, through the cool forests of fern-clad evergreen oak and silver fir, to the regions of perpetual snow – places a question mark against each plant labelled 'Himalayan'. Such a plant might be finicky and tender, or resiliently hardy. The variation in site aspect from a north to a south-facing slope, on the same contour, can mean a difference between, on the one hand, almost desert-dry conditions which support deciduous, thorny, wiry shrubs and, on the other hand, a densely covered, shaded environment and humus-rich soil which, though it may only shallowly overlie the same rock, has resulted in a moisture-loving flora typified by such large-leaved evergreen plants as the early-flowering rhododendrons.

It is on the north-facing slopes which experience monsoon rains that we find these Himalayan rhododendrons, in forest mixture with, mainly, birch trees, though there is little of timber size; dwarfish, scrubby trees with a low, dense canopy. Thus the natural habitat is a moist, shady place which lies each winter under a fair depth of snow; as the slopes are typically very steep and the soil overlying the rock rather poor and shallow, they drain quickly, giving rise to many streams which feed the Himalayan rivers. Those rhododendrons that

Polygonum affine comes from the lower slopes of the Himalayas

are dwarf enough for the rock garden occupy mainly the more exposed, less shaded sites in these forests. They appreciate the protection that their north-facing aspect offers against too rapid a drying-out of the soil, and a south-facing slope would not suit them, for the sun's rays striking at such an angle would quickly desiccate their shallow, fibrously matted root systems.

Tallest of the dwarf rhododendrons is *R. anthopogon,* its tiny, evergreen, aromatic leaves closely set in a compact mound, in April bearing clusters of trumpet flowers which vary from a pale creamy blush to dark pink. In late spring or early summer, the much smaller grey-leaved evergreen *R. calostrotum* produces a brilliant show of broadly flat, crimson flowers. As a result of garden selection, this species has given rise to a magnificent dwarf cultivar, Gigha, with deep wine-red flowers. *R. campylogynum* is a very useful plant, half the height of Gigha, a compact cushion of bright green leaves, with nodding purple flowers in the spring, bearing well when still very young. This has also produced an improved variety – or, rather, a selection of the best consistent variations – with flowers of that peculiar milky pink that suggested the name Crushed Strawberry to its introducers, Hilliers. The somewhat taller *R. chamaethomsonii* is still dwarf and prostrate enough for the smallest rock gardens, with bright clusters of peony-crimson flowers in early spring. Taller again, *R. chryseum* is one of the most unusual dwarf rhododendrons on account of its bright lemon-yellow flowers, conspicuous among the wide range of reds and pinks. The summer-flowering *R. forrestii* is one of the dwarfest of the Himalayan rhododendrons, a creeping, prostrate evergreen which never reaches more than a few centimetres high – seeming taller only by the comparatively large size of the brilliant scarlet flowers which appear in pairs during the spring. This is one of the genus that appreciates shade, for its modest height will rarely allow it to see direct sunlight on its native mountainside. The name *R. forrestii* commemorates the famous plant collector, George Forrest, who was responsible for its introduction to the West, along with many others of the genus. Another of Forrest's introductions, equally dwarf and even more prostrate a carpeter, is *R. radicans,* an evergreen cover of tiny, bright green leaves to run over the rocks, with solitary, almost bowl-shaped flowers of pale purple-pink in late spring. Another true spreader among the evergreens, suckering as it goes – a unique habit among the rhododendrons – is *R. pemakoense,* an early flowerer with a good show of large purple trumpets. The grey-leaved *R. pumilum* is a far more modest spreader, with small, drooping clusters of pale pink flowers in the late spring.

Northwards towards Tibet, the country becomes increasingly arid, with intense sunlight and strong winds which can blow the thin soil into a dust. With this overall dryness and the tendency towards erosion, the craggy peaks here are still very much in the making. There are no large trees, and such shrubs as there are tend to be prostrate, with flexible branches and deciduous leaves. A typical woody plant of this type is *Rhamnus procumbens,* a dwarf buckthorn which makes a useful rock garden shrub with its glossy foliage and black berries. Even grasses are few, and the vegetation as a whole is sparse—only near the streams and in low-lying marshy areas, where there are willows and bog plants, is any lush greenery to be seen. On such moist sites there may be *Dracocephalum hemsleyanum,* a dragon's head with hairy grey leaves and attractive spikes of clear blue flowers in the summer; the trailing, autumn-flowering St John's wort *Hypericum reptans,* with 5cm wide orange-yellow cups; drifts of *Trollius acaulis,* a tiny globe flower which spreads in tufts of finely-cut foliage with buttercup-yellow flowers in the late spring and summer.

Several of the dwarf junipers make natural bonsai shapes on the lower slopes. *Juniperus chinensis* is extremely widespread over much of Asia and, as a garden tree, it has given us *J.c.* Japonica and *J.c.* Mountbatten – the latter a pleasant little glaucous grey column raised in Canada soon after World War II. *Juniperus squamata* occurs in these mountains, as it does over vast tracts of Asia, and, like the common juniper of Europe and America, it is an extraordinarily variable tree, ranging in stature from dwarf mountain specimens to the sizable trees that occur in parts of China. The mountain forms have given rise to a few very valuable rock garden shrubs: Blue Star, a densely foliaged, silvery blue mound-forming bush with soft needle-shaped leaves; Meyeri, which represents an older variety that has been cultivated in Chinese gardens for many years, and makes a large, upright-angular bush somewhat similar to a pfitzer juniper, with attractively blue-grey leaves – rather large for the average rockery, it has nevertheless become very popular in the West and is widely planted; and Wilsonii, which originated from seed collected in the wild on the eastern edge of the Himalayas at the turn of the twentieth century. Buddhist monks are reputed once to have collected the fragrant wood of the so-called drooping juniper, *Juniperus recurva*, to burn as incense. It was seed from this species that gave rise to the English garden form, Embley Park, known originally as Viridis – a reference to the brightness of the green, needle-like leaves which contrast well with the reddish brown bark of the mounding, spreading branches.

The higher western slopes of the Himalayas comprise a dry-cold region with little rain, but a heavy snowfall in the winter, and a fairly low temperature all the year round. In these high, dry areas, the deodar cedar ventures to an altitude considerably above the range normal to it in the moister, warmer extremes on the east. Below the cedar zone, forests of Himalayan cypress occur and, above them, species of mountain pine which have not, apparently, produced any dwarf varieties that have found their way to the West. *Cedrus deodara*, on the other hand, has a few garden forms, and one which was raised in the United States is Pygmy – a tiny, extremely close-growing mound of glaucous-blue foliage that, after ten years or so as a rock garden specimen, will scarcely attain more than 15cm in height.

Above the pines, some of the mountain plants are closely related to the European Alpine counterparts. The Himalayan edelweiss, *Leontopodium haplophylloides*, is at least as attractive as the more familiar *L. alpinum*, with starry flowers in a compact head above the pointed bracts, and a strong lemon scent to its woolly white leaves. The frozen snow which covers these plants during the winter months hints at their appreciation of dryness around the leaves, and the discomfort they exhibit during mild, wet winters; damp weather also often prevents satisfactory seed setting. Nevertheless, they will grow well in the West during most seasons, provided the soil is gritty and well-drained. If there is no seed, mature plants may be divided into replantable crowns as soon as growth starts in the spring.

There are two gentians from the Tibetan edge of the mountains, both well known in the West. Since its introduction to Europe and America before World War I, *Gentiana farreri* has given rise to numerous garden forms, most of them unnamed. It is notably a spreader among gentians, later flowering than almost any other of the genus, and paler in its blue colour than most. *Gentiana sino-ornata* is another spreader, also autumn flowering, when the dense mats of bright green tufted leaves become well covered with brilliant sky-blue trumpets. It is one of the easiest gentians to increase by division of the roots in early spring. Neither *G. farreri* nor *G. sino-ornata* will do well where there is lime in the soil.

The genus *Cassiope* includes species from a wide range over Asia, America and Europe, and some of these spreading, heath-like shrubs occur naturally on these dry, cool slopes. They should be given similar treatment to the heathers, including a strictly lime-free soil but, inhabiting as they do the north-facing slopes, unlike heathers they can tolerate and indeed appreciate a modicum of shade. They bear small, nodding pinkish white flowers in the spring, and some of the best hybrid varieties – not all of Himalayan origin – with their varied heights of flower stem, will be found listed in the Table of Rock Plants.

Tulipa chrysantha is one Himalayan tulip at least that has found its way into Western rock gardens. Bright in April with its six-rayed star-like flowers of brilliant yellow – the petals have a reddish reverse which gives the opening buds a bicolor appearance – a clump of this species strikes the eye forcibly when viewed against a background of grey rocks.

Few stonecrops originate in the Himalayas, for although they might be thought typical plants of the bare rock face, in the main, they appreciate a warmer mountain climate. *Sedum crassipes* is a herbaceous species which enjoys Alpine meadow conditions rather than the dryness of the upper slopes. The thick, upright stems arising from flat, orpine-like leaves bear pale yellow flowers in the summer, darkening as the seed heads ripen into a vivid orange; they are well sited adjacent to, if not actually on, the steeper parts of the rockery. More typical sedum rock species are: the spreading, trailing *Sedum ewersii,* whose fluffy, lilac-pink flowers make a quiet show in the autumn; and *S. linearifolium,* summer flowering – though the flat, wine-red flower heads last well into the autumn – and of slender, tufted habit, it enjoys a sunny crevice in the rocks.

From the western Himalayas, and one of the few saxifrages from this region, is *Saxifraga lilacina* – a parent of many garden hybrids. In the wild it prefers moist, shady nooks where its neat, bright green leaf rosettes bear solitary flowers of lilac-blue in the spring. *Sempervivella alba* is a pretty little plant like a houseleek, with sprawling flower stems arising from fleshy, pinkish leaf rosettes. The little seven-petalled flowers in the spring are white, but the buds as they open match the leaves in roseate pinkness. A hardy little plant that has no objection to lime, it deserves a niche in the sun among the rocks.

Cotoneaster microphyllus is perhaps typical of the Himalayan cotoneasters – an exceptionally hardy, low-spreading evergreen which may reach 3m across an average mature specimen. The small, rounded leaves are a deep glossy green above and downy grey beneath, and the tiny white flowers appear in May and June, to be followed by very beautiful bright scarlet berries. A much dwarfer form of the species is *C.m.* Cochleatus, found wild in the mountains of eastern Tibet – a creeping bush barely more than ankle-high and very slow-growing. Although so much smaller overall than the type, it has larger leaves of a brighter green. Another variety of *C. microphyllus* is Thymifolius, a very effective rock garden shrub with narrow, thyme-like, dark glossy green leaves, dainty and dwarf enough not to damage a dry stone wall. *Cotoneaster congestus* is sometimes said to be another variety of *C. microphyllus*, but most botanists class it as a separate species. More mounded than spreading, it forms a curiously congested series of humps, with leaves broader and flatter than those of Thymifolius, and with berries similar in size and appearance to the full-sized *C. microphyllus*. The foliage has a slight bluish tinge, and the flowers usually show a faint pink blush. *C. conspicuus*, another wild cotoneaster found in Tibet, is potentially rather large for the rockery, but it has a completely prostrate form, Decorus, which spreads densely and is excellent for covering steep areas in large gardens. It is later flowering by a month than the others, and the flowers are large for a cotoneaster, very popular with bees, pretty on close inspection with purple anthers in contrast with the white petals, and followed by brilliant red fruits that last well through the winter months – possibly they are less palatable to birds than some other kinds.

All the cotoneasters seed themselves fairly readily, especially when seeds fall into inaccessible places such as the gaps between paving stones, where no creature can find them. The berries can easily be collected for sowing, but they usually take a year or more to germinate unless they have first been stored in moist sand over winter. Cotoneaster berries that have been digested by birds are said to germinate rapidly, through the action of digestive juices on the hard seed coat, but it is sometimes more convenient – and more certain when named varieties are being propagated – to take cuttings during the late summer, just as the current season's growth is firming and darkening at the shoot bases. Side-shoots should be pulled off with a heel, trimming away any strip of bark that may be attached, and it is best to raise cotoneasters in small individual containers, as they do not take kindly to open-root planting.

The trailing knot grass, *Polygonum vaccinifolium,* is an autumn-flowering plant that looks good on the rockery and is equally valuable for a sunny wall, where suitable autumn-flowerers are few, for its cheerful heather-like spikes of bright pinkish-purple put on an attractive display. This plant, in my view, should be one of the key members of any rock planting scheme, for it reliably carries the design over a difficult end-of-season period and, as it takes very eagerly from cuttings, there need never be any shortage of plants.

From the lower slopes in the shadier, moister ground comes *Polygonum affine,* a very fine carpet-forming plant, also autumn flowering, with brilliant pink flower spikes that mellow to a deep red as they die. This creeping knot grass is deciduous, but the leaves, after taking on gold and scarlet autumn tints, remain attached dead and brown to their prostrate stems during the winter, and have an attractive, warm appearance, besides protecting the soil against winter erosion. Propagation is a matter of simple division. Creeping knot grass looks fine if it is allowed to cascade and trail over large rocks, but the garden must be large enough to accommodate it, or it will overbalance the design. In small rock gardens it is admissible when allowed to clothe the ground level slopes and venture up the valleys as far as the lowest rocks. There are two named varieties with brighter, more compact flowers – Darjeeling Red and Lowndes Variety – and the latter is best for all-round small garden use.

Solomon's seal belongs to a similarly named but unrelated genus – *Polygonatum* – and the spring-flowering *Polygonatum hookeri* is a Himalayan plant that appreciates much the same sort of situation as the creeping knot grass, and its crowded tufts of lily-like leaves should be limited to the lower reaches of the moraine, where they can revel in the shade and moisture. The pinkish purple flowers in May, like erect trumpets on short stems, are not beautiful but they have a certain air of distinction. *Corydalis diphylla* is an unusual subject for this type of site, with its tufted, grey, lobed leaves and spikes of white and purple, tubular, lipped flowers in the late spring. It is a bulbous plant that slowly spreads by producing offsets at its base.

Also preferring moist, gritty situations is the summer-flowering *Androsace sarmentosa,* a spreader by nature, forming mats of white-hairy leaf rosettes which run happily between small rocks. The wild flowers are pink, in short clustered heads, but there are many garden forms and named cultivars which vary in flower colour from pale apple blossom to deep red. More vigorous and, perhaps, less particular about site and climate, is *A. lanuginosa*, a trailer which will revel in a niche high up on the rockery, where the silver-hairy leaves and summer-long pink flowers can be seen to advantage. *A. sempervivoides* also appreciates a gritty soil, but will tolerate most conditions found in the average rock garden. Its tiny, closely overlapping leaves form dwarf rosettes as a base for the short-stemmed clusters of bright pink flowers, which make a good display in the spring.

A little spreading plant that rejoices in a gritty, lime-free soil is *Cyananthus lobatus*, with small fleshy leaves and gentian-blue flowers, each 2.5cm wide, making a bright splash of colour in the late summer. It is a plant for the dividing line between scree and moraine or, on a more modest scale, between rockery and moist border, for its questing roots will run here and there, establishing a clump wherever fancy takes it. It is unlikely to become a problem in this respect, however, and need not be feared as a weed. Shoot cuttings root very readily at any time during the growing season, but a deadline should be set for June, because those rooted later in the year often fail to survive their first winter.

Stream margins are the natural habitat of the Himalayan *Primula rosea*, an interesting little bog plant which sheds its leaves for the winter and commences growth in early April by thrusting its closely packed heads of flower buds through the silted mud. While the leaves develop and the stem lengthens, the flowers open and expand as soon as the spring sunshine warms the air, with as many as a dozen 2cm wide bell-like flowers of yellow-eyed bright pink. There are several garden varieties of the species, with flower colours ranging from pale pink to deep red, and all are excellent for the contrived boggy patch, or for a shady, moist hollow at the base of the rockery. Other Himalayan primulas are: the spring-flowering *P. bracteosa*, a dusty-leaved species with pale lilac, yellow-eyed flowers; and *P. ageniana*, with strongly fragrant flowers of the palest yellow – there is also a pale pink variety of *P. ageniana*, and a very bright yellow one from the southern Himalayas. *P. alpicola* is a Tibetan cowslip-like species with fragrant, late spring flowers that vary over a wide range of colours – white, yellow, purple and violet. Seeds that come true to colour can be bought, and all the forms are excellent for the lower, moister reaches of the moraine, for they revel in light shade and a peaty soil. *P. bellidifolia*, another Tibetan species, bears a tight cluster of as many as fifteen bright violet-blue flowers, and leaves which, as the specific name implies, are somewhat similar to those of the common daisy *Bellis perennis*.

A spring-flowering primula of the darkest purple – a colour set off by its clear yellow eye, like an African violet – *Primula calderiana* thrives in average conditions, and has been cultivated in Western gardens for a century or more. *P. capitata* has dusty leaves and flattened, crowded heads of bell-shaped violet flowers in the summer; *P chungensis* is a summer-flowering species of the candelabra type, with tall stems of whorled, bell-shaped orange-flowers – too tall for elevated positions on the rock garden, but it will fill a narrow gulley adjacent to the rockery. Contrastingly dwarf among the Himalayan primulas is *P. edgeworthii,* a modest spring-flowerer with clusters of pale mauve flowers held barely above the leaf rosettes. During the winter, the leaves are heavily dusted white, and much smaller than the bright green summer crop. This is a primula that could well be planted at near eye level among the rocks. The seeds lose their viability very quickly, and should be sown as soon as they ripen. Similar to *P. edgeworthii*, from the western Himalayas, *P. scapigera* has very bright pink flowers in the spring, and the two grown together make a charming colour blend. *P. scapigera* can be propagated from leaf cuttings: the basal leaves when fully grown are gently detached by pulling sideways, and dibbled into a sandy compost – not under a polythene bag, but preferably within the shelter of a propagating frame – when young plants are formed at the base of the leaves, in the same way as saintpaulia leaf cuttings.

The Tibetan *Primula sonchifolia* is noted for the earliness of its flowering season. The impressively large clusters of drooping, almost bell-shaped flowers, purple-blue with a yellow eye, appear in February, the buds opening before the stem starts to grow, and continue to expand as the sturdy scape lengthens during March. *P. sonchifolia* releases its seed early – often before it appears to be fully ripe – but nevertheless it should be collected and sown immediately if new plants are needed, for it continues to mature and ripen in the compost, and germinates freely the following spring. This primula grows best in districts which experience decisive seasons – where the winters are cold and the spring weather reliable.

11
Chinese Mountain Plants

The cool, moist conditions that many primulas enjoy are to be found over much of China, and many species are native to the region. One of the best known of these is the drumstick *Primula denticulata,* with tightly arranged globular heads of flower in the spring – the flowers opening in March while the rather powdery leaves are still small, and blooming until May, by which time the leaves are all of 30cm long. In the typical species, the flowers are lilac-blue with a yellow eye, but there are several cultivated varieties, and selected strains have flower colours ranging through violet and crimson shades. The species and its varieties are unusual among primulas in their ability to grow from root cuttings – firm pieces of root about 2-3cm long, dibbled upright into a sandy compost during the autumn. Quite as hardy and easy to grow are the Chinese candelabra primulas, *P. aurantiaca, P. beesiana* and *P. bulleyana.* All these species revel in moist, slightly shady sites, and they associate well with water, making a substantial tufty carpet if allowed to naturalise themselves in marshy ground. Their flowering season extends through June and July as successive tiers of candelabra flowers open and fade, and their bright colours stand out well in the shade – especially if viewed against a dark background. *Primula aurantiaca* is a bright reddish orange, with as many as six whorls of up to twelve flowers in each appearing during the season; *P. beesiana* is a yellow-eyed carmine-purple, with more flowers than *P. aurantiaca* to each whorl, though fewer whorls may be produced; and *P. bulleyana,* a deep, glowing orange with apricot shading, also produces about six whorls, each containing numerous flowers.

Another species for moist, moderately shaded positions is the very beautiful *Primula chionantha,* whose fragrant white flowers open early in May. The flowering stems often bear more than one cluster, sometimes as many as four, each containing perhaps twenty or twenty-five large and distinctively shaped flowers. Other Chinese primulas which enjoy cool, moist conditions are: *P. melanops,* of the same type as *P. chionantha,* though perhaps not as easy to grow, and

Cotoneaster horizontalis

with only one or two short-stemmed clusters of black-centred flowers of the deepest violet; *P. polyneura*, with almost nettle-like, softly downy, prominently veined leaves, and short-stalked clusters of somewhat drooping, unusually lobed flowers, the colour varying in individual plants from pale pink through the richest rose-red, to crimson and purple; and *P. vialii*, one of the most distinctive of primulas, bearing its flowers in a dense, tall spike reminiscent of a kniphofia red hot poker, and composed of numerous small flowers, scarlet in the bud, opening to a rich bluish violet.

These mountain primulas by nature inhabit shady spots in the more fertile valleys that separate the peaks, and are accustomed to a winter's covering of snow, which keeps them comparatively dry and frost-free during the dormant months. As the snow melts, they start to flower and put out new growth, so that their spring and early summer seasons are characterised by the soaking wet conditions brought about by the melting snow – the soil barely starting to dry until towards the close of the growing season. One of the worst perils that faces them when transferred to Western rock gardens, therefore, having survived a wet winter, is the risk of spring and early summer drought. England is notorious also for producing warm spells too early in the spring, which tempt buds to break into growth, only to be cut back by frost. Plants which are especially susceptible to these dangers and to the strain of wet winter months present the greatest challenge to the Alpine enthusiast, who traditionally grows the most difficult subjects in pots within an airy, unheated Alpine house. The question of adequate moisture outside during the early growing season is one which can be answered quite readily by artificial watering, and all the plants mentioned here are well capable of surviving outdoors in all temperate zones. Some will be short-lived however, and *Primula nutans* falls within this category: it sets seed only very rarely, but is worth growing for the delicate beauty of its pyramidal clusters of fragrant violet flowers.

An exception to the moist soil rule is found in *Primula forrestii*, for this species prefers a dry, gritty site. It bears cowslip-like clusters of orange-eyed, yellow flowers in May and June and, unlike *P. nutans*, is a most tenacious plant, with a woody rootstock that likes to establish itself firmly between rocks, or the stones of an earth-backed dry wall, from where it sends out rosettes of long-stalked, somewhat heart-shaped, dark green leaves.

A few dwarf conifers have originated in China over the years. The silver fir *Abies delavayi* from the western and central mountains has several closely allied geographical variations, few of which are ever seen in the West. Only one variety, Nana, is suitable for the rock garden, and this is an upright little tree which will take perhaps fifteen years to grow a metre in height, quite handsome with its bristly needles, dark glossy green above and silvery on the reverse, contrasting with the orange-brown shoots and buds. The Chinese arbor vitae, *Thuja orientalis*, has produced a wider range of varieties, if for no other reason than that it has been grown under cultivation in the West for the past three hundred years. *T.o.* Rosedalis is perhaps the best known – a tightly spherical little bush that will still be under half a metre in height after ten years on the rock garden. The soft, feathery foliage changes colour with the seasons – a dark olive green during high summer, darkening to greyish purple for the winter, becoming brightly yellow when growth recommences in the spring. *T.o.* Conspicua is a much older variety, a densely compact, spherical bush of similar size to Rosedalis, but with bright bronzy yellow foliage throughout the summer. Another with coloured foliage is the waist-high *T.o.* Aurea Nana, with upright, ferny sprays of yellowish green. Neatest, perhaps, of the Chinese arbor vitae group is *T.o.* Minima Glauca, a similarly sized bush of densely spherical shape, with soft foliage that changes from its summer sea-green to a warm tawny yellow in the winter.

Plant cultivar names should never be quoted in isolation, without their parent species, or mistakes will certainly occur, as the more descriptive among them are duplicated again and again. There must be dozens of dwarf conifers called 'Nana', for example – and *Chamaecyparis lawsoniana* Minima Glauca and *Thuja orientalis* Minima Glauca are two very different trees.

Many rhododendrons have been introduced from China, and a few of these are of the dwarf mountain type. *Rhododendron hanceanum* Nanum is a variety which occurs in the wild, an evergreen which displays tiny but very numerous primrose-yellow trumpet flowers in the spring, in striking contrast with the dark green upper surface of the leaves. *R. impeditum* is another evergreen of low, twiggy growth, dainty and charming among the rocks, where it forms intricately tangled carpets of tiny rounded leaves, almost covered in the spring with faintly fragrant lilac-blue flowers. *R. lepidostylum* is taller growing, making a dense waist-high thicket of stout branchlets, and loses its foliage in hard winters. The tiny leaves are very ornamental in the summer, however, and have a distinctive blue-grey shade which gives the shrub great ornamental value on larger rock gardens, where it grows happily in moderate shade. The wide flowers are of a very pale greenish yellow, and appear in the late spring.

From the island of Taiwan, *Rhododendron nakaharai* is a truly dwarf creeping mountain evergreen, with tiny pointed leaves, and clusters of trumpet-shaped flowers in an unusual shade of dark red, open from June to early August. If it sets seed, this will be the simplest means of propagating it; but like all rhododendrons, it will eventually strike roots from earthed-up layers, and will also take from cuttings. June or July is the best time to pull off firm little shoots, with a slight heel of older wood attached – the length of cutting will depend on the amount of growth the specimen has made in the spring – and these should be set in a sandy-peat mixture under polythene. All rhododendron seed is tiny, but it germinates fairly readily. Finely sifted sphagnum moss peat is a very useful sowing medium. If a proprietory compost is used, it must be free from lime – the type known as ericaceous seed-sowing compost is suitable. Whichever kind is used, it should be moistened well before sowing, as overhead watering while germination is taking place might well damage the tiny emerging shoots. The seeds should be covered very lightly with a sifting of the same material, and the containers can be covered with paper until the seedlings show. They should not be exposed to direct sunlight for at least the first year, as they are apt to scorch very easily.

Cotoneaster horizontalis must be one of the best known garden shrubs, with its ornamental qualities – the brilliant berries, the red autumn tints of its tiny leaves and, in the spring, the white, bee-favoured flowers – but *C. horizontalis* is apt to grow a little too vigorously for many sites. Its variety Saxatilis is equally tenacious but much more prostrate, with smaller leaves, and tending not to mound to the same extent as the species. Other Chinese cotoneasters include: *C. adpressus*, a similar wide-spreading dwarf bush with comparable foliage and berries; and *C. dammeri*, an evergreen with bright red berries, even more prostrate but also more vigorous, with its long, trailing shoots which will rapidly clothe a large wall or cover the ground beneath shrubs and tall trees. A similarly spreading but dwarfer variety is Skogholm, which also originated in mountainous western China, a good summer-flowering wall plant with exceptionally large, pinkish red berries.

Although they may be found in the wild, there is no guarantee that all cotoneasters will come true from seed, for they are notorious cross-breeders. They are very interesting to grow from seed, however; if space can be spared for a small experimental nursery area, a few years will clearly show how a seedling is going to behave when transplanted to the rock garden. Chinese cotoneasters should preferably be raised in pots or other containers, as open-rooted plants do not take readily. To be sure of obtaining true varieties, vegetative propagation will be necessary. For this, small side-shoot cuttings may be taken as soon as the wood starts to harden around July; a slight heel of older wood at the base will ensure callusing and prevent rotting. Very often, rooting will have taken place before the autumn. Alternatively, longer shoots can be taken in the autumn – also with a heel, or they will probably rot before spring – and set in a sandy compost under glass. Most of them will be ready for potting up after a full year.

(Above) Silene schafta makes a useful patch of carpet for a sunny, rocky spot.
(Below) Primula juliae, a well known carpeter, revels in light shade

(Above) Sedum spurium, a selected red-flowered form of this Caucasian stonecrop. *(Below)* A Siberian stonecrop, *Sedum kamtschaticum,* sharing its site with a campanula

12
The Bonsai Influence

Many dwarf mountain trees have originated in Japan. The white pine, *Pinus parviflora*, growing wild in its native habitat, resembles the Scots pine in becoming picturesquely flat-topped as it matures, and the species is popular not only as a garden tree in Japan, it is also a favourite bonsai subject, lending itself readily to this method of artificial dwarfing. Something of the bonsai appearance, without the need for any special treatment, can be obtained with the *P. parviflora* variety, Adcock's Dwarf, which originated from seed sown in England. A very compact, bushy little tree with short, bluish green needles, it will still be well below waist height after ten years of average rock garden growth. The same remarks apply to the dwarf form of the Japanese red pine, *Pinus densiflora* Umbraculifera, a very useful miniature tree with a dense, umbrella-shaped crown and gnarled, copper-barked branches. Its rate of growth in the garden is about the same as Adcock's Dwarf but, whereas the latter will tolerate lime in the soil, Umbraculifera will not.

If these varieties set viable seed, the resultant seedlings are likely to grow to the full specific size and, as with other pines, it is almost impossible to persuade cuttings to root. The only practical means of propagating dwarf pines such as these is to graft them on normal pine seedlings, and the simplest method, which I have found to give excellent results, is the wedge insert. In late summer, select a stock seedling of near pencil thickness and behead it smoothly where the wood is still soft; choose the plumpest terminal shoot from the tree to be propagated, as nearly as possible the same diameter as the stock – it need be no more than 2.5cm long – and trim the base to a wedge shape; slit the stock across the top and slip the scion in, so that it matches evenly on at least one side of the bark, and tie with raffia or plastic strip. Low melting-point wax – such as match manufacturers sometimes use to make their matches burn more easily – is very useful in this type of grafting; a pot-grown stock with newly grafted scion can simply be inverted and dipped in the melted (but reasonably cool) wax,

Cryptomeria japonica

and the resultant seal will be airtight, watertight, and one hundred per cent effective. As soon as new growth starts, of course, the wax will break its seal.

The Japanese cedar, *Cryptomeria japonica*, is often thought of as the most Japanese of trees but, in fact, the species also occurs in China, and most of the specimens in the West probably originated from Chinese seed. The symmetrical outline typical of cryptomeria, with its well spaced branches, tends to be lost in the dwarf forms, which are usually compact and densely foliaged. Smallest of all is Compressa, a tiny, flat-topped bun of a bush whose tightly packed leaves become purple in the winter. Similar in colouring and foliage is Vilmoriniana, while Globosa, whose foliage takes on a reddish tinge, has a looser arrangement of leaves and attains a rather larger size – though it will still barely exceed a metre after ten or fifteen years. Nana Albospica has creamy white tips to the young leaves. A slightly larger bush is Jindai Sugi, a bright green and somewhat contorted plant with a picturesquely windblown appearance. Pygmaea is a wild form of the species and a truly dwarf tree, which lends itself well to artistic pruning – the practice of opening up the crown and removing some of the branches so as to expose the reddish-brown, shreddy bark, to encourage a weatherbeaten silhouette to develop, and bring home a genuine touch of mountain landscape – but only for the largest gardens, for Pygmaea will top a metre with ease after ten or twelve years.

Pygmaea usually comes true from seed, but the others, though they often bear cones, will seldom reproduce the dwarf characteristics in their seedlings. Varieties of Japanese cedar, however, lend themselves more readily than most conifers to propagation from cuttings. The best time of the year to take cryptomeria cuttings is during August and September, when the season's new wood is becoming firm, and they may be of any convenient length, depending on the variety. A sandy rooting compost is best, and it is a good idea to spread a thin layer of sharp sand on the surface, so that when the cuttings are dibbled in, this falls down around their bases. The polythene bag method is effective, and new growth will normally be seen the following spring. The first transplanting stage is the crucial period, and the young trees need to be sheltered very carefully from direct sunshine or draughts, and allowed to establish themselves in their new containers without any kind of shock.

Two cypresses native to Japan have found their way into our rock gardens – the Hinoki cypress, *Chamaecyparis obtusa*, and the Sawara cypress, *Chamaecyparis pisifera*. Both make large trees in their wild habitat, and both have given rise to numerous garden forms. One of the best known varieties of *C. obtusa* is Nana Gracilis – the 'slender dwarf' to be seen in gardens everywhere, with its distinctive, flat sprays of bright green foliage, and picturesquely sinuous outline. Though very slow growing, it will eventually reach a height of 3m or more. Older specimens often produce cones with fertile seed, but seedlings will not come true to form – variously shaped dwarf trees might result from sowings, but most of the progeny will grow to the height normal for the species. Cuttings from varieties of both Hinoki and Sawara cypresses root fairly readily, and this is always the most reliable method to use with them.

Among other varieties of *Chamaecyparis obtusa*, Chabo Yadari originated in Japan and has not often been planted in the West. It grows almost as tall as Nana Gracilis, but makes a much more compact bush-like dome, and some of the leaves are of the feathery, juvenile type, so that the flattened sprays have a soft texture. Nana Aurea is almost as tall, taking perhaps fifteen years to reach waist height. A very beautiful golden-leaved variety, it too has the distinctively rounded flat 'tennis ball' leaf sprays, many of them cupped at various angles and arranged around the branches in a rough spiral – but it is more of a bush than Nana Gracilis: where the latter ultimately forms a typical tree shape, Nana Aurea retains its flat-topped mounding silhouette into maturity. Mariesii and Kosteri are both very well tried varieties for Western gardens, making somewhat flat-topped cones of densely dwarf foliage. In the summer, Mariesii becomes a rather chlorotic pale yellow, darkening to a healthy bright green for the winter; Kosteri is bright green during the summer, becoming a bronzed metallic purple in the winter. The tiniest and most compact dwarfs are: Minima – growing barely 1cm a year, and making a congested bun of a tree with grotesquely mounding foliage – one of the best conifers for the sink garden; Densa, which grows a little faster and becomes slightly larger, with miniature fans of dark green, densely dwarf foliage; Bassett, which is suitable as a trough plant – an upright dome of congested, cup-shaped whorls in a healthy dark green; and Caespitosa, another pretty little trough garden conifer, equally at home on the small rock garden, where it displays a patch of cheerfully bright green foliage. It was an offspring early in the twentieth century of Nana Gracilis seed, so it is sometimes worthwhile experimenting in this line. Another seedling from Nana Gracilis of about the same vintage is the creeping Repens, almost juniper-like in its prostrate habit, but with loosely rounded fan-shaped sprays of un-juniper-like bright green, which become lighter and more yellowish during the winter months.

Sawara cypress, *Chamaecyparis pisifera*, has given rise to the very popular Boulevard, which eventually makes a sizable tree, reaching perhaps 2m in fifteen years or so, but with so densely soft a mass of foliage – metallic blue in the summer and purple-grey in the winter – that it deserves to be used even in the smallest garden. There is no reason, beyond sheer economics, why such trees should not be grown on the rock garden until they become too large, for even at this size they will transplant comparatively easily and, if there is nowhere else to put them, they often make very acceptable gifts. *C.p.* Squarrosa Aurea Nana and *C.p.* Squarrosa Sulphurea are rather similar, with loosely held sprays of soft, feathery yellow leaves. There are many yellow-leaved forms of Sawara: Aurea Nana is a very richly coloured bush; Filifera Nana Aurea has long branchlets drooping from a tightly formed mound of bright golden foliage; Nana Aureovariegata is a slow-growing, squat dome of a tree, with flattened sprays of golden-tinged foliage; Plumosa Aurea Compacta is a very soft yellow; and

Plumosa Compressa Aurea forms a tight sphere of tiny yellow-tinged leaves which become green during the winter. Smallest of the *C. pisifera* cultivars commonly seen in our rock gardens is Nana, which has the endearing habit after many years – when it will still be no more than knee-high – of forming a distinctive upper tier like a cottage loaf, sculptured in yew-like dark green foliage. It has been grown in the West for a century or so, and has rarely become too large for its site. Filifera Nana is another fascinating century-old introduction, with long whip-like sprays drooping from a squat, dark green, flat-topped bush, rarely exceeding 1m in height; and Plumosa Compressa makes an evenly rounded bush, with densely compact foliage of a soft texture and bright green colour.

Two juniper species from Japan that have proved themselves suitable for Western rock gardens originate not from the mountains, but along the seashore. The shore juniper, *Juniperus conferta*, forms a prickly carpet of bright green sprays arising to a fair height from the prostrate stems. It is too exuberant and vigorous for small gardens but, as a large-scale ground cover plant, it has proved very useful in Britain and the United States, valued especially for its ability to thrive in poor, sandy soils. *Juniperus procumbens,* the creeping juniper, occupies a similar habitat in the wild, and equally enjoys poor soils, where it makes a great sprawling carpet of glaucous grey-green – a good foliage colour-blend with the shore juniper. The wild dwarf form *J. procumbens* Nana is better suited than either species to garden use, for its grey-green prickly shoots grow outwards and downwards to hug the ground; but these Japanese junipers are really too vigorous for the small rock garden, even in their dwarf forms, and we should look to some of the European and American species for dwarf varieties that will not exceed their allotted bounds. Junipers like this are easy to propagate, and take readily from cuttings of any length. If only one or two specimens are required, it is worth exploring among the prostrate shoots to see if any convenient pieces have rooted themselves and are shapely enough to be detached and grown on as young plants.

Common yew has several favourite garden varieties, but the Japanese yew, *Taxus cuspidata*, is less well known. This species, introduced from the Japanese mountains midway through the nineteenth century, is hardier than the more familiar *T. baccata* – a hardy enough tree itself – but it is far too large for the rock garden. The dwarf form *Taxus cuspidata* Nana, on the other hand, has been grown in the West almost as long as the species, and makes an upright mound of a bush with gracefully arching shoots, rarely exceeding 1.5m or so in height. It has the distinctively black-green foliage typical of the genus but, as Nana is a male form, it cannot bear berries. It can be grown from cuttings, when it is usually best to select the thickest terminal shoots available, and keep them in a fairly close atmosphere under glass until they have rooted, as the callusing process takes some time.

Finally, among Japanese dwarf conifers, there is *Thujopsis dolobrata* Nana. The history of its introduction to the West is similar to that of the Japanese yew, for this cypress-like species first arrived midway through the nineteenth century – the compact, flat-topped Nana following a few years later. It is a very slow-growing bush, and I have known a forty year old specimen that was well below 1m in height. It may be propagated from short, leafy cuttings in exactly the same manner as the cypresses, taking convenient shoots in the summer and setting them in a sandy compost, preferably under a frame where they can remain undisturbed.

Japan is famous for its azaleas, and there are several large rhododendron species popular in Western gardens that originated here, among them the winter-flowering *Rhododendron mucronulatum.* Wild dwarf rock species are fewer in number, and outstanding among them is the semi-evergreen *Rhododendron keiskei,* with clusters of broad, trumpet-shaped flowers of clear lemon-yellow, opening in the spring and lasting for several months. Introduced at the turn of the twentieth century, it has usually been found to appreciate a sheltered spot between rocks, preferably on a slope so that any cold spring air can roll freely away. A true mountain rhododendron of Japan is the Kyushu azalea, a forerunner of the cultivated Kurume azaleas, but this bush is too coarsely vigorous for the rock garden and, for sites where it would be in scale, the named Kurume varieties are to be preferred.

A charming Japanese shrub sometimes used to form miniature hedges, but perfect as a little clump in isolation on the rock garden, is the dwarf red barberry, *Berberis thunbergii* Atropurpurea Nana. Its rich purple-red foliage makes a perfect foil for many plants of a bluish or yellowish tinge, and it can be clipped hard back in the spring if it threatens to become too bulky for its site. The variety only rarely sets seed but, if any can be sown, a fair percentage of seedlings should come true to type – any with green leaves can be discarded, although those with the best colour will probably attain a larger ultimate size than their parents. The seed should be gathered as soon as it ripens, mixed with moist sand in a sealed container to stand over winter, and sown in the earliest spring in open beds, sand and seed together, chafing the pulp off the seeds by rubbing them between the hands.

Euonymus radicans is a useful little trailing shrub, not limited to Japan but found also on the mainland of China and Korea; its coloured foliage varieties – Coloratus, with a purple tinge; Variegatus, with white, yellow and pink markings; and the very dwarf form Minimus – are all excellent for fronting shady parts of the outcrop, or acting as the go-between carpet where a sunny rockery merges into a shady border. All these varieties have the advantage of being very easily increased by cuttings of shoot tips, taken at any time of the year – preferably between spring and late summer. Well established plants root themselves as they trail, and rooted pieces can often be lifted and replanted elsewhere, but mature specimens form a distinct type of flowering foliage in the manner of English ivy, and cuttings or layers taken from this type of growth will result in non-trailing, compactly bushy plants.

The herbaceous, early spring-flowering *Polygonum tenuicaule* creeps about slowly and revels in moist, shady situations, where it makes an ankle-deep carpet of small leaves rising like the lily of the valley direct from the soil surface, and numerous spikes of tiny white flowers with prominent stamens. If there are shady lower reaches to a moist moraine, this is one of the plants to clothe it. It is easily increased by simple division of the spreading stolons. A similar site suits the Japanese counterpart of the Western dog's tooth violet, *Erythronium japonicum,* with rounded, bright green leaves and violet flowers in April. It is a bulbous subject and, if a group is planted fairly close together, a small colony will quickly establish itself and increase year by year.

A good carpeting species for where there is shade and moisture, low and neat enough for a place between paving stones, is *Lysimachia japonica* Minuta, which has tiny green leaves and a sprinkling of starry yellow flowers in the summer. The plant needs dividing and replanting every three years or so, using the younger, outside portions and discarding the old central part.

Some of the Japanese primulas are useful for the marginal-moraine type of site – for example, the beautiful *Primula sieboldii,* a plant which revels in light shade and a moist, peaty soil, and which has given rise to many garden forms. The clump of toothed, soft-downy leaves dies back every year, but appears again in time to sheath the 18cm high stalk of large, clustered flowers, as many as ten to the stem, ranging in shade according to variety from pure white through pink to purple, with a conspicuous white eye. Some of the garden forms have developed very attractively fringed petals, and seed will often produce an interesting range of flowers. *Primula japonica* is, perhaps, the best known of the tall, spreading candelabra primulas, and one of the easiest to grow. Hardly a rock garden plant – but ideal for any low-lying areas or boggy patches nearby, *P. japonica* makes a marvellous wine-red drift in the late spring. The plant grows easily from seed sown in the autumn – its two popular varieties Miller's Crimson and Postford White usually come true from seed – and the huge tufted crowns lend themselves so readily to division in the late summer, simply by lifting and teasing apart the separate rosetted portions, and replanting, that increasing stock rarely presents any problem.

One stonecrop species from Japan has been well known in the West, and especially in Britain, for many years, although it is only marginally hardy. This is *Sedum sieboldii,* an old-fashioned favourite pot plant, with arching stems of round, pink-margined leaves, and pale pink flower clusters during October. It will survive outdoors in sheltered spots. *Sedum cauticolum* is very closely related, hardier and more ornamental, its trailing stems making it very suitable for use as a wall plant. It produces sizable clumps of these trailers, clad in rounded leaves of a soft blue-grey, with fist-size clusters of bright crimson flowers in the autumn. To increase these late-flowering sedum species, leafy cuttings need to be taken as early in the spring as possible, just as annual growth is commencing. Late spring and summer cuttings tend to dissipate their energy trying to produce flowers, and fail to become established in time for the winter.

13
The Southern Hemisphere

Among the plants from the southern hemisphere that have found a permanent place in rock gardens of northern climes, perhaps the shrubby veronicas spring first to mind – dwarf bushes of the genus *Hebe,* mostly natives of New Zealand, which are often a feature of seaside planting schemes in Britain and America. The lower-growing evergreen kinds more suitable for the small rock garden are usually the hardiest, and they can all be propagated fairly easily – some species more readily than others – from cuttings taken during the growing season. *Hebe buchananii* is a neat little rounded bush, often no more than ankle-high, with small, leathery, closely arranged leaves of glossy green; a shrub noted not so much for its flowers – though when they appear in June and July they make pleasant white clusters – as for its neat foliage which, in common with that of other hebes, blends well with stone outcrops of all shades and textures. *Hebe epacridea* is prostrate, with trailing shoots closely pressed to the ground, clothed with stiff little leaves in overlapping pairs, and decorated in July with round clusters of tiny white flowers. This is a very distinctive shrub that looks right on the scree, or when given a site high among boulders, where its unusual foliage and low, juniper-like manner of growth give it almost the appearance of a dwarf conifer. *Hebe pinguifolia* makes a neat, rounded bush of clear blue-grey foliage, with spikes of white flowers from June to August; a beautiful plant, but the typical species is too large for even the moderately sized rock garden. In modest surroundings, its place may be taken by the variety *H.p.* Pagei, which makes a low, wide mat of waxy, rounded, blue-grey leaves; it produces fewer flowers than the species and has a shorter flowering season in the spring, but it is a first-class foliage plant with a useful colour. *Hebe rakaiensis* also makes a splendid ground-covering dwarf shrub for a sunny site, with low mounds of pale green leaves forming a neatly compact contour, and a fair display of clustered white flowers in June and July.

Some of the hybrid dwarf hebes are not so reliably hardy as the species, and may need a sheltered, sunny spot that is not liable to become too frosted in the winter or spring. The hardiest of those suitable for the rock garden include: Bowles Hybrid, with clusters of mauve flowers in May and June; Edinensis, a ground-covering shrub with tiny grey leaves and rather sparse pinkish-mauve flowers in July; and Blue Gem, one of the hardiest of the genus, which has been recommended for coastal planting and makes a pronounced dome, below knee-high, covered in late spring and early summer with clusters of bright blue flowers. All these shrubs grow in any well drained soil, and their leathery foliage makes them moderately resistant not only to salt-laden seaside gales but also to industrial pollution and roadside exhaust fumes.

The closely related *Parahebe catarractae* is also a dwarf shrub which makes low, spreading mounds of small, pointed green leaves, and carries spikes of mauve, crimson-streaked flowers from July to September. There is a dwarfer variety, Diffusa, which has smaller leaves and makes a lower, denser mat, well covered in the late summer with clusters of white, red-streaked flowers. Like the hebes, these two shrubby veronicas are plants for a sunny, dryish spot, and will not stand the shade. *Pimelea prostrata* is another shrub from New Zealand which makes flat, evergreen mats of tiny grey leaves in a tangled mass of prostrate stems, and which bears fragrant white flowers in the late spring – but this is rarely to be seen in gardens. It is usually hardy, but is always liable to succumb during very hard winters.

The New Zealand burs are completely hardy and very commonly grown in northern gardens, for they are among the most useful of the dwarf ground-covering herbs because of their ability to grow well in heavy shade – *Acaena microphylla* especially will do this. If given the choice, however, they will opt for sunny, open sites, even in the poorest of soils, where they can make valuable, if rather bulky, paving plants. Their foliage is attractive and, although the flowers themselves are inconspicuous, the spiky red or purplish bur-heads in the late summer are very ornamental. *Acaena microphylla* is probably the best known of the genus, and makes compact, evergreen mats of bronzy-red leaves, usually about 5cm high, with bright crimson spiky burs. The more vigorous *A. novae-zelandiae* has a stout, woody, creeping rootstock, silky-hairy foliage, and dark red spiky burs. It will swamp neighbouring plants if allowed to grow over them, but can be very useful when it is necessary to form a thick, weedproof cover between tall plants or at the base of a rockery. *A. glauca* has the most attractive foliage, with soft, silky, blue-grey leaves, but inconspicuous flower heads. Most acaenas can be grown quite readily from seed, and this is usually easier than attempting to find rooted pieces for replanting.

Cotula squalida is a vigorous mat-forming herb with long, trailing stems bearing tiny, much-divided bronzy leaves and inconspicuous flowers – not a prize rock plant, but it provides a useful cover which will keep the ground clear for small bulbs to come through, and is of use both between paving stones and as a path-former, for it grows as readily as chamomile from small, rooted pieces. It has been used experimentally as a lawn plant, but the stems are a little too woody for this purpose. Needless to say, it will grow well in any garden soil.

If the lowland vegetation of New Zealand is typically luxuriant, evergreen, and sometimes only semi-hardy, the upland flora is typified by sun-loving mat-formers which are usually hardy in temperate climes. Native species are frequently closely related to others in South Africa and South America and, where a genus is widely represented in the northern hemisphere as well, the New Zealand representatives tend to exhibit some distinctive characteristic that speaks of long isolation. New Zealand gentians, for instance, usually have white flowers: *Gentiana saxosa* is an example. The whiteness of its broad trumpets from July to September is only intensified by the dark puce veining of the petals, and the purplish shading in the dark green rosetted leaves. This is a gentian that loves the sun, and needs a gritty, well drained site on the scree, but it is small and neat enough to behave well in a trough garden, too. Another trough or scree plant from the same habitat is *Scleranthus biflorus,* a tiny relative of the sandworts, with minute, downy leaves. It has no flowers worthy of notice, but makes a very compact little cushion for a gritty, well drained soil.

A creeping plant closely related to the lobelias, with little white flowers followed by purple berries, *Pratia angulata* spreads rooting trailers of slender stems, clothed with neat little rounded leaves; it will readily invade a lawn and establish itself in the turf. It is not a mountain plant, but hardy nevertheless, and a lover of moisture and light shade. A rather similar, but unrelated plant, found both in New Zealand and the temperate regions of South America, is *Selliera radicans,* which also sends out long creeping stems, rooting at the nodes wherever they touch the ground, with small rounded leaves and little white flowers. It is not keen on shade, but needs moisture, and a place at the foot of the moraine will give it the coolness it needs. These are both plants which naturally choose a south-facing aspect in their native homes, and their requirements would be well suited in the northern hemisphere by allotting them a north-facing site.

New Zealanders are familiar with their 'vegetable sheep', a species of raoulia which mounds itself up over the years into a woolly-grey mass that looks from a distance like a reclining sheep. There are several hardy species of the same genus that form downy mats of much more manageable proportions, and which have found their way to northern rock gardens. Among these is *Raoulia australis,* which makes a silvery-silky carpet of tiny rosetted leaves, sprinkled in the spring with minute yellow flowers – a plant attractive enough for a place in the trough garden, though it will need curtailing when it outspreads the site. *Raoulia tenuicaulis* also makes a wide-spreading mat of greyish green downy leaves, easily grown on any sunny site, not noted for its inconspicuously tiny yellow spring flowers, but a useful ground cover which small bulbs can penetrate happily. Both these mat-formers are easy to grow in northern gardens, but some of the New Zealand raoulias are temperamental – and prized by Alpine specialists as fascinating miniatures of the tender, sheep-like mounds. They are closely related to the genus *Helichrysum,* some of which, like *H. bellidioides,* are mat-forming plants of the warmer mountain sites, needing a sunny but sheltered spot on a gritty scree if they are to do well in northern gardens. *H. bellidioides* develops a shrubby mat of prostrate stems whose small, rounded leaves are covered with a white, cottony down, and which produces its white everlasting flowers in the summer. *H. milfordiae* is a South African species that is also moderately hardy in north temperate zones, provided it is given a sunny scree facing south. It is less shrubby than *H. bellidioides,* and makes a prostrate carpet of rosetted, silver-silky leaves, and also produces white everlasting flowers in the summer.

Few South African plants are fully hardy in north temperate gardens; some, like many of the native everlastings, are grown as greenhouse plants; others, like the pelargoniums, are limited to summer bedding schemes. The South African asters usually fall into one or other of these categories, but the mat-forming *Aster natalensis,* coming as it does from the high Drakensberg Mountains, is reasonably hardy in temperate zones, provided it is given a warm, sunny scree where it can imagine it is at home. Most of the wild South African asters are given the vernacular name 'blue daisy', and *A. natalensis,* being no exception in this respect, produces clear blue, yellow-centred flowers in the summer, carried on short stems above a hairy-leaved, grey-green carpet.

Selaginella kraussiana, a curiously moss-like carpeter that is often used as a trailing pot plant, is another South African mountain species that will manage to survive outdoors in Britain if it is allocated a reasonably sheltered spot. A stone wall will often give it the protection it needs to be able to survive the hardest winters and, if no wall is available, a sheltered, lightly shaded site will help it to avoid the extremes. It may, however, be propagated very easily, merely by taking convenient portions of the plant as cuttings, and setting them direct into their planting positions; if a supply is kept overwinter in a frame or greenhouse, the species can be used to good effect as a filler wherever a bright green mossy trail of foliage is needed on the rockery,

Oxalis acetosella

and replaced as necessary. The same principles apply to a creeping South American plant, *Lippia canescens*: this may be grown on walls and also between paving stones, and it is usually quite hardy in northern gardens; it will grow easily from cuttings, and its bright green carpet of tiny leaves, sprinkled in the summer with rounded heads of little yellow-throated lilac flowers, can be used on the rock garden for small bulbs to spear through.

The genus *Oxalis* has a worldwide distribution, and is especially well represented in South America, where many of the most useful rock garden species originate. While the British *Oxalis acetosella* enjoys a cool, woodland site, and the American *O. oregana*, also thriving in woodland, is perfectly happy in a dry, sunny spot, the South American species suitable for our use without exception enjoy a sunny site. The spreading *O. magellanica* in particular likes dry, stony places, and is able to flourish on a stone wall, where its long stolons can creep between the rocks and emerge here and there, to weave a tapestry of dark bronzy trefoil leaves, with dainty white flowers in the spring. Also white-flowered, and fragrant, with a somewhat creeping rootstock, is *O. enneaphylla*, from the tip of South America and the Falkland Islands. It does well in moist peat and, if this can be combined with the cool support of a stone wall or rockery, so much the better; a raised bed with a peaty section will probably be ideal for this species, allowing it to form a thick cover of silvery grey-green double shamrock leaves. Another summer-flowering carpeter is the yellow-flowered *O. chrysantha*, with bright green trefoil leaves arranged in ground-hugging rosettes. A sheltered moraine between boulders is the ideal site, for *O. chrysantha* is not so hardy as the others, and is liable to perish during hard weather. The creeping species are easily propagated by grubbing out small lengths of rhizome with shoots attached, and a few spare pieces can be overwintered under a frame, in case replacements are needed in the spring. The tuft-forming *O. adenophylla* is a taller plant which makes a pleasant clump of folded, greyish leaves, with large, bright pink flowers in the spring, and is well at home in a moist moraine where it can see the sun.

Similar conditions, perhaps, will please *Calceolaria darwinii,* provided there is plenty both of grit and of peat in the soil, so that the rootrun will be cool and moist, without ever becoming too cold and wet. It is not a shade-loving plant but, since it comes from the Strait of Magellan, a north-facing site in the northern hemisphere might help to avoid the sudden extremes which can kill a healthy subject. It makes a pleasant little tuft of dark green leaves, with typically pouched lady's slipper flowers of chrome yellow, conspicuously marked in chestnut and white, opening in June or July. It may be grown from seed like a primula or, alternatively, small pieces of rhizome with shoots attached may be removed and potted up.

The monkey flowers are closely related to calceolarias – a relationship that shows in the shape of the flower. One species, *Mimulus cupreus* from Chile, has not only found its way into our gardens, but has given rise since its introduction in the mid-nineteenth century to numerous named varieties with a wide range of flower colours. The typical species has yellow flowers which darken to a coppery shade as they mature. Like the common northern monkey flower, *M. cupreus* enjoys a moist, cool site, and looks well by the water: perhaps a site to suit it best would be a sunny but sheltered boggy patch adjacent to the rockery, and, if there is a drainage point for a watered moraine, this is one of the plants to inhabit it. Cuttings of non-flowering shoots root readily in moist, but not wet, soil, and will strike in the open ground.

A very useful little evergreen shrub from the high Andes is the pearl berry, *Margyricarpus setosus,* with finely divided leaves and tiny green flowers that cover the bush all summer, to be followed by conspicuous pearl-white berries that last well during the winter. It needs a sunny and very well drained spot, on the scree or between the rocks, and has been known to succumb during bitter winter weather. It will grow quite readily from cuttings under a polythene bag, however, and the seed germinates well, so that replacements can be held in reserve. It makes a dark green alternative to the dwarf shrubby veronicas, and contrasts well with silver-leaved carpeting herbs.

Less hardy, but more spectacular, is the Chilean *Philesia magellanica,* an evergreen shrub with narrow, stiff, dark green leaves, and beautiful 5cm long roseate crimson lily-like flowers in June. In northern climes it needs a sheltered, lightly shaded or north-facing site, with a soil that contains at least fifty per cent peat. It is a suckering plant, and propagation is a simple matter of removing and replanting convenient suckers. Another Chilean bush that has translated well to northern rock gardens is *Fabiana imbricata*, in general appearance like one of the heaths, and covered in June with tiny white flowers. The variety Prostrata is hardier than the type and equally floriferous, but with mauve-tinted flowers. It will succeed in northern gardens if it is given a sunny site in a well-drained lime-free soil. Planted on the rock garden, it eventually forms a dense mound as much as 2m across the spread, and is a suitable subject also for a large wall – a site which should ensure its survival even during severe winter weather.

Several of the *Berberis* species originate in South America, but most of them are too large for the rock garden. The result of a cross between *Berberis darwinii*, soon after its introduction to Britain in the nineteenth century, and a small Chilean barberry, *B. empetrifolia*, resulted in the popular *Berberis* × *stenophylla*, and two dwarf varieties of this hybrid are Corallina Compacta, and Gracilis Nana. Both are evergreen with densely crowded branches, spectacular in their small way when in flower during April – Corallina Compacta coral pink in bud, opening yellow, and Gracilis Nana a bright golden yellow. They are among the easiest shrubs to grow in any garden, and will tolerate acid or alkaline soil in sun or shade, never suffering damage even during severe winter weather. They may be propagated from cuttings of firm side-shoots pulled off with a heel in the autumn, and set in a sandy compost – a glass-covered frame as a rule gives better results than the polythene bag.

Few dwarf conifers have originated in the southern hemisphere. Among those that have done so are *Podocarpus nivalis*, the Alpine totara from New Zealand, and the closely related *Podocarpus alpinus* from Australia and Tasmania – yew-like trees which both form a spreading mound of dense, prostrate branches covered with leathery, dark green foliage. The Australian species, *P. alpinus*, spreads eventually into a dense, shin-high carpet almost 2m across. *P. nivalis* is capable of an even greater spread; a lighter green than *P. alpinus*, it has the appearance of a smooth-spreading juniper, and there is a bronzy-yellow leaved form, Aureus, which contrasts well with the dark *P. alpinus*. In the colder areas of Britain and the United States they will probably fail to survive any particularly harsh winter and, in these districts, the spreading junipers and some varieties of *Taxus baccata* would be better.

14
Canada and the North

The North American subcontinent has been divided, for convenience of classification, into seven life zones, each recognised by the relative uniformity of its characteristic plant and animal life. Three of these regions are classed as cold: the Arctic, the Hudsonian and the Canadian zones. Regions that are temperate include the Transitional, the Upper Austral and the Austral zones. The remaining region comprises Tropical North America. All these may again be divided into eastern and western sub-zones – differences which depend chiefly on the degree of moisture available to each.

These zone boundaries are traced by lines not only of latitude, but also of altitude. Mountain tops in the United States are often classified as Arctic, and sometimes collectively called the Arctic-Alpine zone. The peaks of the Rockies, the Cascades and Sierra Nevada in the west, and the uppermost peaks of the White Mountains in New Hampshire in the east fall within this category. The Hudsonian zone includes more extensive areas of these mountain ranges, and embraces the tops of mountains in New England, New York and North Carolina. The Canadian zone also crosses into the USA to include the northern parts of Maine, New Hampshire, Michigan, Minnesota and North Dakota, with the Adirondack and Catskill Mountains, and the lower slopes of the northern Rockies and Sierras – further south, only the upper slopes of these ranges are included. The Appalachians fall mainly within the eastern humid sub-zone of the Transitional zone.

A map of North America divided into zones and sub-zones takes on an intricately patterned appearance, and it would be confusing to follow the system too closely in attempting to classify garden plants. The truly Alpine flora of North America is found only above the altitudinal tree limit, although, as in many other parts of the world, plants normally growing well below this altitude, and within the more temperate climatic zones, are freely admissible to our rock gardens. Some of them are lowland plants which, by their stature and habit of growth, are admirably suited to the surroundings of rock and scree.

(Above) Primula clarkei is neat enough for a sink garden. *(Below) Rhododendron forrestii,* one of the dwarfest of the Himalayan rhododendrons

(Top left) Gentiana sino-ornata, a popular autumn-flowering gentian. *(Top right) Rhododendron impeditum* forms an intricately tangled carpet. *(Centre left) Sedum cauticolum,* a trailing stonecrop, is excellent for growing on a wall. *(Centre right)* This everlasting flower, *Helichrysum bellidioides,* develops a shrubby mat of prostrate stems. *(Bottom left) Iris innominata,* a garden form of this mountain iris

Others are at home in the mountain forests, where they form a carpet beneath the more widely spaced trees. It is usually possible to supply the special needs of a particular plant by means of thoughtful siting within the garden, and the wide variety of natural habitats from which our selection is drawn only makes the gardener's task more interesting.

When trees are introduced into a foreign environment for the purpose of timber production, for example, and are therefore expected to perform at maximum efficiency, their zone of origin is bound to have great significance. In the case of garden plants, however – and perhaps more especially Alpine plants – it is less important to match their climatic preferences exactly, because rapid and vigorous growth is not the prime consideration. In the first place this is so because we want our plants to remain within the bounds allotted to them, and in the second place, because we are able to give them the individual attention, encouragement or curtailment, that their progress demands. If an introduced plant performs too well – especially if its nature is to spread and colonise – there is always the danger that it may become a weed. Initial introductions, therefore, should always be made cautiously, and on a limited, easily controlled scale. When enterprising people first planted the Jamaican *Lantana camara* in South Africa, the American prickly pear in Australia, or even, if we go back far enough in time, the Continental ground elder in Britain, they could scarcely have foreseen the harvest of exasperation that would be reaped by generations to come. Of latter years, even such an unsuspected potential invader as the Japanese honeysuckle *Lonicera japonica halliana* has been the cause for concern in the United States.

Dwarf conifers, especially, tend to transcend climatic zones, and we usually, though not invariably, find that the dwarf variety of a tree which by nature grows, for example, within a cold zone on an acid soil, will perform satisfactorily in a warm climate and on a somewhat alkaline soil – simply because a high standard of production is not required of the garden form. Such a species from the northern forests is the white spruce, *Picea glauca*, and its several dwarf varieties. Of these Albertiana Conica is well known in European as well as American gardens – the original tree was found in the Canadian Rockies early in the twentieth century, and makes a perfect upright cone of bright apple green; Echiniformis makes a globular bush reaching less than knee-high after twenty years of growth, with dense, prickly needles of a quiet grey-green; another that has been cultivated in gardens since early in the nineteenth century is the familiarly named Nana, which also makes a dense, rounded bush of extremely slow growth, intermediate in size between Echiniformis and Albertiana Conica, with attractive blue-grey foliage. *Picea mariana* is the black spruce from the forests of the north-west, and this has also given rise to a dwarf cultivar, Nana – a sea-green bush, dense and compact, which will still be under half a metre after ten or fifteen years.

Douglas fir, *Pseudotsuga menziesii,* from the forests of Oregon, Washington and British Columbia, is a magnificent timber tree which will not thrive on chalky or limy soils, and even its dwarf varieties are much happier when lime is absent. They will all eventually become too large for any but grand-scale rock gardens, although the most shapely of them – Brevifolia – will take many years to exceed 2m in height. It is a miniature, bushy version of the species in silhouette, with short leaves which lend it the proportions of a bonsai tree, and it may be trimmed in imitation of that style to expose the trunk and main limbs. In those cases where the mini-landscape is truly self-contained, this attention to detail can bring dramatic results, but the effect will be lost if there are full-sized trees nearby which, by their overpowering proportions, give the lie to any intended false perspective. Other dwarf varieties of Douglas fir are: Fletcheri, which makes a pleasantly greenish blue table-topped bush approaching 1m in height after about ten years; Holmstrup, a miniature tree similar in size and rate of growth to Brevifolia, but with longer leaves; and Nana, a bush similar in height to Fletcheri, of rounded silhouette, with full-sized bluish green leaves.

Cornus canadensis

A northern forest tree which extends into the Arctic is the balsam fir, *Abies balsamea*, and its variety Hudsonia is a favourite rock garden dwarf which has been in cultivation since early in the nineteenth century. It forms a somewhat bowl-shaped, densely foliaged and aromatic bush of a glossy dark green, that will take many years to reach knee-height. It has often been used as a sink garden plant, though, in my view, too-tiny specimens of Hudsonia in these surroundings are unconvincing, and tend to give the impression that some kind of seedling tree has been used as a temporary stopgap.

Thuja plicata, the western red cedar, though limited by nature to the forests of the west, has a wide range north to south, and is well known as an introduced timber species in Britain and north-west Europe. It is noteworthy in the present context chiefly for its golden-leaved varieties: Cuprea, a densely foliaged, rounded bush, each feathery leaf spray tipped with yellow, cream or coppery gold; Rogersii, a compact, dwarf cone with bronzy gold foliage – both this and Cuprea are very old cultivars; and Stoneham Gold, which was raised after World War II, and forms a dense, feathery ball of bright golden bronze. None of these three varieties will have topped half a metre after ten years of rock garden growth, and they will grow in any soil, given an open, sunny position, provided they are not subjected overlong to cold, drying winds. Typically, *Thuja plicata* will stand a certain amount of shade, but the yellow-foliaged varieties, as with most other conifers, will retain their colour better in full sunlight. They can be propagated fairly easily from cuttings during late summer, taking firm young sprays which will be in the region of 5-6cm long, and setting them under shaded glass. If the polythene bag method is to be used, the operation should not be delayed until after July, or the cuttings will tend to rot in the moist atmosphere before they can callus over and root.

Canadian juniper is *Juniperus communis* Depressa, a natural wild form of the common juniper – the variable species to be found across the northern hemisphere from Alaska through Europe and Asia to Japan. Depressa is quite as effective in the garden as any of the more recently selected forms, and makes a densely spreading thicket, rarely reaching more than knee-high. *J.c.* Dumosa is a much smaller cultivar of this wild form, and originated in Europe. The spreading junipers are noted for their range of subtle coloration, and 'forty shades of green' is an expression which could well be applied to the genus. The Canadian juniper has a tawny tinge to its light green leaves, bronzing as growth hardens for the winter, but with a glaucous silvery bloom beneath each needle. The tendency to bronze has become pronounced in the variety Depressa Aurea, a very similar plant in growth, but whose young spring foliage is canary yellow, darkening quickly to the familiar tawny green and bronze. Another variety of the common juniper, Effusa, retains a deep olive-green during the winter months, contrasting, when the bush is disturbed, with the silvery white undersurface of the leaves. Of similar dimensions to the wild Canadian juniper, its neat plume-like sprays harmonise well in colour and texture when the two varieties are planted close together.

Juniperus horizontalis is a native creeping juniper that makes deep, wide carpets of feathery foliage, and there are several wild strains which vary slightly in colour from fairly bright grass-green to almost pure blue, sometimes taking on a striking purple tint for the winter. Named varieties selected to illustrate this range of natural variation will include: Bar Harbor, a particularly ground-hugging form, with waxy, sea-green leaves; Coast of Maine, a spreading, mounding form with feathery sea-green leaves which become warmly purple in the winter; Douglasii, sometimes known as the Waukegan juniper, a waxy olive-green, becoming purple in the winter, with long, spreading plume-like sprays; Montana, with long, feathery plumes of a startling grey-blue; and Wiltonii, one of the lowest of the carpeting junipers, an old and popular garden variety well suited to the smaller rock garden, with prostrate, waxy blue sprays. These junipers are comparatively easy to propagate from cuttings taken in the autumn and early winter, and the more prostrate varieties can be encouraged to provide rooted layers by the simple expedient of earthing-up any convenient extensions.

The willow genus *Salix* and the dogwood genus *Cornus* include many tree species in their ranks but, in the northern United States and Canada, they have produced on the one hand a completely prostrate willow, *Salix uva-ursi,* and, on the other, the completely prostrate creeping dogwood, *Cornus canadensis.* Both are plants of value in their particular context. The bearberry willow forms dense carpets of creeping stems, pretty when the catkins are out in the spring, and handsome during the summer when covered with small, glossy, bright green leaves – a useful addition to the large rock garden which might have rough, dry corners to fill, for it will maintain a healthy cover without taking on an unkempt or overgrown appearance.

Salix uva-ursi is not to be confused, through its specific name, with *Arctostaphylos uva-ursi,* the bearberry – a creeping shrub which occurs not only in North America but also in many other northern regions of the world. The latter needs an acid soil and a sunny site and, provided these two conditions are satisfied, will grow almost anywhere and make an attractive carpet of glossy, leathery leaves, with tiny pale pink flowers in the spring, followed by brilliant red berries, which bears are said to enjoy. They have a very tough seed-coat which makes germination a slow and erratic process; when they

Arctostaphylos uva-ursi

are eaten by bears, the action of digestive juices and internal heat is said to allow germination to take place evenly after they have been deposited in the bear's droppings, and experiments with heat plus acid treatment have given good results. For garden use, it is more convenient to rely on division as a ready means of increase.

The creeping dogwood has some features which make it resemble more closely a herbaceous plant than a shrub, for it dies back and sends up new shoots annually, and it is now placed botanically in a genus of its own, *Chamaepericlymenum*; but however it is classified – and the dividing line between shrub and herb is one of convenience rather than botanical dogma – it has proved to be of great value during the two centuries or more of its garden cultivation, readily forming a useful, weed-smothering carpet for acid, peaty soil in a shady spot, attractive in June with its white flower-like bracts, succeeded by handsome scarlet berries.

A creeping plant unmistakably herbaceous in character, a native of Canada and Greenland, which has found its way into gardens throughout the northern and temperate world, is *Viola labradorica*, a tiny carpeter which revels in shade, and runs around and between larger plants very happily. The tiny, heart-shaped leaves are dark – almost purple – and the little deep violet flowers appear profusely in the spring and last well into summer. Portions of rooted stems can be lifted and moved, but *V. labradorica* usually seeds itself annually and establishes a colony contentedly if the site is reasonably moist and shady. *Viola adunca*, the hooked-spur violet, is also widespread in northern regions, and will grow in similar conditions.

Like a miniature lily of the valley for peaty, shady sites, *Maianthemum bifolium* produces its fragrant white flowers in the spring. It is usually thought of as a ground cover plant to carpet between tall rhododendrons and similar shrubs, but on or near the rockery it will make an attractive drift on its own.

A few stonecrops from the northern regions have been introduced from time to time into our rock gardens. *Sedum pulchellum* is such a plant, and a typical North American in its tastes for, unlike most of its genus, it enjoys a peaty, damp, lightly shaded site, and is happiest when allowed to sprawl among shady rocks, low down on the north-facing slope. It has reddish stems, bright green, somewhat pointed leaves, and spreading heads of bright rosy-purple flowers in July and August. More typical of the *Sedum* species from this region are: *S. purdyi*, which makes low, rounded cushions of bright green fleshy rosettes, with clusters of dark yellow flowers; and *S. stenopetalum*, a tufted plant with upright stems of pointed, fleshy dark green leaves, conspicuous in June with flat heads of bright yellow flowers. A native of the northern Rockies, this hardy stonecrop will thrive in any exposed, north-facing site high on the rockery. As an associate plant for carpeting such exposed pockets of soil, one of the sandworts, *Arenaria ciliata*, is a useful acquisition. It forms a tangle of twiggy stems and little rounded leaves, with clusters of starry white flowers throughout the summer months. Like the stonecrops, it may be increased easily by division, and can be arranged as the backcloth for more colourful plants.

15
Wild Western Plants

Several of the rock plants native to the western USA grow naturally on the Rocky Mountains, but most of the dwarf conifers, in their typical, specific form, at least, are found in the forests of the Pacific Coastal strip from the Cascades to the Sierra Nevada. An important exception is the Rocky Mountain juniper, *Juniperus scopulorum* – important not, of course, from the standpoint of timber production, for *J. scopulorum* is a scrubby little tree, but because of the cultivars which are greatly valued in rock gardens in both America and Europe: Hill's Silver is a narrow spire of a tree, approaching waist height after ten years' growth, with fine, scale-like silvery blue leaves; Pathfinder is faster growing, and makes a broader cone than Hill's Silver, attaining a metre in about seven or eight years, with cypress-like sprays of bluish grey foliage; Springbank is similar in size and rate of growth, a column of arching sprays in green tinged with silvery grey, capable of bringing an air of distinction to the large rock garden; and the much smaller Repens is a dwarf carpeter in the tradition of *J. horizontalis,* with prickly bluish green foliage and prostrate, spreading branches.

A tree with a desert tradition, and one that appreciates a warm, dryish situation when planted in other climatic zones, is *Cupressus glabra* from Arizona and northern Mexico. Its variety Compacta makes a round ball of a bush, rarely more than 25cm high, with sea-green leaf sprays which barely conceal the peeling red bark so characteristic of the species. Its natural adaptation to the dry-lands fits it admirably for a south-facing spot high on the scree where, anyway, more columnar trees would look out of place.

The Colorado spruce, *Picea pungens,* has a wide range over the dry states, from Wyoming south to Utah, Colorado and New Mexico, and its garden varieties are well capable of flourishing over a wide range of site types. The most important varieties are: Globosa, which takes about twenty years to approach a metre in height, and makes a thick, prickly-foliaged, bun-shaped bush of a striking waxy blue; Montgomery, almost equally dwarf and slow growing, a compact and bristly grey-blue bush – both excellent dwarf conifers for the fairly large rock garden; Procumbens, which is an older variety, and probably occurs in the wild – an arching, spreading bush reminiscent of the pfitzer juniper with its pendulous sprays, although, with its clear waxy blue, needle-sharp leaves, it could only be a spruce. After ten years it will have attained perhaps 30cm in height, and it makes an unusual and effective alternative to the more commonly planted junipers.

A few of the western silver firs have given rise to rock garden dwarfs, among them the red silver fir, *Abies amabilis,* whose variety Spreading Star is named after its habit of growth, with radiating, wide-spreading branches, seldom reaching more than a metre in height. The leaf sprays have a bristly appearance, with the needles crowded towards the upper surface, each a dark glossy green above and waxy white beneath, and the foliage gives off a pleasant, orangey smell if it is crushed, reminiscent of the western red cedar. Spreading Star is rather too expansive for the small rock garden and, like its full-size parent, it needs an acid soil in which to thrive. Of more petite proportions, and capable of growing in a limy soil, is *A. lasiocarpa arizonica* Compacta, a compact globe which should still be well under a metre tall after ten years or so, with pleasantly soft foliage of an almost startling blue-grey. *A. magnifica* is the Californian red fir – in its native forests a large and impressive tree with long 'bottle-brush' leaves of a soft bluish green. It has given rise to the natural form *A.m.* Nana, a true dwarf with wide-spreading branches, attaining perhaps half a metre after twenty years or so. *A. procera* is the noble fir, better known in the UK than the others in this section, for it has been planted there to some extent as a timber tree, and grows well in lime-free soils. Its dwarf variety Glauca Prostrata is a neat little bush with low-spreading branches and waxy, bluish green crowded leaves.

Lawson Cypress, *Chamaecyparis lawsoniana,* from the Pacific States, is a very variable tree with numerous cultivars, and of these, no fewer than seventeen are eminently suitable for the rock garden. All will approach a metre in height at between seven and twenty years, depending on variety, and some like Ellwoodii, although well known to outgrow most rockeries after several years, are so popular that they are planted anyway, and allowed to grow until they start to overbalance the whole design, when they can be dug up and replaced. Ellwood's Gold is also a very popular little tree, slower to grow and better suited to the small rock garden than Ellwoodii itself, neat and compact, with a gold tinge to each leaf spray. Of the Ellwoodii group, Chilworth Silver is an eye-catching column with the typical, densely arranged juvenile type of foliage in bright silvery blue, matching Ellwood's Gold in rate of growth, but tending to broaden out after ten years or so, and eventually taking up more room than the others. Gardeners who like white and cream variegated conifers will like Ellwood's White, of similar slow-growing size and compact shape to Ellwood's Gold. Personally, I find such variegations unsatisfying – their unevenly blotched leaf sprays sometimes have the look of a virus about them, and my instinct is to throw them on the bonfire. Many people love them, but few could prefer them to the best all-over gold and blue varieties. Pygmaea Argentea is also a white-variegated cultivar but, in this case, the white flecks are limited to the spray tips, instead of being scattered randomly through the deep sea-green foliage. It is very dwarf and well adapted to the small rockery, and I can recommend it.

In colour of foliage, there is often very little difference between the two popular Lawson cypress varieties, Minima and Minima Glauca; the latter has a sea-green look, but it is not glaucous in the usual sense of the word. It is more compact than Minima itself, and slower growing – I have known thirty year old specimens of Minima Glauca which are still under a metre in height, when Minima would be approaching the two metre mark. Minima Aurea has soft, bronzy yellow foliage, and a rate of growth somewhere between the other two. All three have densely compact foliage which includes both vertically and horizontally angled sprays – with some specimens tending more completely to one or the other type – well clothed down to the ground in a perfectly globular shape which harmonises admirably with the taller, pyramidal type of tree. Minima and Minima Glauca have been planted in our gardens for well over a century, and the dark sea-green Nana is almost as old; not so globular in shape, it is less a bush and more a dwarf tree than Minima, though the rate of growth is about the same. While Minima has multiple ascending stems hidden beneath the foliage, Nana produces a clearly defined central s tem which gradually thickens into a gnarled trunk, with branches held at right angles, the foliage becoming progressively less dense as the tree matures. It joins the ranks of those dwarf trees which seem to call for the Japanese bonsai treatment, not to curtail root development, but to enhance the impression of gnarled bole and weathered limb by removing the bushier branches and encouraging the development of a tree-like crown.

Nana Argentea is not, despite its name, a silver-foliaged version of Nana, but a very dwarf, bun-shaped bush. It lacks chlorophyll to such a degree that only the very youngest leaf sprays have the faintest tinge of green, and even this fades, after the first year, to an unblemished cream. Though it seems to hover thus on the brink of disaster, it is nevertheless an attractive little bush, and looks very fine against a background of dark rocks. Another dwarf, globe-shaped tree of similar size, and a colour that harmonises with the cream and silver varieties, is Gimbornii, whose tightly packed foliage is a bluish green, shading to purple on the spray tips. It will stay below a metre in height for twenty years or more, and retains its compact shape into maturity. A similarly sized globe of tightly packed foliage arranged in tiny, ferny sprays, is Forsteckensis; it also has a bluish tinge, but lacks the purple of Gimbornii.

One of the most striking yellow-leaved Lawson cypress cultivars with proportions suitable for the medium sized rock garden is Aurea Densa, an upright cone which will have reached waist height after twelve or fifteen years; it has a very neat, compact shape, with short, stiff sprays of bright bronzy yellow. A partner for this is Parsonsii, of similar size and shape but with a completely different type of foliage: each large, soft spray arches and droops gracefully, overlapping the ones beneath in bright grass-green tiers. Rogersii is another conical bush of matching size and rate of growth, but it is not so compact, and broadens out in maturity, the greyish blue foliage being softer and more loosely arranged. Duncanii is smaller and more spreading, making a knee-high globe by the time it is ten years old, with compact, sea-green foliage. Nidiformis makes a very graceful little tree, but it will eventually outgrow all but the most spacious rockery sites, passing 3m in twenty years and at least doubling this height in maturity. It has very attractive bright green foliage and, while it is still small, is rather similar to Parsonsii, but has a more distinctly tree-like shape.

All the Lawson cypress varieties can be propagated from cuttings taken in early October and set preferably in a frame, under glass or polythene. Some varieties root more readily than others, and the slower ones may be left where they are until the following autumn. The polythene bag method is not very satisfactory for them, as the stems need to form a callus at the rooting point before growth can start and, if the atmosphere is excessively damp, the leafy top of the cutting is apt to rot before this stage is reached.

Cupressus macrocarpa is the Monterey cypress from California, most of whose varieties are full-sized trees, but it has two – Minima and Pygmaea – which stay within rock garden limits. Minima has prickly, juvenile-type foliage, and forms a rounded mound, rather shapeless but pleasantly green, which will still be under a metre in height after ten years or so. Pygmaea has the spray-like, dark green adult foliage, but on a smaller scale than the type, and arranged along the twigs in a strangely stiff, square sequence; it makes an unusual and attractive little tree, likely to be still below half a metre in height after twenty years.

Incense cedar, *Calocedrus decurrens*, has a dwarf form, Nana, which resembles the typical species both in silhouette and in the dark green, flattened leaf sprays, but they are distinctively arranged on intricately twisted and intertwined branchlets. The main attraction of the variety lies in its dwarf stature and slow rate of growth but, as it is not readily available from nurseries, other dark-leaved columnar dwarfs are normally used on the rock garden in preference to *C. decurrens* Nana.

Several North American creeping shrubs are associated with conifers. *Arctostaphylos nevadensis*, the pine-mat manzanita from California and Oregon, forms a pleasant, small-leaved evergreen mat overlying a miniature thicket of downy shoots, with clusters of tiny pink or white flowers in the spring, followed by bright pink berries. It needs an acid soil and appreciates shade. Like many creeping shrubs, pine-mat manzanita may easily be increased by division as soon as it has become properly established, but a good stock can be produced from a single plant by taking tip cuttings: if 5cm long soft tips are removed in August, they will root readily, and give time for a fresh crop of shoots to grow, and these may also be taken as cuttings to root under glass or inside the polythene bag. Some creeping shrubs like *Arctostaphylos uva-ursi* and *Vaccinium vitis-idaea* are found in other northern countries in Europe and Asia as well as America. Others are limited longitudinally, but range widely in latitude – *Luetkea pectinata*, for example, is found in many western states and as far north as Alaska; given a cool site in lime-free soil, this dwarf shrub makes an attractive ankle-high carpet, dotted in early summer with

Vaccinium vitis-idaea

clustered white flowers; in its tiny leaf it bears some resemblance to the mossy saxifrages and, like them, will tolerate a degree of shade. As mossy saxifrages need a limy soil to thrive, *Luetka* can be said to provide a satisfactory alternative for sites which have an acid soil.

The vanilla leaf, *Achlys triphylla*, is a shade-loving woodland plant that enjoys peaty conditions free from lime, and bears trefoil leaves and tiny white flowers. The leafy mats often take on a purplish tinge, especially where the sun strikes through the shade, and the vernacular name is derived from the scent of the dried leaves, which are sometimes cut for use as a potpourri ingredient. Propagation is a simple matter of division. Another typical western woodlander is the star flower *Trientalis borealis*, which runs with creeping rootstock under the light shade between shrubs, revelling in a peaty soil. The vernacular name could just as accurately be 'star leaf', for the upright leaf stalks each bear a symmetrical whorl of pointed leaves, and it is from the tops of the stalks that the tiny white starry flowers appear in ones and twos. Star flower can be divided readily by severing the creeping roots, and it usually sets seed, which can be collected and sown in the spring. The star-flowered lily of the valley, *Smilacina stellata*, is a more typically western North American plant than the very widely cultivated *Convallaria*, the true lily of the valley. It is not a subject for the rock garden proper, but it will make a dainty carpet at the foot of an outcrop, where there is some shade and the soil is peaty and acid, producing dense spikes of tiny, starry white flowers above leaves like a Solomon's seal.

The vancouverias are typical Pacific Coastal States woodland ground coverers: *Vancouveria hexandra* forms a deciduous carpet of trefoliate leaves, with clusters of small white flowers in the spring, and creeps through peaty, acid soil in cool, shady spots, with slender roots which may be dug up, divided and replanted; *Vancouveria planipetala* is the redwood ivy, an evergreen with somewhat stiff leaves and clusters of little white or lilac flowers in the spring, and this also makes a very pleasant ankle-deep cover, easy to establish, quick to spread, and readily increased by division.

A pretty little mountain iris from Oregon is *Iris innominata*, a slender, wiry dwarf, flowering in early summer. The type has honey-coloured petals veined with brown but, during half a century of cultivation, seedling selection has produced a variety of colours ranging from apricot to orange, mauve and violet. It spreads quite quickly into wide tufts, and enjoys a gritty but moist soil, such as one hopes to find low down on the moraine bed of a rock garden, where it will have no objection to light shade.

A Californian plant which really revels in hot, dry situations is the so-called Californian fuchsia, *Zauschneria californica*. It makes a hummock of crowded, pointed leaves of a downy grey-green, arising from an almost shrubby base of woody stems. The narrowly tubular, bright scarlet flowers open in July and extend into October, their appearance giving the plant its alternative name of humming bird's trumpet. The flower spikes grow and the flowers open successionally in the manner of the 'fireweed' willow herb and, like that ubiquitous flower, while the last buds at the top of the spike are opening in the autumn, the lowest clusters of fluffy parachute seeds are being released from their pods. Geographic variations of this striking plant are to be found in the wild from Mexico north along the Pacific seaboard to Oregon. It is not altogether hardy in cooler parts of the world and, for this reason, should be given the warmest, most sheltered spot in the garden. If seeds fail to germinate, it may be propagated by means of side-shoot cuttings taken as the flowers fade, and rooted under a polythene bag.

Some of the penstemons, or beard tongues, are splendid plants on the rock garden, and many are native to the Pacific States of the USA. With their showy spikes of tubular flowers, they form a fine summer feature on open, sunny spots that are well drained but not dry. The genus is much hybridised and the classification sometimes confused. The plant sold as *Penstemon roezlii* has rose-pink flowers; *P. menziesii*, violet; *P. newberryi*, bright pink; *P. scouleri*, rose-purple. Penstemons are perhaps more popular in America than Europe, and the American Penstemon Society has been formed to cater for enthusiasts. Accustomed to the warm Pacific winds of their native environment, these beard tongues are liable to sicken and die if subjected to cold winds in other parts of the world, and they should be given a reasonably sheltered site. Propagation can be achieved by taking cuttings from the numerous side-shoots that appear as flowering finishes in the summer, and these root fairly readily.

The lewisias have a comparable natural range, and a similar degree of popularity. They love a warm site, a sharply gritty, well drained, but richly fed soil and, when well suited, are among the most spectacular of rock plants, their bright, fleshy, multi-petalled flowers springing almost from the soil on the shorter-stemmed varieties, and lasting over a long period, from spring often until autumn. They may be propagated from short side-shoot cuttings taken during the summer. Some of the best rock garden varieties are; *Lewisia* Birch Hybrids, in colours ranging from pink to apricot and yellow; George Henley, with dark red flowers; Rose Splendour, with clear pink flowers; the Sunset Strain, ranging from apricot to red; Trevosia, with deep orange-red flowers; and Winifred Herdman, with deep pink flowers.

The stonecrops are often thought typical plants of rocks and arid sites, and most of them prefer warm, dry situations. One of the taller growing kinds, *Sedum rhodanthum*, is perhaps more suitable for the border than the rock garden, but it is a good 'link-up' subject to phase the rock garden smoothly into its surroundings. It is a particularly leafy-stemmed plant, with orpine-like, fleshy leaves and rose-pink flowers in June. A more typical species from the western states is *Sedum douglasii*, a tufted plant with crowded, sharp-pointed leaves that are often tinted with red, and compact clusters of bright yellow flowers. All the stonecrops are easy to propagate by using pieces of leafy stem as cuttings, but *S. douglasii* sends out shoots from the leaf axils of the flowering stems, and these drop off at the end of the season and take root independently. A specimen of *S. douglasii* planted high among the rocks will eventually establish a colony, extending slowly downhill among the stones, and it is just this type of natural spread whose appearance we often try to imitate when planting clumps and drifts of rock garden plants. A true spreader is *S. oreganum*, which makes flat mats of fleshy leaves, glossy green overall but with a tinge of red, and produces bright yellow flowers in small, flat clusters. Best known, perhaps, of all the American stonecrops is *S. spathulifolium*, which sends out runners well clothed with tiny, flatly rosetted, pointed leaves, typically of a dusty, purplish green, often tinged with red – but there are several cultivated varieties: Capa Blanca has powdery, almost white leaves; Purpureum forms a rich purple mat. The flowers in both cases are of a clear, bright yellow, but it is in the weed-smothering ground cover that its chief value lies; the plant is vigorous enough to be used beneath light shrubs such as roses, and hardy enough to cover poor, dusty sites that would support little else.

Pulsatilla is usually thought of as a true mountain plant, and *Pulsatilla occidentalis*, the American counterpart of the Alpine lady of the snows, needs a sunny, open spot where it can enjoy moisture in the spring, and the comparative dryness afforded in nature by a covering of snow during the winter. It has anemone-like, deeply divided leaves, and charming white flowers, the petals backed with purple shading, followed later in the season by long, feathery seedheads. It tends to flower a month later than most of the other pasque flower species.

A dwarf fleabane from the mountains is the pretty *Erigeron aureus*, a tiny, round-leaved, golden-yellow daisy suitable for the trough, or a favoured spot high on the scree. More rampant, but rather less hardy, is the Mexican *E. mucronatum*, which spreads itself energetically, given rock-face protection, and is fine in a retaining wall if it can be allowed to explore without invading choicer plants; larger than *E. aureus*, it flowers profusely with pink or white daisies in the summer. The Mexican species especially can be grown easily from seed, and they may both be divided in the spring.

Phlox douglasii from the western states is a mountain phlox with several popular varieties: Boothman's Variety, a tiny, tufted plant with mauve flowers; May Snow, pure white; Rose Cushion, silvery pink. They all make petite mats, and are eminently suitable for the trough garden. They are not as vigorous for the open rock garden as varieties of the eastern states species *P. subulata* and *P. stolonifera*, but they may be propagated in the same way, using short shoot cuttings taken after flowering is finished, and set in a sandy compost – the polythene bag method should be ideal.

Eriophyllum lanatum is a dry-site plant, with tufted leaves and masses of tiny yellow daisies in the summer. It usually sets seed prolifically but, anyway, can easily be divided – a reliable plant for a small site high on the drier part of a rock outcrop, or the top of a retaining wall.

An easy and very attractive plant from Utah and Colorado is *Polemonium confertum*, found on the moister slopes of dry hills, and settling well into most rock gardens, though rarely obtainable from nurseries. The tiny leaves are arranged in tiered whorls along the rosetted stems, giving a fern-like appearance to the whole plant, and a central stem bears an almost primula-like cluster of blue flowers from June to August. Seed can be collected as the capsules ripen, and sown in the spring, and well developed plants can have their woody rootstocks divided in the autumn.

A rather precious semi-woodland plant for moist, gritty sites is the American monkey flower, *Mimulus primuloides*, which makes tufted, downy mats of tiny rosetted leaves, with brilliant yellow, almost pansy-like flowers from late spring onwards. It grows best while still young, and should be divided every two years and the older, central parts discarded. As an alternative means of propagation, and as it usually sets seed well, it may be sown and planted afresh annually, to ensure a healthy, free-flowering stock.

Oxalis oregana is an all-rounder from the western states that grows well both in semi-shaded conditions and on the higher rock garden, and makes an excellent wall plant. The long-stalked shamrock leaves form a cheerful clump, and the bright purple-pink flowers make a good show in the summer, lasting over a long season.

16
East of the Missouri

The American arbor-vitae, *Thuja occidentalis*, also known as the northern white cedar, is in effect the colder-climate equivalent of the very similar western red cedar, *Thuja plicata*. The latter is better suited climatically to planting in Britain, and the former adapts itself best to more extreme climatic zones. Such preferences as these tend to be of less importance where the dwarf forms of the species are concerned for, if a timber tree performs badly and remains stunted, it is bound to create an unprofitable situation, but similar stunting or slowness of growth in a dwarf form is a desirable trait – at least, while the tree remains green and healthy. Several varieties of *Thuja occidentalis* have proved eminently suitable for rock garden use, in both North America and Britain. The smallest of these is probably Hetz Midget, a tiny globe of dense green foliage, suitable for the trough garden, and seldom growing beyond knee height after many years. Best known, perhaps, and a top buy for garden-centre customers, is the cultivar Rheingold; it is outstanding for its striking colour – a metallic bronzy gold during the winter months, becoming a rich honey yellow as active growth resumes in the spring and summer – and for its foliage texture, part flattened leaf spray of the typical adult form, and part feathery juvenile leaf, which gives it an almost heather-like appearance. A good choice for siting against a dark background, from which it glows warmly during the barren months of the year, Rheingold makes a somewhat ragged dome in outline, slowly growing to pass a metre in about ten or fifteen years, eventually surpassing 2m or more.

Other *Thuja occidentalis* varieties include: the dark green Caespitosa, smaller than Rheingold, and slower of growth, but with a similar shape, spreading after a decade or two to a metre in width; Compacta, of comparable size and shape, with densely packed upright sprays of glaucous grey-green; Globosa, which is wider than high, takes about twenty years to reach waist height, and is distinctly globular and compact in shape, with dark green foliage composed of

(Above) The American monkey flower, *Mimulus primuloides,* is a semi-woodland plant. *(Below) Erigeron aureus,* a dwarf fleabane, can be planted in a favoured spot high on the scree

(Top left) Thuja occidentalis Rheingold is a popular variety of the American arbor-vitae. *(Top right)* A tenacious spreader, *Sisyrinchium angustifolium* belongs to the iris family. *(Bottom left) Iris cristata* loves a moist, cool site below a moraine. *(Bottom right) Phlox subulata* Temiscaming, the lowest-growing variety of this mountain phlox

small, densely packed leaf sprays, paler green on their reverse face; the expressively named Cristata, with dark green foliage of short and distinctive fern-like crests – it makes a rather shapeless bush that will still be below knee height after ten or fifteen years' growth, but it has a naturally dramatic appearance that goes well with rugged rocks; Ericoides, named from the heather-like appearance of its feathery foliage, which has a soft, loose texture, greyish green in spring and summer, becoming bronzy buff for the winter; the variety Filiformis, which makes a dense, rounded bush of dark green, perhaps a metre high after ten years, with whip-like leaf sprays to give it an odd, drooping appearance.

The eastern or spruce hemlock, *Tsuga canadensis*, is found in the mountain forests over a wide range of the eastern states, from Nova Scotia and the Great Lakes southwards to Georgia and Alabama. It has a very bad name among foresters for, unlike its close relative the western hemlock, *T. canadensis* in its typical form almost invariably develops a forked trunk with heavy lower branches. This is no bad thing from the gardener's point of view, however: through this trait, it has given rise to many dwarf, bushy varieties, some of them very small and suitable for the trough garden. Such a tree is Minuta, which makes a tiny ball of congested foliage, each individual leaf dark green on the face and backed with twin blue-grey lines which give the tree a bright, healthy appearance. Jervis is also tiny, with spiky, congested shoots – less symmetrical than Minuta, but no less ornamental. For the sizable rock garden, the completely prostrate Cole sends out sprawling branches in all directions, and eventually carpets a large area. It makes an unusual change from the creeping junipers, but has never become very well known. It may take many years to build up a cover thick enough to exclude weeds, unlike the more vigorous junipers, but the eventual effect is mellow and pleasing. The variety Pendula also needs a fairly large garden if it is to keep in scale, although it will take twenty years or so to reach waist height. Pendula has been grown in American and British gardens for well over a century, and makes a slowly mounding, solid umbrella of overlapping, soft, dark green sprays, drooping after the manner of a deodar cedar. Dwarf Whitetip makes a broad cone that, although still below a metre after fifteen years or so, will eventually attain a fair size. The new spring leaves are a rather chlorotic creamy white but, as summer progresses and growth hardens, the foliage takes on a dark green overall colour. *T.c.* Many Cones is named from its habit of early and prolific coning – *Tsuga* cones are small and neat, about 2cm long, and brown-buff when they mature. Many Cones is rather too bulky for any but the largest rock gardens, as it will surpass a metre in less than ten years, making a spreading bush with somewhat arching, drooping leaf sprays. All these dwarf varieties of eastern hemlock can be grown from cuttings: short side-shoots should be pulled off with a heel in July or August, and set in a sandy compost, either under glass or within a polythene bag.

A variety of the white cypress, *Chamaecyparis thyoides* Ericoides, has been grown in gardens for close on two hundred years. Latterly it has been superseded to some extent by the Sawara cypress cultivar Boulevard – which also originated in the USA and has rapidly become popular in British gardens – but it is still much admired. It makes an upright cone of soft, feathery sea-green, changing during the autumn to a bronzy shade which deepens to purple for the winter months.

The pencil cedar, *Juniperus virginiana*, is a somewhat variable species both in form and habit, and this variability is reflected in the range of garden varieties that have arisen from time to time. The species has a very wide natural distribution over the eastern and central states – a characteristic which points to the tree's hardiness and ability to grow well when planted abroad. A few cultivars are of special importance on the rock garden, and some of them have become very well known in Britain and on the European continent, as well as in the United States: Skyrocket is one of the narrowest, most upright small trees known, and it originated as a wild seedling. The Irish juniper, *Juniperus communis* Hibernica, is often used where an evergreen spire is needed to balance a design, and Skyrocket is similar, but proportionately much narrower, with fine blue-grey foliage. It may reach waist height about five years from planting, and will eventually top 5m or more, but its elegant proportions are such that it will seldom seem out of place on any but the very smallest rock garden outcrop. A much older cultivar of the pencil cedar is Hillii, which makes a very slow-growing, compact spire, never so tall as Skyrocket and rather thicker across the base, with finely pointed blue-green leaves which take on a metallic purple sheen during the winter. Manhattan Blue is a neat little tree of more recent introduction, and makes a pyramidal cone of densely compact blue-green foliage – after fifteen years, specimens have reached not more than 150cm in height, and the rate of growth is slow and steady. As a contrast to this miniature tree, the variety Globosa is very much a bush – a feathery, tufted ball of bright grass-green. It was introduced during the nineteenth century and, after many years of healthy growth, specimens are rarely seen exceeding a metre in height. Grey Owl is a popular variety, very similar in appearance to the pfitzer juniper, with its ascending branches in a radially splayed, shuttlecock arrangement, but with soft, silvery blue foliage. All these varieties of *Juniperus virginiana* grow well from cuttings – preferably short side-shoots taken with a heel early in September, and set in sandy compost under a closed frame.

The American white pine, *Pinus strobus*, is known in Britain as the Weymouth pine, not because it has more connections with the seaside resort of Weymouth than elsewhere, but because the English Lord Weymouth planted the species at Longleat early in the eighteenth century. There is a dwarf form, Nana, which makes a somewhat variable, ragged-outlined bush, with densely arranged needles of a slightly bluish green. There is also a completely prostrate form, Prostrata – a stemless tree with a peculiarly collapsed appearance, its branches spreading along the ground in all directions, rising slightly at their tips and eventually making a low mound. It is not a tree for the small garden but, like the spruce hemlock variety Cole, it is of great value where there is room enough for it to be seen from above, or from a facing bank, or where it can weave a deep carpet between rocks on a steep slope. Like other pines, *P. strobus* varieties are practically impossible to raise from cuttings, and they have to be grafted on seedling stocks of the species. The wedge and cleft method described on page 157 gives perfectly satisfactory results with these densely foliaged or prostrate dwarf types.

One of the most unusual of dwarf conifers is Hursley Park, a variety of *Taxodium distichum*, the bald or swamp cypress from the Everglades of Florida, and other southern swamp areas. It forms a small, compact bush of intricately tangled twigs, bare in the winter, clothed in the summer with feathery, bright green leaves which turn tawny yellow for the autumn. Planted in a boggy patch at the foot of the moraine, Hursley Park is able to carry the dwarf tree theme from the mountains of the rockery into the lowland swamps of the bog garden. It does not need boggy conditions in which to thrive, however, and this hardy tree is equally willing to grow on drier sites. It is normally increased by grafting on to seedling stocks of the species, as it is unlikely to give successful results with cuttings.

A suitable plant, provided the soil is not too damp, to associate with the dwarf bald cypress is the creeping evening primrose, *Oenothera missouriensis*, which forms low mats of trailing stems and variably shaped little leaves, adorned from June to August with spectacular primrose-yellow flowers, up to 10cm across the petals. Increase by division is possible once the plants have established themselves, otherwise short cuttings of new growth may be taken during April and May, and rooted in a sandy compost under a polythene bag.

A charming flower of the iris family is *Sisyrinchium douglasii*. It enjoys a cool, moist spot at the base of a moraine, with plenty of peat and coarse sand in the soil so that the site neither dries out nor becomes waterlogged. It makes an ideal partner for any spreading plant which is not too rampant and which forms only a thin cover, for it dies down completely after flowering, and runs sedately in the summer, producing grass-like tufts here and there, with wine-red bell flowers. Another of the genus is *Sisyrinchium angustifolium*, which produces pale violet-blue flowers from June to August – a tenacious spreader which is less fussy about soil and site conditions, it has naturalised itself in many places, including Britain.

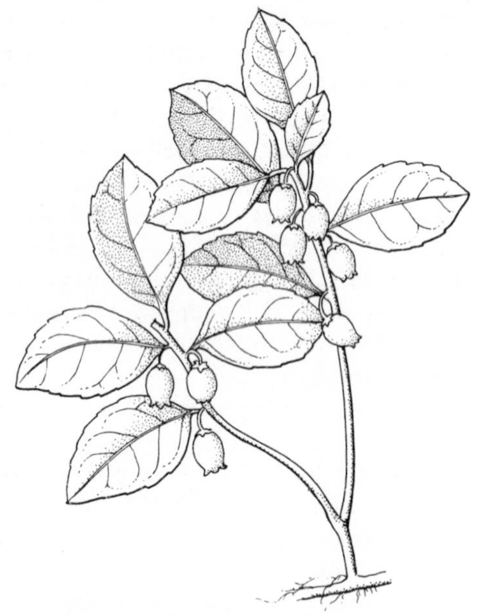

Gaultheria procumbens

Several plants native to the eastern states, and which have become popular for garden use, are happiest in woodland conditions – a moist, acid, peaty soil in a shaded or semi-shaded site. Such a plant is *Gaultheria procumbens*, the partridge berry – though it has several other popular names, and is sometimes called creeping wintergreen checkerberry – a shrub with ankle-high ascending stems spreading to form a very even carpet, with little rounded evergreen leaves clustered at the top of each shoot. It bears tiny white or pinkish heath-type flowers in late summer, followed by bright red berries. Where the height is apt, this is the ideal subject for running around the base of tufted or mounding plants in peaty, shaded places, and propagation is easily effected by division in the spring.

Mitchella repens is also sometimes called partridge berry, and requires similar conditions in a shaded, peaty soil. An evergreen carpeter like gaultheria, its manner of spreading is quite different, for it is a trailer, the long stems rooting as they trail, and bearing tiny, dark green glossy leaves in pairs, with the small fragrant white flowers and the scarlet berries that follow also in pairs.

Other plants for damp, lightly shaded sites include one of the onions, *Allium uniflorum*, with large clusters of bright pink flowers that last well in the summer; and two dog's tooth violets – *Erythronium albidum* and *E. americanum*, spreading plants of the lily family which produce their cyclamen-like flowers in the spring, rising from tufts of broad leaves which are oddly mottled in shades of green, violet and white. These two eastern North American species associate well together – *E. americanum* with bright yellow, and *E. albidum* with pale, milky bluish flowers; the bulbs should be set close together in a moist, peaty soil, at about a finger's depth, and they will soon establish a permanent colony.

The celandine poppy, *Stylophorum diphyllum*, is an unusual herb for moist shady spots. It is occasionally invasive but attractive, with deeply cut, rosetted leaves and 3cm wide deep buttercup-yellow single flowers in May. It is usually possible to divide established clumps, or seed may be collected as soon as the capsules ripen and harden, to be sown the following spring. A member of the same family enjoying similar conditions is the bloodroot, *Sanguinaria canadensis,* which ranges in nature from Canada down the eastern states. To grow satisfactorily, seeds need to be subjected to prolonged cold spells both before and after germination, but the mature plant develops a thick, fleshy rootstock which may be divided into pieces, each with some roots attached, and transplanted in the late summer. The leaves, in an attractive shade of grey, are large, rounded, and symmetrically lobed, and the beautiful white flowers – like many-petalled 8cm wide waterlilies on 15cm stems – open in the spring just as the leaves are unfurling. There is also a multi-petalled double variety, Plena, of quite exquisite beauty.

Like an evergreen lily of the valley, *Galax urceolata* carpets damp, shady, peaty places with a thick cover of heart-shaped leaves, bright glossy green in spring and summer, becoming bronzed for the winter – especially in more open sites. The dense spikes of tiny flowers appear in June. It is a plant which looks equally at home covering the ground beneath and around acid-loving shrubs, or climbing the lower north-facing slopes of the rock garden, where the bronzed winter leaves look especially handsome among the rocks.

Other plants of the eastern states which enjoy cool, moist situations include members of the lily family: *Streptopus roseus*, a tufted plant with arching sprays of nodding, broad bells in bright carmine pink, at its best in June; and the wake robin, *Trillium grandiflorum*, which bears three-petalled pure white flowers in May, each blossom about 8cm across. On their 25cm stems, these wake robins may be too tall for the rock garden proper, but should be planted within sight of it if there is a shady, moist place nearby to suit them. The varieties Roseum and Rubrum have pink flowers and are eye-catching. Wake robins set seed readily, and sowings often produce attractive colour breaks – mainly variations of pink – but germination is erratic unless the seed is first exposed to cold winter weather. To this end, sowing is best carried out in the autumn, leaving the containers to stand outside until the spring. Another eastern states woodland plant which will make an ankle-high drift of unspectacular but useful fresh green foliage, and cover the ground in moist, shady places, is the snakeroot *Asarum canadense.* Closely related to the European asarabaca, with similar kidney shaped leaves and inconspicuous brown flowers, it is easily increased by division in the spring.

The dwarf *Iris cristata* is native to the eastern states, and also loves a moist, cool site below a moraine, where the creeping rhizomes can produce thick mats of tufted, pointed leaves. The short-stalked flowers are usually in pairs, very pretty in pale lilac with a deep yellow throat. If the district normally experiences very wet winters without long-lasting snow, it is as well to lift the rhizomes in the autumn and store them like dahlias until March, when they can be planted out again.

The foam flower, *Tiarella cordifolia*, spreads by means of creeping stolons into low but rather untidy mats – another example of a plant which looks well near, but not actually on, the rockery. The lobed leaves bronze handsomely in the autumn, and the starry flowers create a fluffy white cloud from April to June. In the variety Purpurea the flowers are pink and the leaves bronzy purple, and this is an exceptionally fine plant.

Bluets, *Houstonia caerulea*, is a plant of the eastern states that has been grown in Europe and Britain for two hundred years. A mat-forming perennial that falls into a category between the extremes of moist shade and dry rock, it has been used in Britain as a counterpart of aubrieta where the site is shaded. It looks particularly good on stone steps, provided there is a cool rootrun of moist soil, and makes a bright splash of clear colour in the early summer, with its saucers of pale blue against a background of tiny, glossy green leaves. The plant will usually divide satisfactorily, or it may be grown from seed.

Plants of the open mountains – mat-forming dwarfs for a sunny spot on the rockery – include an eastern stonecrop, *Sedum ternatum*, which produces loose clusters of white flowers in May and June, above pale pea-green rosettes of flat, rock-hugging leaves. Other mat-formers for full sun are the mountain phloxes. *Phlox stolonifera* has an outstanding variety, Blue Ridge, with flowering stems over 20cm high, bearing masses of 2-3cm wide soft blue flowers in April and May. *Phlox subulata* has several excellent varieties, and all make magnificent wall plants: lowest-growing of these is Temiscaming, with crimson-pink flowers extending from late spring into the summer months; Sensation has deep pink flowers; Atropurpurea, wine-red; Betty, salmon-pink; and G. F. Wilson, mauve. They all range between 10 and 15cm in flowering height, and all are easily grown in any sunny spot. Propagation is best achieved by taking cuttings of short shoots in the summer after flowering has finished, setting them in a polythene bag, but keeping them shaded from full sunlight until active new growth can be seen.

17
Fifty Easy Plants for Year-round Colour

Alyssum – *Alyssum saxatile*, with familiar yellow flowers in the spring, has a few dwarf varieties such as Tom Thumb.

Anemone – *Anemone blanda* flowers very early in the spring and enjoys light shade. There are varieties with blue, red, white and pink flowers.

Aubrieta – *Aubrieta deltoides* is one of the best loved spring flowerers, with many varieties, such as the purple Dr Mules.

Auricula – *Primula auricula*, the spring-flowering 'dusty miller', has many varieties, the flowers ranging in colour from yellow to blue.

Barberry, dwarf red – *Berberis thunbergii* Atropurpurea Nana is a dwarf shrub whose leaves are purple-red from spring to autumn.

Bugle – *Ajuga reptans* has many coloured-leaf varieties, such as Burgundy Glow, which are useful to carpet the rockery surrounds.

Campanula – *Campanula portenschlagiana*, with purple-blue flowers in the summer, is one of the easiest and loveliest of this large genus.

Candytuft – *Iberis sempervirens* is an evergreen shrubby plant with white flowers in the spring. Several varieties are available.

Cobweb houseleek – *Sempervivum arachnoideum* makes clustered rosettes of cobwebby green and red leaves, and bears pink flowers in the summer.

Cotoneaster – *Cotoneaster conspicuus* Decorus is one of the many charming shrubs which belong to this genus; red-berried in the winter.

Creeping Jenny – *Lysimachia nummularia* Aurea is the yellow-leaved variety of a native British plant, with yellow flowers in the summer.

Edelweiss – *Leontopodium alpinum*. This famous Alpine flower is very easy to grow in a sunny situation. It flowers in the spring.

Ellwoodii, and Ellwood's Gold – popular varieties of the cypress

Chamaecyparis lawsoniana. They grow very slowly, but eventually become too large for the rock garden.

Ferns – the smaller kinds such as the hart's tongue, *Phyllitis scolopendrium*, are easy to please and always look good on the rockery.

Gentian – one of the easiest to grow of this huge genus is *Gentiana septemfida*, with glorious blue flowers in the summer.

Glory of the Snow – *Chionodoxa luciliae*, with sky-blue flowers in early spring. The small bulbs should be planted in drifts.

Grape hyacinth – *Muscari armeniacum* and *M. tubergenianum* are excellent species, with intensely blue flowers in the spring.

Gromwell – *Lithodora diffusa (Lithospermum prostratum)* Grace Ward is easy to grow, and produces its clear blue flowers during spring and summer.

Heath – *Erica* species. The varieties Springwood White and Springwood Pink are prostrate, and flower in late winter and early spring.

Heather – *Calluna vulgaris*. Among the many dwarf and creeping varieties, Prostrate Orange has coloured foliage throughout the year.

Houseleek – *Sempervivum tectorum* is one of the easiest to grow of these curious, fleshy-rosetted plants.

Iris, winter-flowering – *Iris unguicularis* produces its purple flowers in midwinter. It needs a sunny spot at the foot of the rockery.

Juniper, miniature – *Juniperus communis* Compressa is a perfect dwarf evergreen tree, remaining tiny for many years.

Juniper, spreading – there are many excellent kinds, including *Juniperus horizontalis* Bar Harbor, and *J. virginiana* Grey Owl.

Knotgrass, creeping – *Polygonum affine* Lowndes Variety is useful to clothe the foot of a rockery, with bright pink flowers in late summer and autumn.

Knotgrass, trailing – *Polygonum vaccinifolium* is an easy autumn-flowering rock plant with mauve-pink flowers.

Lamb's tongue – *Stachys lanata* Silver Carpet makes a thick, woolly carpet for the sunny foot of the rockery.

Maiden pink – *Dianthus deltoides* has several good, easily grown varieties with pink or red flowers during the summer.

Milfoil – *Achillea tomentosa*, or the hybrid variety King Edward, produce flat heads of yellow flowers in the summer, for any sunny spot.

Moss phlox – *Phlox subulata* Temiscaming is easy to grow, and produces its bright pink flowers throughout the spring and summer.

Mossy saxifrage – there are numerous *Saxifraga* hybrids, all easily grown, covered in the spring with red, pink or white flowers.

Nana Gracilis – a variety of the cypress *Chamaecyparis obtusa*, this graceful evergreen takes many years to outgrow the average rock garden.

New Zealand bur – *Acaena microphylla* is an easy carpeting plant that will grow in the shade. It produces spiky red burs in the late summer.

Primrose – *Primula vulgaris* is the well loved British wild flower. There are many seedling varieties of various colours, all spring-flowering.

Primula – among the many species available, *Primula juliae* is a useful spring-flowering carpeter which revels in light shade. It is a parent of several hybrid varieties, all beautiful and easy to grow.

Rheingold – *Thuja occidentalis* Rheingold is one of the most popular of conifers, slow-growing, but eventually becoming too large for the rockery.

Rock campion – *Silene schafta* is an easy carpeter which becomes covered with pink flowers in late summer and autumn.

Rockrose – the numerous colourful varieties of *Helianthemum nummularium* flower throughout the summer months when given a sunny, south-facing site.

Skyrocket – *Juniperus virginiana* Skyrocket is the slenderest of all trees, and seldom outgrows the average rock garden.

Snowdrop – *Galanthus nivalis* is the old favourite, flowering in winter and early spring. The bulbs are best planted in drifts.

Soapwort – *Saponaria ocymoides* is a useful sprawling plant, easy to grow on a dry, sunny site or a stone wall. It produces its pink flowers in the summer.

Spruce, Alberta – *Picea glauca* Albertiana Conica. A very slow-growing conifer, it takes many years to outgrow the rock garden.

Squill – *Scilla sibirica*, like a miniature bluebell, produces its rich blue flowers in the spring.

Stonecrop – varieties of *Sedum acre, S. spurium*, and *S. spathulifolium* are among the easiest plants to grow, and produce sheets of colour during the summer months.

Thyme, lemon-scented – *Thymus citriodorus* Aureus is a beautiful golden-leaved variety of thyme, excellent for a sunny spot low down on the rockery, and useful in the kitchen.

Thyme, shepherd's – *Thymus serpyllum* has several excellent, dwarf varieties, flowering throughout the spring and summer in pink, purple or white, perfect for planting between paving stones and easily grown in any light soil.

Veronica – *Veronica prostrata* has several good varieties such as Spode Blue, which produces its pale blue flowers in the spring, but some veronicas such as *V. filiformis* can become invasive in the garden.

Winter aconite – *Eranthis hyemalis* has bright yellow flowers in midwinter. The bulbs are best planted in small groups.

Wood anemone – *Anemone nemorosa* is a native British wild plant whose starry flowers in the early spring are white, faintly backed with purplish blue.

Wood sorrel – *Oxalis acetosella* is another native British plant with white, purple-veined flowers in the spring. The variety Rosea has pink flowers.

Table of Rock Plants

All the plants discussed in the book are classified under headings chosen to describe briefly their characteristics, and any special requirements they may have.

Form notes whether a plant is a herb, a shrub, a bulbous subject or a dwarf tree, and whether its habit of growth is upright, mounding or tuft-forming, or prostrate and spreading.

Flower indicates the flowering season, and points out those – such as dwarf conifers – that are planted not for their flowers but for their foliage effect.

Soil differentiates between those plants that need gritty or peaty conditions, and those that are happy in normal, average soil. Lime-lovers, acid-lovers, and those that will grow in a neutral soil are easily picked out, and so are those – the majority – that will thrive in all three types.

Site Those plants marked as enjoying a general site are the easiest to please. Scree and moraine-lovers are noted; those that will be happy on a wall, in a trough or between paving slabs; those – usually the larger or more vigorous kinds – which are best sited nearby, but not actually on the rockery ('Surrounding'); and those useful subjects which are able to flourish in the shade, are all indicated.

Height Plant heights are noted in centimetres. In the case of dwarf conifers, the figure is the average attained after about ten years of growth on the rock garden. In the case of small plants, the height includes flowering stems. Thus, a prostrate plant which is, say, 5cm high throughout most of the year, but which produces 10cm flowering stems in the spring, will be shown as 10cm – for comparisons on the ground will be made most readily during the flowering season.

	Page No.	FORM							FLOWER					SOIL						SITE								HEIGHT
		HERB	BULB	SHRUB	DWARF TREE	SPREADING	MOUND OR TUFT	UPRIGHT	SPRING	SUMMER	AUTUMN	WINTER	FOLIAGE EFFECT	GRITTY	NORMAL	PEATY	ACID	NEUTRAL	LIMY	GENERAL	SCREE	MORAINE	SURROUNDING	WALL	TROUGH	PAVING	SHADE	(cm)
Abies amabilis Spreading Star	182				*	*							*		*		*			*								75
balsamea Hudsonia	177				*		*						*		*		*	*		*								60
cephalonica Nana	117				*	*							*		*		*	*	*	*								38
delavayi Nana	152				*			*					*		*		*	*	*	*								90
lasiocarpa arizonica Compacta	182				*			*					*		*		*	*	*	*								45
magnifica Nana	182				*	*							*		*		*			*								38
nordmanniana Golden Spreader	125				*	*							*		*		*	*	*	*								30
procera Glauca Prostrata	182				*	*							*		*		*	*		*								45
Acaena glauca	166	*				*				*					*		*	*	*	*						*		5
microphylla	166	*				*				*					*		*	*	*	*				*		*	*	5
novae-zelandiae	166	*				*				*					*		*	*	*	*						*		8
Acantholimon glumaceum	125	*					*			*					*		*	*	*	*								10
Achillea King Edward	67	*				*				*					*		*	*	*	*								15
tomentosa	67	*				*				*	*				*		*	*	*	*								15
Achlys triphylla	186	*				*				*					*	*	*	*		*							*	23
Adiantum capillus-veneris (FERN)	80, 82	*				*							*		*			*	*									25
Aethionema grandiflorum	128			*			*			*				*				*	*					*				22
pulchellum	128			*			*			*				*				*	*					*				18
Warley Rose	128			*			*			*				*				*	*					*				10
Ajuga pyramidalis	93	*				*				*			*		*		*	*	*				*					15
reptans	93, 94	*				*				*			*		*		*	*	*				*					15
Burgundy Glow	93	*				*				*			*		*		*	*	*				*					15
Multicolor (Rainbow)	93	*				*				*			*		*		*	*	*				*					15
Pink Elf	93	*				*				*			*		*		*	*	*				*					15
Alchemilla alpina	105	*				*	*			*			*		*		*	*	*	*				*				15
conjuncta	105	*				*	*			*			*		*		*	*	*	*				*				10

		FORM							FLOWER					SOIL						SITE								HEIGHT
	Page No.	HERB	BULB	SHRUB	DWARF TREE	SPREADING	MOUND OR TUFT	UPRIGHT	SPRING	SUMMER	AUTUMN	WINTER	FOLIAGE EFFECT	GRITTY	NORMAL	PEATY	ACID	NEUTRAL	LIMY	GENERAL	SCREE	MORAINE	SURROUNDING	WALL	TROUGH	PAVING	SHADE	(cm)
Allium karataviense	140		*			*			*						*		*	*	*	*								25
moly	118		*				*			*					*		*	*	*	*								23
napolitanum	118		*			*	*		*						*		*	*	*	*								24
oreophilum	130		*			*	*			*					*		*	*	*	*								10
pedemontanum	113		*				*			*					*		*	*	*	*								20
pulchellum	119		*				*			*					*		*	*	*	*			*					40
Album	119		*				*			*					*		*	*	*	*			*					40
triquetrum	118		*			*	*		*	*					*		*	*	*	*							*	30
uniflorum	197		*				*			*					*		*	*	*	*			*					38
Alyssum olympicum	115	*					*			*					*		*	*	*	*				*				7
saxatile	109, 124			*		*			*						*		*	*	*					*				22
Citrinum	124			*		*			*						*		*	*	*					*				22
Dudley Neville	124			*		*			*						*		*	*	*	*				*				15
Tom Thumb	124			*		*			*						*		*	*	*	*				*				8
Anacyclus depressus	106	*					*			*				*	*		*	*	*	*	*							5
Anagallis tenella Studland	91, 104	*				*				*					*		*	*	*	*		*						5
Anchusa caespitosa	112	*					*		*					*			*	*	*		*							8
Androsace×*aretioides*	44	*					*		*					*			*	*			*				*			5
carnea	46	*					*		*	*					*		*	*	*	*		*			*			8
hausmannii	44	*					*		*					*				*	*	*								10
lanuginosa	148	*				*				*					*		*	*	*	*				*				10
pyrenaica	44	*					*			*				*	*		*	*	*		*							12
sarmentosa	147	*				*	*			*				*			*	*	*		*							10
sempervivoides	148	*					*		*					*			*	*	*	*								5
villosa	44	*				*			*					*			*	*	*		*				*			5
Anemone apennina	62		*			*	*		*						*				*	*								15
Alba	62		*			*	*		*						*				*	*								15

		FORM							FLOWER					SOIL						SITE								HEIGHT
	Page No.	HERB	BULB	SHRUB	DWARF TREE	SPREADING	MOUND OR TUFT	UPRIGHT	SPRING	SUMMER	AUTUMN	WINTER	FOLIAGE EFFECT	GRITTY	NORMAL	PEATY	ACID	NEUTRAL	LIMY	GENERAL	SCREE	MORAINE	SURROUNDING	WALL	TROUGH	PAVING	SHADE	(cm)
biflora	140		*				*		*			*			*				*	*								15
blanda	116		*			*	*		*						*		*	*	*	*								15
Atrocoerulea	116		*			*	*		*						*		*	*	*	*								15
Rosea	116		*			*	*		*						*		*	*	*	*								15
nemorosa	93, 95		*			*	*		*						*		*	*	*	*							*	15
Alba Plena	93		*			*	*		*						*		*	*	*	*							*	15
Allenii	93		*			*	*		*						*		*	*	*	*							*	15
Blue Bonnet	93		*			*	*		*						*		*	*	*	*							*	15
Robinsoniana	93		*			*	*		*						*		*	*	*	*							*	15
Rosea	93		*			*	*		*						*		*	*	*	*							*	15
Royal Blue	93		*			*	*		*						*		*	*	*	*							*	15
palmata	108		*				*		*						*		*	*	*	*								15
ranunculoides	126		*			*	*		*							*	*	*	*	*							*	18
Antennaria dioica	71	*				*				*			*		*		*	*	*	*								8
Anthemis nobilis	89, 90	*				*				*					*		*	*	*				*			*		20
Anthyllis hermanniae Compacta	110			*		*			*						*		*	*	*	*								30
montana	45			*		*				*					*		*	*	*	*								8
Carminea	45			*		*				*					*		*	*	*	*								8
Rubra	45			*		*				*					*		*	*	*	*								8
vulneraria Coccinea	89			*		*				*					*		*	*	*	*								8
Arabis androsacea	124	*					*			*				*			*	*	*	*	*				*			5
caucasica	124	*				*			*					*			*	*	*	*				*				22
Variegata	124	*				*			*				*	*			*	*	*	*							*	22
Arctostaphylos nevadensis	185			*		*			*				*		*		*			*			*				*	18
uva-ursi	178, 179			*		*			*				*			*	*			*			*				*	15

		FORM							FLOWER					SOIL						SITE								HEIGHT
	Page No.	HERB	BULB	SHRUB	DWARF TREE	SPREADING	MOUND OR TUFT	UPRIGHT	SPRING	SUMMER	AUTUMN	WINTER	FOLIAGE EFFECT	GRITTY	NORMAL	PEATY	ACID	NEUTRAL	LIMY	GENERAL	SCREE	MORAINE	SURROUNDING	WALL	TROUGH	PAVING	SHADE	(cm)
Arenaria balearica	111	*				*			*	*					*		*	*	*	*		*				*	*	2
ciliata	90, 180	*				*			*						*		*	*	*	*								15
montana	45	*				*			*					*	*		*	*	*	*				*				8
tetraquetra	111	*					*		*					*			*	*	*		*							8
Armeria maritima	84, 87	*				*	*			*					*		*	*	*	*								10
Asarina procumbens	108	*				*			*	*					*		*	*	*	*				*				15
Asarum canadense	198	*				*				*			*		*	*	*	*	*	*			*				*	20
europaeum	75. 76	*				*				*			*		*	*	*	*	*	*			*				*	30
Aster alpinus	45, 51	*				*	*			*					*		*	*	*	*								15
natalensis	168	*				*				*				*			*	*	*		*							14
Astragalus alpinus	115	*				*				*					*		*	*	*	*								15
angustifolius	115			*			*			*					*		*	*	*	*								5
Aubrieta deltoides Bressingham Pink	108	*				*			*						*		*	*	*	*				*				14
Dr Mules	108	*				*			*						*		*	*	*	*				*				14
Greencourt Purple	108	*				*			*						*		*	*	*	*				*				14
Red Carpet	108	*				*			*						*		*	*	*	*				*				14
Barbarea vulgaris Variegata	90	*						*		*			*		*		*	*	*				*					35
Bellis perennis	89	*				*			*	*					*		*	*	*	*								10
Alice	89	*				*			*	*					*		*	*	*	*								12
Dresden China	89	*				*			*	*					*		*	*	*	*								10
Victoria	89	*				*			*	*					*		*	*	*	*								15
Bellium minutum	32, 128	*				*				*					*		*	*	*	*						*		2
Berberis×*stenophylla*																												
Corallina Compacta	171			*		*				*			*		*		*	*	*	*								25
Gracilis Nana	171			*		*				*			*		*		*	*	*	*								35

	Page No.	FORM							FLOWER					SOIL						SITE								HEIGHT (cm)
		HERB	BULB	SHRUB	DWARF TREE	SPREADING	MOUND OR TUFT	UPRIGHT	SPRING	SUMMER	AUTUMN	WINTER	FOLIAGE EFFECT	GRITTY	NORMAL	PEATY	ACID	NEUTRAL	LIMY	GENERAL	SCREE	MORAINE	SURROUNDING	WALL	TROUGH	PAVING	SHADE	
thunbergii Atropurpurea Nana	162			*			*			*			*		*		*	*	*	*								38
Betula nana	100, 102			*	*	*	*						*		*		*	*	*	*								100
Bruckenthalia spiculifolia	122			*		*	*		*	*						*	*			*								18
Calceolaria darwinii	170	*					*			*				*		*	*	*	*			*						10
Calluna vulgaris CULTIVARS:																												
Alba Minor	99			*		*	*			*						*	*			*								15
Alba Plena	99			*		*	*				*					*	*			*								30
Alportii	99			*		*	*			*	*					*	*			*								60
Californian Midge	98			*		*	*			*						*	*			*						*	*	8
County Wicklow	99			*		*	*			*	*					*	*			*								22
Cuprea	99			*		*	*						*			*	*			*								30
Elegantissima	99			*		*	*				*	*				*	*			*								60
Foxhole Wanderer	32, 98			*		*				*	*		*			*	*			*							*	15
Foxii Nana	32, 98			*		*	*			*	*		*			*	*										*	8
Golden Feather	99			*		*	*						*			*	*			*								45
Gold Haze	99			*		*	*						*			*	*			*								60
Hammondii	99			*		*	*			*	*					*	*			*								90
H. E. Beale	99			*		*	*				*					*	*			*								60
Hibernica	99			*		*	*				*					*	*			*								15
J. H. Hamilton	99			*		*	*			*	*					*	*			*								23
Joan Sparkes	99			*		*	*				*					*	*			*								30
Mair's Variety	98			*		*	*			*	*					*	*			*								100
Mrs Pat	99			*		*	*			*			*			*	*			*								25
Mullion	99			*		*	*			*						*	*			*								22
Peter Sparkes	99			*		*	*			*	*					*	*			*								45
Prostrate Orange	99			*		*	*						*			*	*			*								15
Ruth Sparkes	99			*		*	*				*		*			*	*			*								24

	Page No.	FORM							FLOWER					SOIL						SITE								HEIGHT
		HERB	BULB	SHRUB	DWARF TREE	SPREADING	MOUND OR TUFT	UPRIGHT	SPRING	SUMMER	AUTUMN	WINTER	FOLIAGE EFFECT	GRITTY	NORMAL	PEATY	ACID	NEUTRAL	LIMY	GENERAL	SCREE	MORAINE	SURROUNDING	WALL	TROUGH	PAVING	SHADE	(cm)
Calluna vulgaris CULTIVARS:																												
Sunset	99			*		*	*						*			*	*			*								30
The Pygmy	98			*		*							*			*	*			*						*		5
Tib	99			*		*	*			*	*					*	*			*								38
Tom Thumb	99			*		*	*			*	*					*	*			*					*			15
Calocedrus decurrens Nana	184				*			*					*		*		*	*	*	*								60
Campanula Birch Hybrid	121	*				*				*					*		*	*	*	*				*			*	18
carpatica	120, 121	*				*				*					*		*	*	*	*				*				23
cochlearifolia	120	*				*				*					*		*	*	*	*				*				10
garganica	114	*				*			*	*					*		*	*	*	*				*				10
Hallii	120	*					*			*					*		*	*	*	*				*				8
Peter Nix	120	*				*				*					*		*	*	*	*				*				23
portenschlagiana (syn. *muralis*)	120	*				*				*					*		*	*	*	*				*			*	10
poscharskyana	120	*				*				*					*		*	*	*	*				*				23
rotundifolia	87	*				*				*					*		*	*	*	*				*				20
Cassiope Bearsden	145			*		*	*		*						*	*	*			*							*	13
Edinburgh	145			*		*	*		*						*	*	*			*							*	30
George Taylor	145			*		*	*		*						*	*	*			*							*	12
Kathleen Dryden	145			*		*	*		*						*	*	*			*							*	10
Randle Cooke	145			*		*	*		*						*	*	*			*							*	15
Cedrus deodara Pygmy	144				*		*						*		*		*	*	*	*								15
libani Aurea Prostrata	127				*	*							*		*		*	*	*	*								60
Comte de Dijon	127				*		*						*		*		*	*	*	*								100
Nana	127				*		*						*		*		*	*	*	*								150
Sargentii	127				*		*						*		*		*	*	*	*								75
Cerastium alpinum	105	*				*				*			*		*		*	*	*	*	*							8

	Page No.	FORM: HERB	FORM: BULB	FORM: SHRUB	FORM: DWARF TREE	FORM: SPREADING	FORM: MOUND OR TUFT	FORM: UPRIGHT	FLOWER: SPRING	FLOWER: SUMMER	FLOWER: AUTUMN	FLOWER: WINTER	FLOWER: FOLIAGE EFFECT	SOIL: GRITTY	SOIL: NORMAL	SOIL: PEATY	SOIL: ACID	SOIL: NEUTRAL	SOIL: LIMY	SITE: GENERAL	SITE: SCREE	SITE: MORAINE	SITE: SURROUNDING	SITE: WALL	SITE: TROUGH	SITE: PAVING	SITE: SHADE	HEIGHT (cm)
lanatum	73	*				*				*			*		*		*	*	*	*			*					8
tomentosum	44	*				*				*			*		*		*	*	*	*			*					15
uniflorum	44	*					*			*				*	*		*	*	*	*	*							10
Chamaecyparis lawsoniana CULTIVARS:																												
Aurea Densa	184				*		*	*					*		*		*	*	*	*								120
Chilworth Silver	182				*			*					*		*		*	*	*	*								90
Duncanii	184				*		*						*		*		*	*	*	*								75
Ellwoodii	182				*			*					*		*		*	*	*	*								150
Ellwood's Gold	182				*			*					*		*		*	*	*	*								90
Ellwood's White	183				*			*					*		*		*	*	*	*								120
Forsteckensis	184				*		*						*		*		*	*	*	*								40
Gimbornii	184				*		*						*		*		*	*	*	*								75
Minima	183				*		*						*		*		*	*	*	*								90
Minima Aurea	183				*		*						*		*		*	*	*	*								80
Minima Glauca	183				*		*						*		*		*	*	*	*								70
Nana	183				*		*						*		*		*	*	*	*								150
Nana Argentea	183				*		*						*		*		*	*	*	*								60
Nidiformis	184				*			*					*		*		*	*	*	*								150
Parsonsii	184				*		*						*		*		*	*	*	*								120
Pygmaea Argentea	183				*		*						*		*		*	*	*	*								50
Rogersii	184				*		*						*		*		*	*	*	*								135
obtusa CULTIVARS:																												
Bassett	160				*		*						*		*		*	*	*	*					*			28
Caespitosa	160				*		*						*		*		*	*	*	*					*			23
Chabo Yadari	159				*		*						*		*		*	*	*	*								100
Densa	160				*		*						*		*		*	*	*	*					*			30
Kosteri	160				*	*	*						*		*		*	*	*	*								38

	Page No.	FORM: HERB	FORM: BULB	FORM: SHRUB	FORM: DWARF TREE	FORM: SPREADING	FORM: MOUND OR TUFT	FORM: UPRIGHT	FLOWER: SPRING	FLOWER: SUMMER	FLOWER: AUTUMN	FLOWER: WINTER	FLOWER: FOLIAGE EFFECT	SOIL: GRITTY	SOIL: NORMAL	SOIL: PEATY	SOIL: ACID	SOIL: NEUTRAL	SOIL: LIMY	SITE: GENERAL	SITE: SCREE	SITE: MORAINE	SITE: SURROUNDING	SITE: WALL	SITE: TROUGH	SITE: PAVING	SITE: SHADE	HEIGHT (cm)
Chamaecyparis obtusa CULTIVARS:																												
Mariesii	160				*		*						*		*		*	*	*	*								45
Minima	160				*		*						*		*		*	*	*	*					*			10
Nana	160				*		*						*		*		*	*	*	*								30
Nana Aurea	160				*		*	*					*		*		*	*	*	*								90
Nana Gracilis	159				*		*	*					*		*		*	*	*	*								135
Repens	160				*	*							*		*		*	*	*	*								25
pisifera CULTIVARS:																												
Aurea Nana	160				*	*	*						*		*		*	*	*	*								90
Boulevard	160				*		*						*		*		*	*	*	*								180
Filifera Nana	161				*		*						*		*		*	*	*	*								95
Filifera Nana Aurea	160				*		*						*		*		*	*	*	*								75
Nana	161				*		*						*		*		*	*	*	*								30
Nana Aureovariegata	160				*		*						*		*		*	*	*	*								30
Plumosa Aurea Compacta	160				*		*						*		*		*	*	*	*								60
Plumosa Compressa	161				*		*						*		*		*	*	*	*								90
Plumosa Compressa Aurea	161				*		*						*		*		*	*	*	*								90
Squarrosa Aurea Nana	160				*		*						*		*		*	*	*	*								90
Squarrosa Sulphurea	160				*		*						*		*		*	*	*	*								90
thyoides Ericoides	194				*		*	*					*		*		*	*	*	*								150
Chionodoxa gigantea	131		*			*			*						*		*	*	*	*								15
Alba	131		*			*			*						*		*	*	*	*								15
luciliae	131		*			*			*						*		*	*	*	*								10
Rosea	131		*			*			*						*		*	*	*	*								10
sardensis	131		*			*			*						*		*	*	*	*								15
tmoli	131		*			*			*						*		*	*	*	*								8
Chrysanthemum alpinum	44	*					*			*				*	*		*	*	*		*							8

	Page No.	FORM							FLOWER					SOIL						SITE								HEIGHT
		HERB	BULB	SHRUB	DWARF TREE	SPREADING	MOUND OR TUFT	UPRIGHT	SPRING	SUMMER	AUTUMN	WINTER	FOLIAGE EFFECT	GRITTY	NORMAL	PEATY	ACID	NEUTRAL	LIMY	GENERAL	SCREE	MORAINE	SURROUNDING	WALL	TROUGH	PAVING	SHADE	(cm)
Cistus×cyprius	107			*			*			*				*	*		*	*	*	*			*					180
laurifolius	107			*			*			*				*	*		*	*	*	*			*					180
Pat	107			*			*			*				*	*		*	*	*	*			*					120
Peggy Sannons	107			*			*			*				*	*		*	*	*	*			*					90
populifolius	107			*			*			*				*	*		*	*	*	*			*					120
Silver Pink	107			*			*			*				*	*		*	*	*	*			*					75
Colchicum agrippinum	117		*			*					*				*		*	*	*	*			*					15
alpinum	118		*			*				*					*		*	*	*	*			*					15
autumnale	78, 79		*			*					*				*		*	*	*	*			*					24
Album	78		*			*					*				*		*	*	*	*			*					24
byzantium	129		*			*					*				*		*	*	*	*			*					38
speciosum	129		*			*				*					*		*	*	*	*			*					28
Album	129		*			*				*					*		*	*	*	*			*					28
Cornus (syn. *Chamaepericlymenum*)																												
canadensis	176, 178			*		*				*						*	*						*				*	20
Coronilla varia	67	*				*				*	*				*		*	*	*				*					10
Corydalis diphylla	147	*	*			*	*		*						*		*	*	*	*							*	15
solida	121	*	*			*	*		*						*		*	*	*	*							*	15
Cotoneaster adpressus	154			*		*				*			*		*		*	*	*	*								30
buxifolius	136			*		*	*			*			*		*		*	*	*	*								38
congestus	146			*			*			*			*		*		*	*	*	*								25
conspicuus Decorus	146			*		*	*			*			*		*		*	*	*	*				*				15
dammeri	154			*		*				*			*		*		*	*	*	*			*	*				25
horizontalis	151, 153			*		*			*				*		*		*	*	*	*			*	*				30
Saxatilis	153			*		*			*				*		*		*	*	*	*			*	*				25
microphyllus	146			*		*			*				*		*		*	*	*	*			*	*				38
Cochleatus	146			*		*			*				*		*		*	*	*	*			*	*				15

		FORM							FLOWER					SOIL						SITE								HEIGHT
	Page No.	HERB	BULB	SHRUB	DWARF TREE	SPREADING	MOUND OR TUFT	UPRIGHT	SPRING	SUMMER	AUTUMN	WINTER	FOLIAGE EFFECT	GRITTY	NORMAL	PEATY	ACID	NEUTRAL	LIMY	GENERAL	SCREE	MORAINE	SURROUNDING	WALL	TROUGH	PAVING	SHADE	(cm)
Cotoneaster microphyllus																												
Thymifolius	146			*			*		*				*		*		*	*	*	*				*				15
Skogholm	154			*		*				*			*		*		*	*	*	*				*				25
Cotula squalida	32, 166	*				*							*		*		*	*	*							*		30
Crocus ancyrensis	129		*			*	*					*			*		*	*	*	*								15
aureus	129		*			*	*		*						*		*	*	*	*								18
biflorus Alexandri	129		*			*	*		*						*		*	*	*	*								15
Weldenii	129		*			*	*		*						*		*	*	*	*								15
chrysanthus	129		*			*	*		*						*		*	*	*	*								10
Blue Bird	129		*			*	*		*						*		*	*	*	*								10
Blue Peter	129		*			*	*		*						*		*	*	*	*								10
Cream Beauty	129		*			*	*		*						*		*	*	*	*								10
E. P. Bowles	129		*			*	*		*						*		*	*	*	*								10
Lady Killer	129		*			*	*		*						*		*	*	*	*								10
Snow Bunting	129		*			*	*		*						*		*	*	*	*								10
Zwanenberg Bronze	129		*			*	*		*						*		*	*	*	*								10
dalmaticus	129		*			*	*		*						*		*	*	*	*								10
elwesii	117		*			*	*				*				*		*	*	*	*								15
fleischeri	129		*			*	*					*			*		*	*	*	*								15
goulimyi	117		*			*	*				*				*		*	*	*	*								10
imperati	117		*			*	*					*			*		*	*	*	*								18
iridiflorus	129		*			*	*				*				*		*	*	*	*								10
niveus	117		*			*	*				*				*		*	*	*	*								10
salzmannii	117		*			*	*				*				*		*	*	*	*								15
sativus	117		*			*	*				*				*		*	*	*	*								20
sieberi	117		*			*	*					*			*		*	*	*	*								15

		FORM							FLOWER					SOIL						SITE								HEIGHT
	Page No.	HERB	BULB	SHRUB	DWARF TREE	SPREADING	MOUND OR TUFT	UPRIGHT	SPRING	SUMMER	AUTUMN	WINTER	FOLIAGE EFFECT	GRITTY	NORMAL	PEATY	ACID	NEUTRAL	LIMY	GENERAL	SCREE	MORAINE	SURROUNDING	WALL	TROUGH	PAVING	SHADE	(cm)
susianus Cloth of Gold	129		*			*	*					*			*		*	*	*	*								13
tomasinianus	129		*			*	*		*						*		*	*	*	*								13
Whitewell Purple	129		*			*	*		*						*		*	*	*	*								13
versicolor	117		*			*	*		*						*		*	*	*	*								15
zonatus	129		*			*	*				*				*		*	*	*	*								10
Cryptomeria japonica Compressa	158				*		*						*		*		*	*	*	*					*			23
Globosa	158				*		*						*		*		*	*	*	*								45
Jindai Sugi	159				*		*						*		*		*	*	*	*								90
Nana Albospica	159				*		*						*		*		*	*	*	*								75
Pygmaea	159				*		*						*		*		*	*	*	*								150
Vilmoriniana	158				*		*						*		*		*	*	*	*								30
Cupressus glabra Compacta	181				*		*						*		*		*	*	*	*	*							25
macrocarpa Minima	184				*		*						*		*		*	*	*	*								90
Pygmaea	184				*		*	*					*		*		*	*	*	*								30
Cyananthus lobatus	148	*				*				*				*			*	*			*							10
Cyclamen coum	119		*			*						*			*		*	*	*	*							*	10
Roseum	119		*			*						*			*		*	*	*	*							*	10
hederifolium	116, 119		*			*					*				*		*	*	*	*							*	12
Album	119		*			*					*				*		*	*	*	*							*	12
repandum	119		*			*			*						*		*	*	*	*							*	8
Cymbalaria aequitriloba	108	*				*				*					*		*	*	*					*		*		8
hepaticifolia	108	*				*				*					*		*	*	*					*		*	*	8
muralis	80, 81	*				*				*					*		*	*	*	*				*			*	5

	Page No.	FORM							FLOWER					SOIL						SITE								HEIGHT
		HERB	BULB	SHRUB	DWARF TREE	SPREADING	MOUND OR TUFT	UPRIGHT	SPRING	SUMMER	AUTUMN	WINTER	FOLIAGE EFFECT	GRITTY	NORMAL	PEATY	ACID	NEUTRAL	LIMY	GENERAL	SCREE	MORAINE	SURROUNDING	WALL	TROUGH	PAVING	SHADE	(cm)
Cytisus ardoinii	64			*		*	*		*						*		*	*	*	*								15
austriacus	64			*			*			*	*				*		*	*	*	*								90
×*beanii*	64			*		*	*		*						*		*	*	*	*								38
decumbens	64			*		*			*						*		*	*	*	*								25
demissus	116			*		*	*		*						*		*	*	*	*								8
×*kewensis*	65			*		*			*						*		*	*	*	*				*				38
×*praecox*	65			*			*	*	*						*		*	*	*	*								120
prostratus	88			*		*			*						*		*	*	*	*								15
purpureus	65			*		*	*		*						*		*	*	*	*								45
Daboecia cantabrica CULTIVARS:																												
Alba	100			*		*	*		*	*	*					*	*			*								50
Atropurpurea	100			*		*	*		*	*	*					*	*			*								50
Bicolor	100			*		*	*		*	*	*					*	*			*								45
Globosa	100			*		*	*		*	*	*					*	*			*								60
Porter's Variety	100			*		*	*			*						*	*			*								15
Praegerae	100			*		*	*			*	*					*	*			*								38
Daphne collina	113			*			*		*	*					*		*	*	*	*								30
Neapolitana	113			*				*	*						*			*	*	*								50
petraea	113, 137			*		*			*	*				*				*	*		*	*			*			6
×*thauma*	113			*			*		*	*					*		*	*	*	*								22
Dianthus alpinus	46	*				*			*	*				*				*	*	*	*							8
callizonus	72	*				*				*				*					*		*	*			*			6
deltoides	72	*				*				*					*			*	*	*								15
gratianopolitanus	89	*				*			*	*					*			*	*	*	*							15
squarrosus	133	*				*				*					*			*	*	*								24
superbus	72	*				*				*					*			*	*	*								20
Digitalis purpurea	97	*					*	*		*					*		*	*		*			*				*	100

		FORM							FLOWER					SOIL						SITE								HEIG
	Page No.	HERB	BULB	SHRUB	DWARF TREE	SPREADING	MOUND OR TUFT	UPRIGHT	SPRING	SUMMER	AUTUMN	WINTER	FOLIAGE EFFECT	GRITTY	NORMAL	PEATY	ACID	NEUTRAL	LIMY	GENERAL	SCREE	MORAINE	SURROUNDING	WALL	TROUGH	PAVING	SHADE	(cm)
Dracocephalum hemsleyanum	143	*					*			*					*		*	*	*	*								30
Dryas octopetala	102, 104, 105			*		*			*						*		*	*	*	*								8
×*suendermannii*	102			*		*			*						*		*	*	*	*								10
Edraianthus pumilio	111	*					*			*				*			*	*	*		*				*			5
serpyllifolius	122	*				*				*				*				*	*		*							8
Eranthis cilicica	119		*			*			*			*			*		*	*	*	*							*	6
hyemalis	78		*			*			*			*			*		*	*	*	*							*	7
Erica arborea Alpina	125			*				*	*							*	*			*			*					200
australis Mr Robert	68			*				*	*							*	*			*			*					200
Riverslea	68			*				*	*							*	*			*			*					200
carnea (syn. *herbacea*) CULTIVARS:																												
Atrorubra	54			*		*	*		*						*		*	*	*	*								22
Aurea	54			*		*	*		*			*	*		*		*	*	*	*								20
December Red	54			*		*						*			*		*	*	*	*								20
Eileen Porter	53			*		*	*		*		*	*			*		*	*	*	*								15
King George V	54			*		*	*		*						*		*	*	*	*								22
Praecox Rubra	54			*		*	*					*			*		*	*	*	*								18
Ruby Glow	54			*		*	*		*						*		*	*	*	*								25
Springwood Pink	53			*		*			*			*			*		*	*	*	*								15
Springwood White	53			*		*			*			*			*		*	*	*	*								15
Vivellii	54			*		*	*		*			*	*		*		*	*	*	*								24
ciliaris CULTIVARS:																												
Maweana	68			*		*	*			*	*					*	*			*								45
Mrs C. H. Gill	68			*		*	*			*	*					*	*			*								30
Stoborough	68			*		*	*			*	*					*	*			*								60

	Page No.	FORM							FLOWER					SOIL						SITE								HEIGHT
		HERB	BULB	SHRUB	DWARF TREE	SPREADING	MOUND OR TUFT	UPRIGHT	SPRING	SUMMER	AUTUMN	WINTER	FOLIAGE EFFECT	GRITTY	NORMAL	PEATY	ACID	NEUTRAL	LIMY	GENERAL	SCREE	MORAINE	SURROUNDING	WALL	TROUGH	PAVING	SHADE	(cm)
Erica cinerea CULTIVARS:																												
Ann Berry	69			*		*	*			*			*		*	*	*			*								30
Apple Blossom	69			*		*	*			*					*	*	*			*								30
Atrorubens	69			*		*	*			*					*	*	*			*								24
Atrosanguinea	69			*		*	*			*					*	*	*			*								15
Coccinea	69			*		*	*			*					*	*	*			*					*	*		10
Domino	69			*		*	*			*					*	*	*			*								23
Eden Valley	69			*		*	*			*					*	*	*			*								15
Golden Drop	69			*		*	*			*			*		*	*	*			*								15
Janet	69			*		*	*			*					*	*	*			*								30
Joyce Burfitt	69			*		*	*			*					*	*	*			*								30
Mrs Dill	69			*		*	*			*					*	*	*			*					*	*		10
P. S. Patrick	69			*		*	*			*					*	*	*			*								38
Rose Queen	69			*		*	*			*	*				*	*	*			*								38
Velvet Night	69			*		*	*			*					*	*	*			*								30
hibernica CULTIVARS:																												
Brightness	100			*		*	*		*						*		*	*	*	*			*					100
Coccinea	100			*		*	*		*						*		*	*	*	*			*					60
W. T. Rackliff	100			*		*	*		*						*		*	*	*	*			*					75
hybrida CULTIVARS:																												
Arthur Johnson	70			*		*	*		*		*	*				*	*			*			*					75
ciliaris Hybrida	70			*		*	*			*	*					*	*			*								22
Darleyensis	70			*		*	*		*		*	*				*	*			*			*					60
Dawn	70			*		*	*			*	*					*	*			*								22
George Rendall	70			*		*	*		*	*		*				*	*			*			*					45
Gwen	70			*		*	*			*	*					*	*			*								15
H. Maxwell	70			*		*	*			*	*					*	*			*			*					45

	Page No.	FORM							FLOWER					SOIL						SITE								HEIGHT
		HERB	BULB	SHRUB	DWARF TREE	SPREADING	MOUND OR TUFT	UPRIGHT	SPRING	SUMMER	AUTUMN	WINTER	FOLIAGE EFFECT	GRITTY	NORMAL	PEATY	ACID	NEUTRAL	LIMY	GENERAL	SCREE	MORAINE	SURROUNDING	WALL	TROUGH	PAVING	SHADE	(cm)
N. R. Webster	70			*		*	*		*		*	*				*	*			*			*					60
Silberschmelze	70			*		*	*		*		*	*				*	*			*			*					60
mediterranea	68			*		*	*		*						*		*	*	*	*			*					135
Superba	68			*		*	*		*						*		*	*	*	*			*					135
tetralix CULTIVARS:																												
Alba Mollis	69			*		*	*			*	*		*			*	*			*								24
Con Underwood	69			*		*	*			*	*					*	*			*								24
L. E. Underwood	69			*		*	*			*	*					*	*			*								24
vagans CULTIVARS:																												
Lyonesse	70			*		*	*			*	*					*	*	*		*			*					75
Mrs. D. F. Maxwell	70			*		*	*			*	*					*	*	*		*			*					75
Pyrenees Pink	70			*		*	*			*	*					*	*	*		*			*					45
St Keverne	70			*		*	*			*	*					*	*	*		*			*					60
Erigeron aureus	188, 191	*					*			*				*			*	*	*		*				*			5
mucronatus	188	*				*				*				*	*		*	*	*	*				*				23
Erinus alpinus	58	*					*		*						*		*	*	*					*		*		15
Eriophyllum lanatum	189	*					*			*					*		*	*	*	*				*				19
Erysimum alpinum	62	*					*		*						*		*	*	*	*			*					15
helveticum	62	*					*			*				*	*		*	*	*	*	*							8
Erythronium albidum	197		*			*			*							*	*	*	*	*							*	13
americanum	197		*			*			*							*	*	*	*	*							*	10
dens-canis	133, 140		*			*			*							*	*	*	*	*							*	15
Rose Beauty	140		*			*			*							*	*	*	*	*							*	15
White Splendour	140		*			*			*							*	*	*	*	*							*	15
japonicum	163		*			*			*							*	*	*	*	*							*	15

	Page No.	FORM							FLOWER					SOIL						SITE								HEIGHT
		HERB	BULB	SHRUB	DWARF TREE	SPREADING	MOUND OR TUFT	UPRIGHT	SPRING	SUMMER	AUTUMN	WINTER	FOLIAGE EFFECT	GRITTY	NORMAL	PEATY	ACID	NEUTRAL	LIMY	GENERAL	SCREE	MORAINE	SURROUNDING	WALL	TROUGH	PAVING	SHADE	(cm)
Euonymus radicans	162			*		*							*		*		*	*	*	*			*	*			*	25
Coloratus	162			*		*							*		*		*	*	*	*			*	*			*	25
Minimus	162			*		*							*		*		*	*	*	*			*	*			*	13
Variegatus	162			*		*							*		*		*	*	*	*			*	*			*	25
Euphorbia myrsinites	104, 108			*		*				*					*		*	*	*	*				*				15
Fabiana imbricata Prostrata	171			*			*		*	*				*	*		*	*		*				*				35
×*Fatshedera lizei*	94			*		*					*				*		*	*	*	*				*			*	30
Festuca alpina (GRASS)	43	*					*						*		*		*	*	*	*								10
glacialis (GRASS)	43	*					*						*		*		*	*	*	*								15
ovina Glauca (GRASS)	102	*					*						*		*		*	*	*	*								23
Frankenia laevis	84	*				*				*				*			*	*	*	*	*					*		3
Fritillaria bithynica	114		*			*	*		*						*		*	*	*	*								23
camschatcensis	140		*			*	*		*					*			*	*	*	*		*					*	23
The Black Knight	140		*			*	*		*					*			*	*	*	*		*					*	23
crassifolia	128		*			*	*		*						*		*	*	*	*								18
Galanthus elwesii	130		*			*						*			*		*	*	*	*								20
Cassaba	130		*			*						*			*		*	*	*	*								20
nivalis	129, 130		*			*			*			*			*		*	*	*	*								13
Plena	129		*			*						*			*		*	*	*	*								13
S. Arnott	129		*			*						*			*		*	*	*	*								13
Viridapicis	129		*			*						*			*		*	*	*	*								13
plicatus	130		*			*			*			*			*		*	*	*	*								15
Galax urceolata	197	*				*				*			*			*	*	*		*			*				*	30
Gaultheria procumbens	196			*		*				*			*			*	*						*				*	12

		FORM							FLOWER					SOIL						SITE								HEIGHT
	Page No.	HERB	BULB	SHRUB	DWARF TREE	SPREADING	MOUND OR TUFT	UPRIGHT	SPRING	SUMMER	AUTUMN	WINTER	FOLIAGE EFFECT	GRITTY	NORMAL	PEATY	ACID	NEUTRAL	LIMY	GENERAL	SCREE	MORAINE	SURROUNDING	WALL	TROUGH	PAVING	SHADE	(cm)
Genista delphinensis	107			*		*				*					*		*	*	*	*				*				8
hispanica	64			*				*		*					*		*	*	*	*								60
lydia	123			*			*		*						*		*	*	*	*								50
pilosa	64			*		*	*		*	*					*		*	*	*	*								30
pulchella	107			*		*	*			*					*		*	*	*	*				*				4
sagittalis	64, 65			*		*				*					*		*	*	*	*				*				10
Minor	64			*		*				*					*		*	*	*	*				*				8
sylvestris	64			*		*	*			*					*		*	*	*	*				*				15
tinctoria Plena	88			*				*		*					*		*	*	*				*					30
Gentiana acaulis	73	*					*		*						*		*	*	*	*		*						10
alpina	44	*					*			*					*		*	*	*	*		*						10
angustifolia	44	*					*			*					*		*	*	*	*		*						9
farreri	145	*				*	*				*			*			*	*				*						10
saxosa	167	*					*			*				*	*		*	*	*		*				*			10
septemfida	201	*				*	*			*					*		*	*	*	*		*						15
sino-ornata	145, 174	*				*					*				*		*			*		*						10
verna	73, 103	*					*		*					*			*	*	*	*					*			8
Geranium celticum	80	*					*			*					*		*	*	*	*				*	*			5
lucidum	80	*					*		*	*	*			*	*		*	*	*	*				*				20
robertianum	80	*					*		*	*	*				*		*	*	*	*				*				20
sanguineum	97, 104	*					*			*				*	*				*	*				*				15
Geum reptans	46	*				*				*				*		*	*	*				*						20
Glechoma hederacea Variegata	93	*				*							*		*		*	*	*				*	*			*	5
Globularia bellidifolia	110	*				*				*					*				*	*	*			*		*		10
cordifolia	41	*				*				*					*				*	*								20

		FORM							FLOWER					SOIL						SITE								HEIGHT
	Page No.	HERB	BULB	SHRUB	DWARF TREE	SPREADING	MOUND OR TUFT	UPRIGHT	SPRING	SUMMER	AUTUMN	WINTER	FOLIAGE EFFECT	GRITTY	NORMAL	PEATY	ACID	NEUTRAL	LIMY	GENERAL	SCREE	MORAINE	SURROUNDING	WALL	TROUGH	PAVING	SHADE	(cm)
Globularia incanescens	110	*				*				*					*				*	*	*			*				20
Gymnocarpium dryopteris (FERN)	95, 96	*				*	*						*		*	*	*	*		*				*				20
Gypsophila repens	46	*				*				*				*	*			*	*			*						15
Hebe Blue Gem	166			*			*		*	*			*		*		*	*	*	*								35
Bowles Hybrid	166			*			*		*	*			*		*		*	*	*	*								25
buchananii	165			*			*		*	*			*		*		*	*	*	*								20
Edinensis	166			*			*		*	*			*		*		*	*	*	*								23
epacridea	165			*		*				*			*		*		*	*	*	*	*							30
pinguifolia Pagei	165			*		*			*				*		*		*	*	*	*								20
rakaiensis	165			*		*	*			*			*		*		*	*	*	*								30
Hedera helix Congesta	94			*		*	*						*		*		*	*	*					*	*		*	10
Conglomerata	94			*		*	*						*		*		*	*	*					*	*		*	10
Helianthemum nummularium	87			*		*	*			*				*	*		*	*	*	*	*			*				18
Ben Dearg	88			*		*	*			*				*	*		*	*	*	*	*			*				18
Ben Fhada	88			*		*	*			*				*	*		*	*	*	*	*			*				18
Ben Hope	88			*		*	*			*				*	*		*	*	*	*	*			*				18
Ben Ledi	88			*		*	*			*				*	*		*	*	*	*	*			*				18
Ben More	88			*		*	*			*				*	*		*	*	*	*	*			*				18
Ben Nevis	88			*		*	*			*				*	*		*	*	*	*	*			*				18
Red Dragon	88			*		*	*			*				*	*		*	*	*	*	*			*				18
Rhodanthe Carneum	88			*		*	*			*				*	*		*	*	*	*	*			*				18
The Bride	88			*		*	*			*				*	*		*	*	*	*	*			*				18
Watergate Rose	88			*		*	*			*				*	*		*	*	*	*	*			*				18
Wisley Primrose	88			*		*	*			*				*	*		*	*	*	*	*			*				18
Helichrysum bellidioides	168, 174	*				*				*				*			*	*	*	*	*							8
milfordiae	168	*				*				*				*			*	*	*		*							8

	Page No.	FORM: HERB	BULB	SHRUB	DWARF TREE	SPREADING	MOUND OR TUFT	UPRIGHT	FLOWER: SPRING	SUMMER	AUTUMN	WINTER	FOLIAGE EFFECT	SOIL: GRITTY	NORMAL	PEATY	ACID	NEUTRAL	LIMY	SITE: GENERAL	SCREE	MORAINE	SURROUNDING	WALL	TROUGH	PAVING	SHADE	HEIGHT (cm)
Hepatica×media Ballardii	75	*					*		*						*				*	*							*	13
Herniaria glabra	89	*				*				*			*	*	*		*	*	*	*	*					*		5
Houstonia caerulea	198	*				*				*					*		*	*	*	*				*			*	8
Hypericum androsaemum	95			*			*			*					*		*	*	*				*				*	75
coris	108			*			*			*					*				*	*				*				15
empetrifolium Prostratum	115			*		*				*				*	*		*	*	*	*	*				*			5
humifusum	96			*		*				*					*		*	*	*	*								13
olympicum	114, 115			*			*			*					*		*	*	*	*								15
Citrinum	115			*			*			*					*		*	*	*	*								15
reptans	143			*		*			*	*					*		*	*	*	*				*				8
rhodopeum	123			*		*			*	*					*		*	*	*	*								13
Iberis sempervirens	108, 109			*		*			*	*					*		*	*	*	*				*				15
Pink Variety	108			*		*			*	*					*		*	*	*	*				*				15
Snowflake	108			*		*			*	*					*		*	*	*	*				*				15
Inula ensifolia	125	*					*			*					*		*	*	*	*								30
Iris cristata	192, 198	*				*			*					*			*	*	*			*						15
innominata	174, 186	*				*				*				*			*	*	*			*						15
pumila	72	*				*			*	*					*				*	*								10
unguicularis	106	*					*					*		*	*		*	*	*	*			*					28
Jasminum parkeri	140			*			*			*					*		*	*	*	*								24
Jovibarba arenaria	122	*					*			*			*		*		*	*	*	*								23
heuffelii	123	*					*			*			*		*		*	*	*	*								15
hirta	42	*					*			*			*		*		*	*	*	*								13
sobolifera	74	*					*			*			*		*		*	*	*	*					*			5

	Page No.	FORM: HERB	BULB	SHRUB	DWARF TREE	SPREADING	MOUND OR TUFT	UPRIGHT	FLOWER: SPRING	SUMMER	AUTUMN	WINTER	FOLIAGE EFFECT	SOIL: GRITTY	NORMAL	PEATY	ACID	NEUTRAL	LIMY	SITE: GENERAL	SCREE	MORAINE	SURROUNDING	WALL	TROUGH	PAVING	SHADE	HEIGHT (cm)
Juniperus chinensis Japonica	144				*	*							*		*		*	*	*	*								100
Mountbatten	144				*			*					*		*		*	*	*	*								200
communis CULTIVARS:																												
Compressa	101				*			*					*		*		*	*	*	*					*			30
Depressa	177				*	*							*		*		*	*	*	*								45
Depressa Aurea	177				*	*							*		*		*	*	*	*								45
Dumosa	177				*	*							*		*		*	*	*	*								45
Effusa	178				*	*							*		*		*	*	*	*								60
Hibernica	100, 194				*			*					*		*		*	*	*	*								100
Hornibrookii	101				*	*							*		*		*	*	*	*								10
Montana	101				*	*							*		*		*	*	*	*								15
Repanda	101				*	*							*		*		*	*	*	*								60
conferta	161				*	*							*		*		*	*	*	*								38
horizontalis CULTIVARS:																												
Bar Harbor	178				*	*							*		*		*	*	*	*								25
Coast of Maine	178				*	*							*		*		*	*	*	*								30
Douglasii	178				*	*	*						*		*		*	*	*	*								45
Montana	178				*	*							*		*		*	*	*	*								37
Wiltonii	178				*	*							*		*		*	*	*	*								25
×*media* CULTIVARS:																												
Blue Cloud	136				*	*		*					*		*		*	*	*	*								120
Old Gold	136				*	*		*					*		*		*	*	*	*								150
Pfitzeriana	136				*	*		*					*		*		*	*	*	*								200
Pfitzeriana Aurea	136				*	*		*					*		*		*	*	*	*								180
Pfitzeriana Glauca	136				*	*		*					*		*		*	*	*	*								125
Plumosa	139				*	*	*						*		*		*	*	*	*								105
Plumosa Aurea	139				*	*		*					*		*		*	*	*	*								100

	Page No.	FORM							FLOWER					SOIL						SITE								HEIGHT
		HERB	BULB	SHRUB	DWARF TREE	SPREADING	MOUND OR TUFT	UPRIGHT	SPRING	SUMMER	AUTUMN	WINTER	FOLIAGE EFFECT	GRITTY	NORMAL	PEATY	ACID	NEUTRAL	LIMY	GENERAL	SCREE	MORAINE	SURROUNDING	WALL	TROUGH	PAVING	SHADE	(cm)
procumbens	161				*	*							*		*		*	*	*	*								25
Nana	161				*	*							*		*		*	*	*	*								23
recurva Embley Park	144				*	*	*						*		*		*	*	*	*								120
sabina CULTIVARS:																												
Blue Danube	56				*	*	*						*		*		*	*	*	*								40
Skandia	55, 56				*	*							*		*		*	*	*	*								20
Tamariscifolia	55, 56				*	*							*		*		*	*	*	*								40
Von Ehren	56				*	*	*						*		*		*	*	*	*								120
scopulorum CULTIVARS:																												
Hill's Silver	181				*			*					*		*		*	*	*	*								95
Pathfinder	181				*		*	*					*		*		*	*	*	*								120
Repens	181				*	*							*		*		*	*	*	*								25
Springbank	181				*			*					*		*		*	*	*	*								120
squamata CULTIVARS:																												
Blue Star	144				*		*						*		*		*	*	*	*								110
Meyeri	144				*			*					*		*		*	*	*	*								180
Wilsonii	144				*		*	*					*		*		*	*	*	*								100
virginiana CULTIVARS:																												
Globosa	194				*		*						*		*		*	*	*	*								60
Grey Owl	194				*	*	*						*		*		*	*	*	*								90
Hillii	194				*			*					*		*		*	*	*	*								180
Manhattan Blue	194				*		*	*					*		*		*	*	*	*								120
Skyrocket	194				*			*					*		*		*	*	*	*								200
Kentranthus ruber	80	*					*			*					*		*	*	*					*				60
Lamiastrum galeobdolon Variegatum	92	*				*			*	*			*		*		*	*	*				*				*	22

		FORM							FLOWER					SOIL						SITE								HEIGHT
	Page No.	HERB	BULB	SHRUB	DWARF TREE	SPREADING	MOUND OR TUFT	UPRIGHT	SPRING	SUMMER	AUTUMN	WINTER	FOLIAGE EFFECT	GRITTY	NORMAL	PEATY	ACID	NEUTRAL	LIMY	GENERAL	SCREE	MORAINE	SURROUNDING	WALL	TROUGH	PAVING	SHADE	(cm)
Lamium maculatum	22, 93	*				*			*				*		*		*	*	*				*				*	25
Larix decidua Corley	49				*		*						*		*		*	*	*	*								45
Lavandula stoechas	110			*			*			*					*			*	*	*			*	*				90
Leontopodium alpinum	41, 43	*					*		*						*		*	*	*	*								15
haplophylloides	144	*					*		*				*		*		*	*	*	*								15
Lewisia CULTIVARS:	187																											
Birch Hybrids	187	*					*		*	*				*			*	*		*		*						19
George Henley	187	*					*		*	*				*			*	*		*		*						19
Rose Splendour	187	*					*		*	*				*			*	*		*		*						19
Sunset Strain	187	*					*		*	*				*			*	*		*		*						19
Trevosia	187	*					*		*	*				*			*	*		*		*						19
Winifred Herdman	187	*					*		*	*				*			*	*		*		*						19
Linaria alpina	42	*				*				*					*		*	*	*	*				*				8
glacialis	73	*				*				*				*			*	*	*		*			*				5
tristis	73	*				*				*				*			*	*	*		*			*				8
Linnaea borealis	101, 102	*				*			*							*	*	*	*				*				*	5
Linum arboreum	112			*			*		*						*		*	*	*	*	*							30
campanulatum	112			*			*			*					*		*	*	*	*	*							30
Gemmell's Hybrid	112			*			*			*				*			*	*	*		*				*			22
narbonense	112			*			*		*	*					*		*	*	*	*	*							50
Lippia canescens	32, 169	*				*				*					*		*	*	*	*				*		*		4
Lithodora diffusa (syn. *Lithospermum prostratum)*	109			*		*			*	*					*		*	*		*	*			*				8
Grace Ward	109, 137			*		*			*	*					*		*	*		*	*			*				8

	Page No.	FORM							FLOWER					SOIL						SITE								HEIGHT
		HERB	BULB	SHRUB	DWARF TREE	SPREADING	MOUND OR TUFT	UPRIGHT	SPRING	SUMMER	AUTUMN	WINTER	FOLIAGE EFFECT	GRITTY	NORMAL	PEATY	ACID	NEUTRAL	LIMY	GENERAL	SCREE	MORAINE	SURROUNDING	WALL	TROUGH	PAVING	SHADE	(cm)
Heavenly Blue	109			*		*			*	*					*		*	*		*	*			*				8
Luetkea pectinata	185			*		*				*					*	*	*	*		*		*					*	20
Lychnis alpina	73	*					*			*					*		*	*	*	*								9
flos-jovis	123	*					*			*					*		*	*	*	*								30
Lysimachia japonica Minuta	163	*				*				*					*		*	*	*					*		*	*	2
nummularia	91	*				*				*					*		*	*	*					*			*	5
Aurea	91	*				*				*					*		*	*	*					*			*	5
Maianthemum bifolium	180	*				*			*						*		*	*	*	*			*				*	9
Margyricarpus setosus	170			*		*				*			*		*		*	*	*	*	*							28
Mentha pulegium	111	*				*				*	*				*		*	*	*	*								15
requienii	111	*				*				*	*				*		*	*	*			*						8
Merendera sobolifera	129		*			*	*		*			*			*		*	*	*	*								15
Micromeria varia	32, 111			*			*			*			*		*		*	*	*		*					*		23
Mimulus cupreus	170	*					*		*	*					*		*	*	*	*			*					25
primuloides	189, 191	*				*			*	*				*			*	*	*			*						10
Minuartia verna	44	*					*		*					*			*	*	*		*				*			3
Mitchella repens	196			*		*			*							*	*	*		*							*	8
Moltkia petraea	110			*			*			*					*		*	*	*	*	*			*				18
Muscari ambrosiacum	130		*			*			*						*		*	*	*	*								23
armeniacum	130		*			*			*						*		*	*	*	*								15
azureum	130		*			*			*	*					*		*	*	*	*								15
macrocarpum	119		*			*			*						*		*	*	*	*								15

	Page No.	FORM							FLOWER					SOIL						SITE								HEIGHT
		HERB	BULB	SHRUB	DWARF TREE	SPREADING	MOUND OR TUFT	UPRIGHT	SPRING	SUMMER	AUTUMN	WINTER	FOLIAGE EFFECT	GRITTY	NORMAL	PEATY	ACID	NEUTRAL	LIMY	GENERAL	SCREE	MORAINE	SURROUNDING	WALL	TROUGH	PAVING	SHADE	(cm)
Muscari neglectum	119		*			*			*						*		*	*	*	*								15
tubergenianum	130		*			*			*						*		*	*	*	*								20
Myosotis alpestris	54, 81	*					*			*					*		*	*	*	*								15
discolor	81	*					*			*				*	*		*	*	*	*								22
hispida	81	*					*		*	*				*	*		*	*	*	*				*				20
Narcissus asturiensis	76		*			*	*		*						*		*	*	*	*								13
Bambi	78		*			*	*		*						*		*	*	*	*								15
bulbocodium Conspicuus	76		*			*	*		*						*		*	*	*	*								15
Nivalis	76		*			*	*		*			*			*		*	*	*	*		*						8
canaliculatus	78		*			*	*		*			*			*		*	*	*	*								18
cyclamineus	76		*			*	*		*						*		*	*	*	*		*					*	18
lobularis	77		*			*	*		*						*		*	*	*	*								20
nanus	77		*			*	*		*						*		*	*	*	*								15
pseudo-narcissus	76, 77		*			*	*		*						*		*	*	*	*							*	30
rupicola	78		*			*	*		*						*		*	*	*	*								15
scaberulus	78		*			*	*		*						*		*	*	*	*								23
triandrus Albus	76		*			*	*		*						*		*	*	*	*								15
Concolor	76		*			*	*		*						*		*	*	*	*							*	15
watieri	106		*			*	*		*						*		*	*	*	*	*							10
Oenothera missouriensis	195	*				*				*					*		*	*	*	*			*					23
Omphalodes cappadocica	124	*				*	*		*	*					*		*	*	*	*		*		*				22
verna	60	*				*	*		*						*		*	*	*	*		*					*	15
Onosma taurica	109	*					*			*				*			*	*	*	*				*				23
Origanum vulgare	87	*					*		*						*		*	*	*	*			*					38
Aureum	87	*					*		*				*		*		*	*	*	*			*					38

	Page No.	FORM							FLOWER					SOIL						SITE								HEIGHT
		HERB	BULB	SHRUB	DWARF TREE	SPREADING	MOUND OR TUFT	UPRIGHT	SPRING	SUMMER	AUTUMN	WINTER	FOLIAGE EFFECT	GRITTY	NORMAL	PEATY	ACID	NEUTRAL	LIMY	GENERAL	SCREE	MORAINE	SURROUNDING	WALL	TROUGH	PAVING	SHADE	(cm)
Oxalis acetosella	97, 169	*	*			*			*						*	*	*	*	*	*							*	8
Rosea	97	*	*			*			*						*	*	*	*	*	*							*	8
adenophylla	170	*	*				*		*						*		*	*	*	*		*						13
chrysantha	169	*	*			*				*					*		*	*	*			*						6
enneaphylla	169	*	*			*			*	*					*	*	*	*	*	*		*		*				5
magellanica	169	*	*			*			*						*		*	*	*			*		*				2
oregana	169, 189	*	*			*	*			*					*		*	*	*	*				*				13
Papaver alpinum	43	*					*		*					*			*	*	*	*								23
Parahebe catarractae	166			*		*				*					*		*	*	*	*								30
Diffusa	166			*		*				*					*		*	*	*	*								23
Paris quadrifolia	91	*				*			*	*				*	*		*	*	*	*			*				*	30
Parnassia palustris	97	*					*			*					*	*	*	*	*				*					20
Penstemon roezlii	187	*				*	*			*					*		*	*	*	*								25
menziesii	187	*					*			*					*		*	*	*	*								25
newberryi	187	*					*			*					*		*	*	*	*								30
scouleri	187	*					*			*					*		*	*	*	*								25
Petrocallis pyrenaica	45	*					*		*					*			*	*	*		*							5
Philesia magellanica	170, 171			*		*				*						*	*	*									*	22
Phlox douglasii Boothman's Variety	189	*					*		*						*		*	*	*						*			5
May Snow	189	*					*		*						*		*	*	*						*			8
Rose Cushion	189	*					*		*						*		*	*	*						*			8
stolonifera Blue Ridge	199	*				*			*						*		*	*	*	*								23
subulata Atropurpurea	199	*				*			*	*					*		*	*	*	*				*				15
Betty	199	*				*			*	*					*		*	*	*	*				*				13

		FORM							FLOWER					SOIL						SITE								HEIGHT
	Page No.	HERB	BULB	SHRUB	DWARF TREE	SPREADING	MOUND OR TUFT	UPRIGHT	SPRING	SUMMER	AUTUMN	WINTER	FOLIAGE EFFECT	GRITTY	NORMAL	PEATY	ACID	NEUTRAL	LIMY	GENERAL	SCREE	MORAINE	SURROUNDING	WALL	TROUGH	PAVING	SHADE	(cm)
Phlox subulata G. F. Wilson	199	*				*			*	*					*		*	*	*	*				*				15
Sensation	199	*				*			*	*					*		*	*	*	*				*				15
Temiscaming	192, 199	*				*			*	*					*		*	*	*	*				*				10
Phuopsis stylosa	124	*				*				*					*		*	*	*	*								25
Phyllitis scolopendrium (FERN)	97, 98	*				*	*						*		*		*	*	*	*							*	30
Picea abies Capitata	50				*		*						*		*		*	*	*	*								90
Doone Valley	49				*		*						*		*		*	*	*	*					*			15
Echiniformis	49				*		*						*		*		*	*	*	*								10
Effusa	50				*		*						*		*		*	*	*	*								38
Gregoryana	50				*		*						*		*		*	*	*	*								40
Humilis	49				*		*						*		*		*	*	*	*								15
Little Gem	50				*		*						*		*		*	*	*	*								45
Nidiformis	50				*	*	*						*		*		*	*	*	*								60
Procumbens	50				*	*	*						*		*		*	*	*	*								38
Pygmaea	49				*		*						*		*		*	*	*	*								15
glauca Albertiana Conica	175				*		*	*					*		*		*	*	*	*								90
Echiniformis	175				*		*						*		*		*	*	*	*								30
Nana	175				*		*						*		*		*	*	*	*								60
mariana Nana	175				*		*						*		*		*	*	*	*								45
omorika Nana	50				*		*						*		*		*	*	*	*								95
pungens Globosa	181				*		*						*		*		*	*	*	*								60
Montgomery	181				*		*						*		*		*	*	*	*								90
Procumbens	182				*	*	*						*		*		*	*	*	*								30
Pimelea prostrata	166			*		*			*							*	*	*			*							6

	Page No.	FORM: HERB	FORM: BULB	FORM: SHRUB	FORM: DWARF TREE	FORM: SPREADING	FORM: MOUND OR TUFT	FORM: UPRIGHT	FLOWER: SPRING	FLOWER: SUMMER	FLOWER: AUTUMN	FLOWER: WINTER	FLOWER: FOLIAGE EFFECT	SOIL: GRITTY	SOIL: NORMAL	SOIL: PEATY	SOIL: ACID	SOIL: NEUTRAL	SOIL: LIMY	SITE: GENERAL	SITE: SCREE	SITE: MORAINE	SITE: SURROUNDING	SITE: WALL	SITE: TROUGH	SITE: PAVING	SITE: SHADE	HEIGHT (cm)
Pinus cembra Jermyns	53				*		*						*		*		*	*	*	*								30
densiflora Umbraculifera	157				*		*	*					*		*		*			*								95
mugo Gnom	51, 53				*		*						*		*		*	*	*	*								60
Mops	53				*		*						*		*		*	*	*	*								45
nigra Hornibrookiana	50				*		*	*					*		*		*	*	*	*								60
Pygmaea	53				*		*						*		*		*	*	*	*								120
parviflora Adcock's Dwarf	157				*		*						*		*		*	*	*	*								95
pumila Compacta	136				*			*					*		*		*			*								150
strobus Nana	195				*		*						*		*		*			*								180
Prostrata	195				*	*							*		*		*			*								60
sylvestris Beuvronensis	101				*		*	*					*		*		*	*	*	*								90
Compressa	102				*		*						*		*		*	*	*	*								100
Doone Valley	102				*		*	*					*		*		*	*	*	*								90
Windsor	102				*		*						*		*		*	*	*	*								45
Platycodon grandiflorus	133	*					*			*					*		*	*	*	*								30
Apoyama	133	*					*			*					*		*	*	*	*								15
Mariesii	133	*					*			*					*		*	*	*	*								25
Mother of Pearl	133	*					*			*					*		*	*	*	*								30
Podocarpus alpinus	171				*	*	*						*		*		*	*	*	*								10
nivalis	171				*	*	*						*		*		*	*	*	*								15
Aureus	171				*	*	*						*		*		*	*	*	*								15
Polemonium cönfertum	189	*					*			*				*	*		*	*	*	*		*						17
Polygala chamaebuxus	59	*				*			*							*	*	*	*	*							*	10
Grandiflora	60	*				*			*							*	*	*	*	*							*	13
Polygonatum hookeri	147	*						*	*						*	*	*	*	*	*							*	10

		FORM							FLOWER					SOIL						SITE								HEIGHT
	Page No.	HERB	BULB	SHRUB	DWARF TREE	SPREADING	MOUND OR TUFT	UPRIGHT	SPRING	SUMMER	AUTUMN	WINTER	FOLIAGE EFFECT	GRITTY	NORMAL	PEATY	ACID	NEUTRAL	LIMY	GENERAL	SCREE	MORAINE	SURROUNDING	WALL	TROUGH	PAVING	SHADE	(cm)
Polygonum affine	142, 147	*				*					*				*		*	*	*	*								23
Darjeeling Red	147	*				*					*				*		*	*	*	*								15
Lowndes Variety	147	*				*					*				*		*	*	*	*								15
tenuicaule	163	*				*			*						*		*	*	*	*							*	13
vaccinifolium	147	*				*					*				*		*	*	*	*				*				15
Polypodium vulgare (FERN)	95	*				*	*						*		*	*	*	*	*	*		*		*			*	25
Potentilla alba	57	*				*			*	*					*		*	*	*	*								8
aurea	57	*				*				*					*		*	*	*	*								8
Fireflame	57	*				*			*	*					*		*	*	*	*								5
fruticosa Beanii	56			*			*		*	*	*				*		*	*	*	*			*					60
Buttercup	133			*			*		*	*	*				*		*	*	*	*			*					90
Gold Drop	133			*			*		*	*	*				*		*	*	*	*			*					75
Hurstbourne	56			*			*		*	*	*				*		*	*	*	*			*					60
Klondyke	133			*			*		*	*	*				*		*	*	*	*			*					65
Longacre	56			*			*		*	*	*				*		*	*	*	*			*					25
mandshurica	133			*			*		*	*	*				*		*	*	*	*			*					25
Minstead Dwarf	56			*			*		*	*	*				*		*	*	*	*			*					30
Moonlight	56			*			*		*	*	*				*		*	*	*	*			*					90
Red Ace	56			*			*		*	*	*				*		*	*	*	*			*				*	60
Tangerine	56			*			*		*	*	*				*		*	*	*	*			*				*	75
nitida	51, 57	*				*				*				*					*		*							8
Lissadell	57	*				*				*				*					*		*							8
Rubra	57	*				*				*				*					*		*							8
tabernaemontani Nana	57	*				*			*	*					*		*	*	*	*					*			2
ternata	57	*				*				*					*		*	*	*	*								7
×*tonguei*	57	*				*				*					*		*	*	*	*								10
Pratia angulata	167	*				*				*					*		*	*	*	*							*	5

	Page No.	FORM: HERB	BULB	SHRUB	DWARF TREE	SPREADING	MOUND OR TUFT	UPRIGHT	FLOWER: SPRING	SUMMER	AUTUMN	WINTER	FOLIAGE EFFECT	SOIL: GRITTY	NORMAL	PEATY	ACID	NEUTRAL	LIMY	SITE: GENERAL	SCREE	MORAINE	SURROUNDING	WALL	TROUGH	PAVING	SHADE	HEIGHT (cm)
Primula agleniana	148	*				*	*		*						*		*	*	*	*								30
alpicola	148	*				*	*		*						*	*	*	*	*			*					*	30
amoena	126	*				*	*		*						*		*	*	*	*								12
aurantiaca	150	*				*	*			*					*		*	*	*	*							*	30
auricula	61, 85, 200	*				*	*		*						*		*	*	*	*								25
beesiana	150	*				*	*		*	*					*		*	*	*	*							*	20
bellidifolia	148	*				*	*		*						*		*	*	*	*								15
bracteosa	148	*				*	*		*						*		*	*	*	*								18
bulleyana	150	*				*	*			*					*		*	*	*	*							*	30
burmanica	134	*				*	*			*					*		*	*	*	*			*					60
calderiana	149	*				*	*		*						*		*	*	*	*								38
capitata	149	*				*	*			*					*		*	*	*	*								23
carniolica	61	*				*	*		*						*		*	*	*	*							*	18
chionantha	150	*				*	*		*						*		*	*	*	*							*	38
chungensis	149	*				*	*			*					*		*	*	*	*			*					50
clarkei	134, 173	*				*	*		*						*		*	*	*	*		*			*			6
denticulata	150	*				*	*		*						*		*	*	*	*			*				*	30
edgeworthii	149	*				*	*		*						*		*	*	*	*								8
elatior	92	*				*	*		*						*		*	*	*	*								15
farinosa	36, 92	*				*	*		*						*		*	*	*	*		*						28
forrestii	152	*				*	*		*					*	*		*	*	*		*			*				20
glutinosa	61	*				*	*		*						*		*	*		*								8
helodoxa	134	*				*	*			*					*		*	*	*				*					90
japonica	163	*				*	*		*						*		*	*	*				*					45
juliae	126, 155	*				*	*		*						*	*	*	*	*	*							*	5
marginata	61, 85	*				*	*		*						*		*	*	*	*								9
melanops	150	*				*	*		*						*		*	*	*	*								20

		FORM							FLOWER					SOIL						SITE								HEIGHT
	Page No.	HERB	BULB	SHRUB	DWARF TREE	SPREADING	MOUND OR TUFT	UPRIGHT	SPRING	SUMMER	AUTUMN	WINTER	FOLIAGE EFFECT	GRITTY	NORMAL	PEATY	ACID	NEUTRAL	LIMY	GENERAL	SCREE	MORAINE	SURROUNDING	WALL	TROUGH	PAVING	SHADE	(cm)
Primula nutans	152	*				*	*			*					*		*	*	*	*								28
palinuri	61	*				*	*		*						*				*	*	*							18
polyneura	151	*				*	*		*						*		*	*	*	*								25
rosea	148	*				*	*		*						*		*	*	*	*							*	8
scapigera	149	*				*	*		*						*		*	*	*	*								8
scotica	92	*				*	*		*						*		*	*	*			*						10
sieboldii	163	*				*	*		*						*		*	*	*	*							*	18
sonchifolia	149	*				*	*		*			*			*		*	*	*	*								25
spectabilis	61	*				*	*		*						*		*	*	*	*								5
veris	91	*				*	*		*						*		*	*	*	*								15
vialii	151	*				*	*			*					*		*	*	*	*			*					45
vulgaris	91, 92, 125	*				*	*		*						*		*	*	*	*							*	10
Prunella vulgaris	91	*				*				*					*		*	*	*	*			*					30
Lilac Loveliness	91	*				*				*					*		*	*	*	*			*					22
Pink Loveliness	91	*				*				*					*		*	*	*	*			*					30
White Loveliness	91	*				*				*					*		*	*	*	*			*					26
Red Riding Hood	91	*				*				*					*		*	*	*	*			*					25
Prunus prostrata	113			*		*	*		*						*		*	*	*	*								60
Pseudotsuga menziesii Brevifolia	176				*		*	*					*		*		*			*								110
Fletcheri	176				*		*						*		*		*			*								95
Holmstrup	176				*		*	*					*		*		*			*								120
Nana	176				*		*	*					*		*		*			*								90
Pterocephalus parnassi	115	*				*	*			*					*		*	*	*	*				*				8
Pulsatilla alpina	47, 48	*					*		*						*			*	*	*		*						25
occidentalis	188	*					*			*					*			*	*	*								30

	Page No.	FORM: HERB	FORM: BULB	FORM: SHRUB	FORM: DWARF TREE	FORM: SPREADING	FORM: MOUND OR TUFT	FORM: UPRIGHT	FLOWER: SPRING	FLOWER: SUMMER	FLOWER: AUTUMN	FLOWER: WINTER	FLOWER: FOLIAGE EFFECT	SOIL: GRITTY	SOIL: NORMAL	SOIL: PEATY	SOIL: ACID	SOIL: NEUTRAL	SOIL: LIMY	SITE: GENERAL	SITE: SCREE	SITE: MORAINE	SITE: SURROUNDING	SITE: WALL	SITE: TROUGH	SITE: PAVING	SITE: SHADE	HEIGHT (cm)
vernalis	47, 48	*				*	*		*						*			*	*	*								10
vulgaris	88	*					*		*						*			*	*	*								18
Puschkinia libanotica	131		*			*	*		*						*		*	*	*	*								18
Alba	131		*			*	*		*						*		*	*	*	*								18
Pyrola minor	91	*				*				*					*		*	*	*	*							*	20
Ramonda myconi	53, 60	*					*		*	*				*			*	*	*					*			*	15
Alba	60	*					*		*	*				*			*	*	*					*			*	15
Rosea	60	*					*		*	*				*			*	*	*					*			*	15
nathaliae	60	*					*		*					*			*	*	*					*			*	15
Ranunculus alpestris	47	*					*		*	*				*			*	*	*			*						10
amplexicaulis	47	*					*		*					*			*	*	*	*		*						15
calandrinioides	106	*					*		*					*			*	*	*			*						18
ficaria Aurantiaca	91	*					*		*						*		*	*	*	*								15
montanus	47, 51	*					*		*	*				*			*	*	*	*								13
Raoulia australis	167	*				*			*				*	*			*	*	*	*	*				*			2
tenuicaulis	168	*				*			*				*	*			*	*	*	*	*							2
Rhamnus procumbens	143			*			*						*		*	*	*	*	*	*								30
pumila	37			*		*	*						*		*	*	*	*	*	*								18
Rhododendron anthopogon	142			*		*	*		*							*	*			*								60
calostrotum	142			*		*	*		*							*	*			*								30
Gigha	142			*		*	*		*							*	*			*								30
campylogynum	142			*		*	*		*							*	*			*								15
Crushed Strawberry	143			*		*	*		*							*	*			*								15
cephalanthum crebreflorum	135			*		*	*		*							*	*			*								25
chamaethomsonii	143			*		*	*		*							*	*			*								29

	Page No.	FORM							FLOWER					SOIL						SITE								HEIGHT
		HERB	BULB	SHRUB	DWARF TREE	SPREADING	MOUND OR TUFT	UPRIGHT	SPRING	SUMMER	AUTUMN	WINTER	FOLIAGE EFFECT	GRITTY	NORMAL	PEATY	ACID	NEUTRAL	LIMY	GENERAL	SCREE	MORAINE	SURROUNDING	WALL	TROUGH	PAVING	SHADE	(cm)
Rhododendron chrysanthum	135			*		*	*		*							*	*			*								23
chryseum	143			*		*	*		*							*	*			*								45
ferrugineum	42			*			*			*						*	*			*								100
forrestii	143, 173			*		*	*		*							*	*			*							*	12
hanceanum Nanum	153			*		*	*		*							*	*			*								38
hirsutum	41, 42			*		*	*			*						*	*	*	*	*								95
impeditum	153, 174			*		*	*		*							*	*			*								28
keiskei	162			*		*	*		*	*						*	*			*								45
lepidostylum	153			*		*	*		*							*	*			*							*	90
nakaharai	153			*		*				*						*	*			*								10
nitens	135			*		*	*			*						*	*			*								45
pemakoense	143			*		*			*							*	*			*								14
pumilum	143			*		*	*		*							*	*			*								25
radicans	143			*		*	*		*							*	*			*								8
Rhododendron HYBRID CULTIVARS:																												
Aspansia	135			*		*			*							*	*			*								30
Bluebird	135			*			*		*							*	*			*								30
Carmen	135			*		*			*	*						*	*			*								150
Chikor	135			*			*		*	*						*	*			*								30
Chink	135			*			*		*							*	*			*								45
Ethel	135			*		*			*							*	*			*								18
Fittra	135			*			*		*							*	*			*								38
Impeanum	135			*		*			*	*						*	*			*								25
Jenny	135			*		*			*	*						*	*			*								10
Lady Primrose	135			*			*		*							*	*			*								30
Little Ben	135			*		*			*							*	*			*								30
Pastel	135			*		*				*						*	*			*								30
Pink Drift	135			*			*		*							*	*			*								25

	Page No.	FORM: HERB	FORM: BULB	FORM: SHRUB	FORM: DWARF TREE	FORM: SPREADING	FORM: MOUND OR TUFT	FORM: UPRIGHT	FLOWER: SPRING	FLOWER: SUMMER	FLOWER: AUTUMN	FLOWER: WINTER	FLOWER: FOLIAGE EFFECT	SOIL: GRITTY	SOIL: NORMAL	SOIL: PEATY	SOIL: ACID	SOIL: NEUTRAL	SOIL: LIMY	SITE: GENERAL	SITE: SCREE	SITE: MORAINE	SITE: SURROUNDING	SITE: WALL	SITE: TROUGH	SITE: PAVING	SITE: SHADE	HEIGHT (cm)
Prostigiatum	135			*		*	*		*							*	*			*								45
Red Cap	135			*			*			*						*	*			*								38
Sapphire	135			*			*		*							*	*			*								28
Sarled	135			*			*		*							*	*			*								23
Scarlet Wonder	135			*		*	*		*	*						*	*			*								38
Treasure	135			*			*		*							*	*			*								25
Rhodothamnus chamaecistus	45			*			*		*						*		*	*		*								20
Sagina boydii	105	*				*				*			*	*	*		*	*	*		*				*			1
glabra	105	*				*				*			*	*	*		*	*	*	*	*							8
Salix×finnmarchica	37			*		*			*						*		*	*	*	*								15
glaucosericea	37			*			*		*						*		*	*	*	*								38
herbacea	37			*		*			*						*		*	*	*	*								8
myrsinites	37			*		*			*						*		*	*	*	*								30
repens	102			*		*			*						*		*	*	*	*								90
reticulata	37			*		*			*						*		*	*	*	*								13
retusa	37			*		*			*						*		*	*	*	*								15
uva-ursi	178			*		*			*						*		*	*	*	*								10
Sanguinaria canadensis	197	*					*		*						*	*	*	*	*	*			*				*	15
Plena	197	*					*		*						*	*	*	*	*	*			*				*	15
Santolina chamaecyparissus	110			*			*			*			*		*		*	*	*	*			*					38
Saponaria Bressingham Hybrid	48	*				*				*					*		*	*	*	*				*				13
ocymoides	48	*				*				*					*		*	*	*	*				*				15
Olivana	48	*				*				*				*			*	*			*				*			10
pulvinaris	128	*				*				*				*			*	*			*				*			10

	Page No.	FORM							FLOWER					SOIL						SITE								HEIGHT
		HERB	BULB	SHRUB	DWARF TREE	SPREADING	MOUND OR TUFT	UPRIGHT	SPRING	SUMMER	AUTUMN	WINTER	FOLIAGE EFFECT	GRITTY	NORMAL	PEATY	ACID	NEUTRAL	LIMY	GENERAL	SCREE	MORAINE	SURROUNDING	WALL	TROUGH	PAVING	SHADE	(cm)
Saxifraga aizoides	38	*				*				*					*			*	*	*								10
aizoon	59	*					*		*	*					*		*	*	*	*				*			*	23
androsacea	39	*					*			*					*		*	*		*		*						6
aspera	40, 59	*				*			*	*					*		*	*	*	*								9
burseriana	34, 39	*					*		*					*	*			*	*		*				*			5
caesia	34, 39	*				*	*		*					*	*			*	*		*				*			5
cochlearis	39	*					*		*	*				*	*			*	*		*			*	*			15
cotyledon	59	*				*	*			*					*		*	*		*			*	*				60
cuneifolia	39	*				*	*		*						*		*	*	*	*							*	8
geranioides	40	*				*				*					*			*	*	*		*					*	15
×*geum*	40	*				*				*					*		*	*	*	*							*	30
grisebachii	116	*					*		*					*	*			*	*	*								18
hypnoides	83	*					*			*					*		*	*	*	*							*	10
lilacina	146	*					*		*					*			*	*				*					*	4
longifolia	40	*					*			*				*				*	*	*				*				45
Tumbling Waters	40, 51	*					*			*				*				*	*	*				*				60
marginata	117	*				*			*						*		*	*	*	*								8
moschata	59	*				*			*						*			*	*	*								5
Cloth of Gold	59	*				*			*				*		*			*	*	*								5
oppositifolia	33, 38	*				*			*						*		*	*	*	*								3
stolonifera	132	*				*				*				*			*	*	*	*							*	25
trifurcata	59	*					*			*					*			*	*	*								15
umbrosa	82, 83	*				*			*	*					*		*	*	*	*			*				*	28
Variegata Aurea	83	*				*			*	*			*		*		*	*	*	*			*					25
Saxifraga MOSSY HYBRID CULTIVARS:																												
Ballawley Guardsman	40	*				*			*					*	*			*	*	*		*		*			*	23
Bob Hawkins	40	*				*			*					*	*			*	*	*		*					*	15

	Page No.	FORM: HERB	FORM: BULB	FORM: SHRUB	FORM: DWARF TREE	FORM: SPREADING	FORM: MOUND OR TUFT	FORM: UPRIGHT	FLOWER: SPRING	FLOWER: SUMMER	FLOWER: AUTUMN	FLOWER: WINTER	FLOWER: FOLIAGE EFFECT	SOIL: GRITTY	SOIL: NORMAL	SOIL: PEATY	SOIL: ACID	SOIL: NEUTRAL	SOIL: LIMY	SITE: GENERAL	SITE: SCREE	SITE: MORAINE	SITE: SURROUNDING	SITE: WALL	SITE: TROUGH	SITE: PAVING	SITE: SHADE	HEIGHT (cm)
Carnival	40	*				*			*					*	*			*	*	*		*					*	10
Diana	40	*				*			*					*	*			*	*	*		*					*	15
Dubarry	40	*				*			*					*	*			*	*	*		*					*	15
Elf	40	*				*			*					*	*			*	*	*		*				*	*	5
Flowers of Sulphur	40	*				*			*					*	*			*	*	*		*					*	18
Four Winds	40	*				*			*					*	*			*	*	*		*		*			*	23
Gaiety	40	*				*			*					*	*			*	*	*		*					*	10
Gnome	40	*				*			*					*	*			*	*	*		*				*	*	6
James Bremner	40	*				*			*					*	*			*	*	*		*		*			*	30
Mrs Piper	40	*				*			*					*	*			*	*	*		*					*	13
Pearly King	40	*				*			*					*	*			*	*	*		*				*	*	8
Peter Pan	40	*				*			*					*	*			*	*	*		*				*	*	8
Pixie	40	*				*			*					*	*			*	*	*		*				*	*	8
Pompadour	40	*				*			*					*	*			*	*	*		*		*			*	23
Red Admiral	40	*				*			*					*	*			*	*	*		*					*	10
Sanguinea Superba	40	*				*			*					*	*			*	*	*		*		*			*	18
Stansfieldii	40	*				*			*					*	*			*	*	*		*		*			*	22
Triumph	40	*				*			*					*	*			*	*	*		*		*			*	20
Winston Churchill	40	*				*			*					*	*			*	*	*		*					*	15
Scabiosa graminifolia	112	*					*			*					*		*	*	*	*								25
Scilla autumnalis	79		*			*	*			*	*				*		*	*	*	*								15
campanulata	79		*			*			*						*		*	*	*	*								25
monophylla	79		*			*			*						*		*	*	*	*								15
siberica	140		*			*			*						*		*	*	*	*								15
Spring Beauty	140		*			*			*						*		*	*	*	*								20
Taurica	140		*			*			*						*		*	*	*	*								15

		FORM							FLOWER					SOIL						SITE								HEIGHT
	Page No.	HERB	BULB	SHRUB	DWARF TREE	SPREADING	MOUND OR TUFT	UPRIGHT	SPRING	SUMMER	AUTUMN	WINTER	FOLIAGE EFFECT	GRITTY	NORMAL	PEATY	ACID	NEUTRAL	LIMY	GENERAL	SCREE	MORAINE	SURROUNDING	WALL	TROUGH	PAVING	SHADE	(cm)
Scilla tubergeniana	130		*			*			*						*		*	*	*	*								23
verna	79		*			*			*						*		*	*	*	*								15
Scleranthus biflorus	167	*					*						*	*			*	*	*		*				*			4
Scutellaria alpina	72	*				*	*			*					*		*	*	*	*								13
hirta	122	*				*				*					*		*	*	*	*								8
macrochlamys	134	*				*				*					*		*	*	*	*								10
orientalis	72	*					*			*					*		*	*	*	*								8
scordiifolia	134	*				*				*					*		*	*	*	*								15
virens	122	*					*			*					*		*	*	*	*								22
Sedum acre	8, 81	*				*				*					*		*	*	*	*								4
Aureum	81	*				*				*			*		*		*	*	*	*				*		*		4
Majus	82	*				*				*					*		*	*	*	*				*		*		8
aizoon	132	*					*	*		*					*		*	*	*	*			*	*				30
album	82	*				*				*			*		*		*	*	*	*								13
alpestre	74	*				*				*					*		*	*	*	*								6
anacampseros	74	*				*				*					*		*	*	*	*								2
anglicum	82	*				*				*					*		*	*	*	*	*			*				2
cauticolum	164, 174	*					*				*				*		*	*	*	*				*				23
crassipes	145	*					*			*					*		*	*	*	*			*					30
dasyphyllum	113	*					*			*					*		*	*	*	*								5
douglasii	188	*				*	*			*					*		*	*	*	*								15
ewersii	145	*				*					*				*		*	*	*	*								18
gracile	126	*				*				*					*		*	*	*	*								5
hirsutum	74	*					*			*					*		*	*	*	*								5
hispanicum	126	*				*				*					*		*	*	*	*				*				2
hybridum	132	*				*	*			*					*		*	*	*	*								9

	Page No.	FORM							FLOWER					SOIL						SITE								HEIGHT
		HERB	BULB	SHRUB	DWARF TREE	SPREADING	MOUND OR TUFT	UPRIGHT	SPRING	SUMMER	AUTUMN	WINTER	FOLIAGE EFFECT	GRITTY	NORMAL	PEATY	ACID	NEUTRAL	LIMY	GENERAL	SCREE	MORAINE	SURROUNDING	WALL	TROUGH	PAVING	SHADE	(cm)
kamtschaticum	132, 156	*				*				*					*		*	*	*	*								10
Variegatum	132	*				*				*			*		*		*	*	*	*				*				15
linearifolium	145	*					*			*	*				*		*	*	*	*								22
lydium	126	*					*			*					*		*	*	*	*								6
multiceps	107	*				*	*			*					*		*	*	*	*				*		*		8
ochroleucum	74	*				*				*					*		*	*	*	*								15
oreganum	188	*				*				*					*		*	*	*	*								8
pruinatum	74	*				*				*					*		*	*	*	*								15
pulchellum	180	*				*				*					*		*	*	*			*					*	10
purdyi	180	*				*	*			*					*		*	*	*	*								8
reflexum	74	*				*				*					*		*	*	*	*								20
rhodanthum	188	*					*			*					*		*	*	*	*			*					30
sediforme	113	*					*			*					*		*	*	*	*			*					38
sempervivoides	126	*					*			*					*		*	*	*	*								15
sexangulare	74	*				*	*			*					*		*	*	*	*					*	*		5
sieboldii	164	*				*					*				*		*	*	*	*								23
spathulifolium	188	*				*				*					*		*	*	*	*								8
Capa Blanca	188	*				*				*			*		*		*	*	*	*								7
Purpureum	188	*				*				*			*		*		*	*	*	*								8
spurium	126, 156	*				*				*					*		*	*	*	*				*				8
Schorbusser Blut	126	*				*				*					*		*	*	*	*				*				8
stenopetalum	180	*				*			*	*					*		*	*	*	*								13
stoloniferum	126	*				*				*					*		*	*	*	*								7
tenuifolium	113	*				*				*					*		*	*	*	*								14
ternatum	198	*					*		*						*		*	*	*	*								8
Selaginella helvetica	134	*				*							*		*		*	*	*	*				*			*	2
kraussiana	168	*				*							*		*		*	*	*	*				*			*	8

	Page No.	FORM							FLOWER					SOIL						SITE								HEIGHT
		HERB	BULB	SHRUB	DWARF TREE	SPREADING	MOUND OR TUFT	UPRIGHT	SPRING	SUMMER	AUTUMN	WINTER	FOLIAGE EFFECT	GRITTY	NORMAL	PEATY	ACID	NEUTRAL	LIMY	GENERAL	SCREE	MORAINE	SURROUNDING	WALL	TROUGH	PAVING	SHADE	(cm)
Selliera radicans	167	*				*				*					*		*	*	*	*		*						10
Sempervivella alba	146	*					*		*						*		*	*	*	*								6
Sempervivum arachnoideum	42	*					*			*			*		*		*	*	*	*					*			8
atlanticum	107	*					*			*			*		*		*	*	*	*								25
dolomiticum	42	*					*			*			*		*		*	*	*	*					*			10
erythraeum	122	*					*			*			*		*		*	*	*	*								18
grandiflorum	42	*					*			*			*		*		*	*	*	*								20
kosaninii	42	*					*			*			*		*		*	*	*	*								18
leucanthum	123	*					*			*			*		*		*	*	*	*								18
macedonicum	122	*					*			*			*		*		*	*	*	*								13
montanum	73	*					*			*			*		*		*	*	*	*					*			10
pumilum	127	*					*			*			*		*		*	*	*	*					*			8
reginae-amaliae	122	*					*			*			*		*		*	*	*	*								15
ruthenicum	123	*					*			*			*		*		*	*	*	*								25
schlehanii	122	*					*			*			*		*		*	*	*	*								10
tectorum	73, 74, 107, 122	*					*			*			*		*		*	*	*	*								20
wulfenii	42	*					*			*			*		*		*	*	*	*								18
Senecio abrotanifolius	58	*				*	*			*					*	*	*	*	*				*					38
adonidifolius	58	*				*	*			*					*		*	*	*	*			*					38
doronicum	106	*				*	*			*					*		*	*	*				*					45
hosmariensis	106	*				*	*			*					*		*	*	*	*								10
incanus	58	*					*			*				*			*	*	*		*							9
uniflorus	58	*					*			*				*			*	*	*		*							8
Sibthorpia europaea Variegata	84	*				*				*			*		*		*	*	*	*	*							5

	Page No.	FORM							FLOWER					SOIL						SITE								HEIGHT
		HERB	BULB	SHRUB	DWARF TREE	SPREADING	MOUND OR TUFT	UPRIGHT	SPRING	SUMMER	AUTUMN	WINTER	FOLIAGE EFFECT	GRITTY	NORMAL	PEATY	ACID	NEUTRAL	LIMY	GENERAL	SCREE	MORAINE	SURROUNDING	WALL	TROUGH	PAVING	SHADE	(cm)
Silene acaulis	33, 38	*				*				*				*			*	*	*			*			*			3
alpestris	58	*					*			*					*		*	*	*	*								15
armeria	58	*					*			*				*			*	*	*	*				*				38
ciliata	58	*				*				*					*		*	*	*	*								13
maritima	84	*				*				*				*	*		*	*	*	*				*				8
schafta	125, 155	*				*				*	*				*		*	*	*	*				*				10
Sisyrinchium angustifolium	192, 196	*				*	*			*					*		*	*	*	*								25
douglasii	195	*					*			*					*		*	*	*	*								19
Smilacina stellata	186	*				*			*						*	*	*	*		*			*				*	30
Soldanella alpina	61	*				*	*		*					*			*	*	*	*		*						8
austriaca	61	*				*	*		*					*			*	*	*	*		*						8
hungarica	61, 121	*				*	*		*					*			*	*	*	*		*						10
minima	61	*				*	*		*					*			*	*	*	*		*						6
montana	61	*				*	*		*					*			*	*	*	*		*						15
pindicola	61	*				*	*		*					*			*	*	*	*		*						9
pusilla	61	*				*	*		*					*			*	*	*	*		*						10
villosa	61	*				*	*		*					*			*	*	*	*		*						8
Spiraea lancifolia	45			*		*	*			*					*		*	*	*		*	*						24
Stachys corsica	110	*				*				*					*		*	*	*	*								8
discolor	123			*		*				*					*		*	*	*	*								22
lanata Silver Carpet	110, 123	*				*							*		*		*	*	*	*			*					9
Stellaria graminea Aurea	90	*				*	*		*	*			*		*		*	*	*	*								15
Sternbergia clusiana	129		*			*	*		*						*		*	*	*	*								20
fischeriana	129		*			*	*		*						*		*	*	*	*								15
lutea	129		*			*	*				*				*		*	*	*	*								20

	Page No.	FORM							FLOWER					SOIL						SITE								HEIGHT
		HERB	BULB	SHRUB	DWARF TREE	SPREADING	MOUND OR TUFT	UPRIGHT	SPRING	SUMMER	AUTUMN	WINTER	FOLIAGE EFFECT	GRITTY	NORMAL	PEATY	ACID	NEUTRAL	LIMY	GENERAL	SCREE	MORAINE	SURROUNDING	WALL	TROUGH	PAVING	SHADE	(cm)
Streptopus roseus	197	*					*		*							*	*	*	*	*							*	23
Stylophorum diphyllum	197	*					*		*							*	*	*					*				*	30
Tanacetum herderi	133	*					*			*			*		*		*	*	*	*								20
Taxodium distichum Hursley Park	195				*		*						*		*	*	*			*		*						45
Taxus baccata Argentea Minor	55				*		*						*		*		*	*	*	*								60
Cavendishii	55				*	*	*						*		*		*	*	*	*								90
Decora	55				*	*	*						*		*		*	*	*	*								60
Fastigiata	101				*			*					*		*		*	*	*	*								180
Fastigiata Aurea	101				*			*					*		*		*	*	*	*								180
Pygmaea	55				*		*						*		*		*	*	*	*								45
Repandens	55				*	*							*		*		*	*	*	*								38
Standishii	101				*			*					*		*		*	*	*	*								120
cuspidata Nana	161				*		*	*					*		*		*	*	*	*								90
Teucrium chamaedrys	72	*				*				*					*		*	*	*	*			*				*	30
marum	106			*			*			*					*		*	*	*	*								25
pyrenaicum	72	*				*				*					*		*	*	*	*				*				15
Thlaspi rotundifolium	45	*				*	*		*					*			*	*	*		*							8
Thuja occidentalis Caespitosa	190				*		*						*		*		*	*	*	*								60
Compacta	190				*		*						*		*		*	*	*	*								60
Cristata	193				*		*						*		*		*	*	*	*								45
Ericoides	193				*		*	*					*		*		*	*	*	*								95
Filiformis	193				*		*						*		*		*	*	*	*								120
Globosa	190				*		*						*		*		*	*	*	*								60
Hetz Midget	190				*		*						*		*		*	*	*	*					*			25
Rheingold	190, 192				*		*	*					*		*		*	*	*	*								105

	Page No.	FORM							FLOWER					SOIL						SITE								HEIGHT
		HERB	BULB	SHRUB	DWARF TREE	SPREADING	MOUND OR TUFT	UPRIGHT	SPRING	SUMMER	AUTUMN	WINTER	FOLIAGE EFFECT	GRITTY	NORMAL	PEATY	ACID	NEUTRAL	LIMY	GENERAL	SCREE	MORAINE	SURROUNDING	WALL	TROUGH	PAVING	SHADE	(cm)
orientalis Aurea Nana	152				*		*						*		*		*	*	*	*								45
Conspicua	152				*		*						*		*		*	*	*	*								45
Minima Glauca	152				*		*						*		*		*	*	*	*								45
Rosedalis	152				*		*						*		*		*	*	*	*								45
plicata Cuprea	177				*		*						*		*		*	*	*	*								38
Rogersii	177				*		*						*		*		*	*	*	*								38
Stoneham Gold	177				*		*						*		*		*	*	*	*								90
Thujopsis dolobrata Nana	162				*	*	*						*		*		*	*	*	*								100
Thymus×*citriodorus*	58			*		*	*						*		*		*	*	*	*						*		22
Argenteus	58			*		*	*						*		*		*	*	*	*						*		22
Aureus	58			*		*	*						*		*		*	*	*	*						*		22
lanuginosus	57			*		*			*	*					*		*	*	*	*						*		6
Hall's Variety	57			*		*			*	*					*		*	*	*	*						*		6
serpyllum	87, 88, 104			*		*			*	*					*		*	*	*	*						*		2
Albus	87			*		*			*	*					*		*	*	*	*						*		2
Coccineus	87			*		*			*	*					*		*	*	*	*						*		2
Elfin	87			*			*		*	*					*		*	*	*	*					*	*		2
Pink Chintz	87			*		*			*	*					*		*	*	*	*						*		2
Tiarella cordifolia	198	*				*			*						*		*	*	*	*			*					23
Purpurea	198	*				*			*						*		*	*	*	*			*					23
Trientalis borealis	186	*				*			*							*	*	*		*							*	24
europaea	95	*				*				*						*	*	*		*							*	15
Trifolium alpinum	63	*				*				*					*		*	*	*	*								10
uniflorum	63	*				*				*				*	*		*	*	*	*	*							5

	Page No.	FORM							FLOWER					SOIL						SITE								HEIGHT
		HERB	BULB	SHRUB	DWARF TREE	SPREADING	MOUND OR TUFT	UPRIGHT	SPRING	SUMMER	AUTUMN	WINTER	FOLIAGE EFFECT	GRITTY	NORMAL	PEATY	ACID	NEUTRAL	LIMY	GENERAL	SCREE	MORAINE	SURROUNDING	WALL	TROUGH	PAVING	SHADE	(cm)
Trillium grandiflorum	197	*					*		*						*		*	*	*	*			*				*	25
Roseum	198	*					*		*						*		*	*	*	*			*				*	25
Rubrum	198	*					*		*						*		*	*	*	*			*				*	25
Trollius acaulis	143	*				*	*			*					*		*	*	*	*		*						10
Tsuga canadensis Cole	193				*	*							*		*		*	*	*	*								15
Dwarf Whitetip	193				*		*						*		*		*	*	*	*								90
Jervis	193				*		*						*		*		*	*	*	*								30
Many Cones	193				*	*	*						*		*		*	*	*	*								120
Minuta	193				*		*						*		*		*	*	*	*					*			25
Pendula	193				*	*	*						*		*		*	*	*	*								75
Tulipa aitchisonii	139		*			*	*		*					*			*	*	*	*								5
biflora	139		*			*	*		*					*			*	*	*	*								15
celsiana	106		*			*	*		*					*			*	*	*	*								15
chrysantha	145		*			*	*		*					*			*	*	*	*								20
fosteriana	139		*			*	*		*					*			*	*	*	*								25
greigii Compostella	139		*			*	*		*					*			*	*	*	*								23
Donna Bella	139		*			*	*		*					*			*	*	*	*								23
Perlina	139		*			*	*		*					*			*	*	*	*								23
Plaisir	139		*			*	*		*					*			*	*	*	*								15
Red Riding Hood	139		*			*	*		*					*			*	*	*	*								20
hageri	127		*			*	*		*					*			*	*	*	*								18
kaufmanniana	139		*			*	*		*					*			*	*	*	*								23
Ancilla	139		*			*	*		*					*			*	*	*	*								10
Fritz Kreisler	139		*			*	*		*					*			*	*	*	*								20
Gluck	139		*			*	*		*					*			*	*	*	*								20

	Page No.	FORM: HERB	FORM: BULB	FORM: SHRUB	FORM: DWARF TREE	FORM: SPREADING	FORM: MOUND OR TUFT	FORM: UPRIGHT	FLOWER: SPRING	FLOWER: SUMMER	FLOWER: AUTUMN	FLOWER: WINTER	FLOWER: FOLIAGE EFFECT	SOIL: GRITTY	SOIL: NORMAL	SOIL: PEATY	SOIL: ACID	SOIL: NEUTRAL	SOIL: LIMY	SITE: GENERAL	SITE: SCREE	SITE: MORAINE	SITE: SURROUNDING	SITE: WALL	SITE: TROUGH	SITE: PAVING	SITE: SHADE	HEIGHT (cm)
Scarlet Elegance	139		*			*	*		*			*		*			*	*	*	*								12
Shakespeare	139		*			*	*		*					*			*	*	*	*								15
linifolia	139		*			*	*		*					*			*	*	*	*								20
pulchella humilis	127		*			*	*		*					*			*	*	*	*								15
violacea	127		*			*	*		*					*			*	*	*	*								13
tarda	139		*			*	*		*					*			*	*	*	*								15
urumiensis	127		*			*	*		*					*			*	*	*	*								14
Tunica graminea	115	*					*			*				*	*		*	*	*	*								22
illyrica	115	*				*	*			*					*		*	*	*	*								13
saxifraga	62	*					*			*				*	*		*	*	*	*				*				15
Umbilicus rupestris	83	*					*		*	*					*		*	*	*					*			*	30
Vaccinium vitis-idaea	102, 185			*		*				*						*	*			*		*					*	22
Valeriana celtica	62	*				*				*					*		*	*	*	*								8
saliunica	72	*					*			*					*		*	*	*	*								10
supina	62	*				*				*					*		*	*	*	*		*						15
Vancouveria hexandra	186	*					*		*							*	*										*	20
planipetala	186	*				*			*							*	*										*	20
Verbascum Letitia	112, 138			*			*			*					*		*	*	*	*	*							20
spinosum	112			*		*	*			*					*		*	*	*	*	*							28
Veronica allionii	62	*				*			*						*		*	*	*	*								5
alpina	62	*				*			*						*		*	*	*	*								15
filiformis	123	*				*			*						*		*	*	*	*			*					5
fruticans	62	*				*				*					*		*	*	*	*								13
nummularia	62	*				*				*					*		*	*	*	*						*		10
pectinata	123			*		*			*						*		*	*	*	*								8

		FORM							FLOWER					SOIL						SITE								HEIGHT
	Page No.	HERB	BULB	SHRUB	DWARF TREE	SPREADING	MOUND OR TUFT	UPRIGHT	SPRING	SUMMER	AUTUMN	WINTER	FOLIAGE EFFECT	GRITTY	NORMAL	PEATY	ACID	NEUTRAL	LIMY	GENERAL	SCREE	MORAINE	SURROUNDING	WALL	TROUGH	PAVING	SHADE	(cm)
Veronica peduncularis Nymans Variety	125	*				*	*		*						*		*	*	*	*								15
prostrata	66	*				*			*						*		*	*	*	*				*				15
Alba	66	*				*			*						*		*	*	*	*				*				15
Mrs Holt	66	*				*			*						*		*	*	*	*				*		*		7
Nana	66	*				*			*						*		*	*	*	*				*				10
Royal Blue	66	*				*			*						*		*	*	*	*				*				15
Silver Queen	66	*				*			*						*		*	*	*	*				*				15
Spode Blue	66	*				*			*						*		*	*	*	*				*				15
teucrium	66, 67	*				*	*			*					*		*	*	*	*			*					25
Rosea	67	*				*	*			*					*		*	*	*	*			*					23
Royal Blue	67	*				*	*			*					*		*	*	*	*			*					28
Trehane	67, 86	*				*	*			*			*		*		*	*	*	*			*					30
Vinca minor	75	*				*			*						*		*	*	*				*				*	15
Alba	75	*				*			*						*		*	*	*				*				*	15
Bowles Variety	75	*				*			*						*		*	*	*				*				*	15
Multiplex	75	*				*			*						*		*	*	*				*				*	15
Variegata	75	*				*			*				*		*		*	*	*	*			*				*	15
Viola adunca	180	*					*		*						*		*	*	*	*								10
alpina	60	*					*		*						*		*	*	*	*								10
biflora	60	*				*			*						*		*	*	*	*			*				*	13
calcarata	60	*				*				*					*		*	*	*	*								11
cornuta	60	*				*				*					*		*	*	*	*			*				*	20
labradorica	180	*				*			*	*					*		*	*	*	*			*				*	9
lutea	92, 93	*				*				*					*		*	*	*	*			*					12
odorata	92	*				*			*						*		*	*	*	*			*					15
Wahlenbergia hederacea	97	*				*				*						*	*	*				*						5
Waldsteinia ternata	134	*				*			*						*		*	*	*								*	10
Zauschneria californica	186	*					*			*	*			*	*		*	*	*	*	*							23

Bibliography

Other comprehensive books to be found on Alpine plants include the *Manual of Alpine Plants* by Will Ingwersen (Ingwersen & Dunnsprint Ltd, East Grinstead, 1978) and *Alpines and Rock Garden Plants* by Anna N. Griffiths (Collins, 1972). In the sphere of dwarf trees and shrubs, *Hillier's Manual of Trees and Shrubs* (David & Charles, Newton Abbot, 1981) is full of information. For guidance on dwarf and ornamental conifers, *Manual of Dwarf Conifers* by Humphrey J. Welch (Garland Press, New York, 1979) and *Ornamental Conifers* by Charles R. Harrison (David & Charles, 1975) are recommended.

The publications of the Royal Horticultural Society are extremely useful, and those of the Alpine Garden Society are indispensable for anyone interested in rock gardens and gardening.

Index